THE
AMERICAN FREEDOM
PRIMER

THE
AMERICAN FREEDOMS
PRIMER

A CITIZEN'S GUIDEBOOK TO
THE MOST CELEBRATED DECLARATIONS
OF AMERICAN LIBERTY

LES ADAMS

Skyhorse Publishing

Skyhorse Publishing books may be purchased in bulk at special discounts
for sales promotion, corporate gifts, fund-raising, or educational
purposes. Special editions can also be created to specifications. For
details, contact the Special Sales Department, Skyhorse Publishing,
307 West 36th Street, 11th Floor, New York, NY 10018 or info@
skyhorsepublishing.com.

Skyhorse® and Skyhorse Publishing® are registered trademarks of
Skyhorse Publishing, Inc.®, a Delaware corporation.

Visit our website at www.skyhorsepublishing.com.

10 9 8 7 6 5 4 3 2 1

Library of Congress Cataloging-in-Publication Data is available on file.

Print ISBN: 978-1-62914-725-3
Ebook ISBN: 978-1-62914-855-7

Printed in United States of America

CONTENTS

THE
AMERICAN FREEDOMS
PRIMER

INTRODUCTION

The last line in this book, taken from President Ronald Reagan's farewell address to the nation on January 11, 1989, is "God bless the United States of America." This statement became especially significant to me as I was working on this book. For as I studied the entire breadth of American history — from, say, George Washington's first inaugural speech to Reagan's farewell address — I found it difficult not to conclude then, and I will take the risk of sounding somewhat maudlin about it now, that the American people, and the American nation, must be especially blessed by God. How else otherwise to explain our extraordinary good fortune? Consider Washington's incredible victory with a poorly trained and ill-equipped ragtag army over the more highly skilled, more heavily musketed British redcoats. . . . Thomas Jefferson's extraordinary purchase from the French, for only fifteen million dollars, of more than eight hundred thousand square miles of prime land that today makes up practically the entire midwestern section of the country. . . . Lincoln's rock-hard determination and raw courage, in the face of harrowing initial Union army defeats, vicious personal criticism, and awesome battlefield injuries and deaths, to save his Union at any cost. How else to explain the growth and development of the United States of America, in just four hundred

*years, from a scattering of small coastal agricul-
tural colonies on the eastern edge of a savage
wilderness into the most powerful, most affluent
nation in the history of the world?*

If there is any other answer, I think it is this:

Before we had power, wealth, or a written constitution, we had a desire for freedom

*Before we had power, before we had wealth, even
before we had a written constitution, we had
something that was to make America unique
among the nations of the world — a burning,
persistent, unquenchable desire for freedom. "We
hold these truths to be self-evident: that all men
are created equal; that they are endowed, by
their Creator with certain unalienable rights;
that among these are life, liberty, and the pursuit
of happiness."* [1]

*Of course, a decade after the Declaration of
Independence, we went on to write the U.S.
Constitution and its accompanying Bill of Rights.
It is the landmark document of our freedoms.*

*But in our heritage, there are a number of
other writings about freedom that are worthy of
your attention. Some of them are really quite
extraordinary. Included in the book are my personal favorites: the two pamphlets of Thomas
Paine; George Washington's humble letter to his
wife, Martha; Justice Harlan's dissent in* Plessy
v. Ferguson; *Theodore Roosevelt's robust exhor-
tation to lead the strenuous life; examples of*

---

[1] From The Declaration of Independence, July 4, 1776.
See page 112 for complete text.

the magnificent though quite dissimilar oratory styles of Daniel Webster and Martin Luther King, Jr.; and most influential of all, at least in my view, the roughhewn speeches of Abraham Lincoln, who I believe is America's greatest hero.

Hopefully, all the writings in the book will provide you with additional valuable insights into the meaning of the freedoms you enjoy as a citizen of the United States: how they came to be, what they mean today, why they are worth preserving and fighting for. I apologize in advance for the inadvertent omission of any of your favorites.

Valuable insights into the meaning of the freedoms you enjoy

LES ADAMS

I
ENGLISH WRITINGS
BEFORE THE
AMERICAN REVOLUTION

Many Americans have the notion that our con-
cepts of freedom were the original, spontaneous
product of a few minds — James Madison, George
Mason, Alexander Hamilton, and the other Found-
ing Fathers who met in Philadelphia in the sum-
mer of 1787 to write the U.S. Constitution. But
the development of these concepts goes back **American**
much further than that: to the state constitutions **concepts of**
freedom go
and declarations of rights written between 1776 **back long**
and 1787; to the first colonial charters granted to **before the**
the individual American colonies by the English **Constitution**
Crown between 1604 and 1732; and, even fur-
ther back, to several important events and writ-
ings in England.

Let's look at events first, with this thumbnail
description of English constitutional history.

Everything starts, of course, with the Magna **Magna**
Carta, King John's royal proclamation of 1215 **Carta**
that granted to his barons certain new rights
they had pressured him into acknowledging.
Although the Magna Carta was a comparatively
rude, medieval document, in it we see the first
faint stirrings of ideas and forces that would ulti-
mately transform England from a monarchy to a

representative democracy. *Thus the Magna Carta has come to be recognized as the cornerstone of English constitutional law. For the American colonists, who were learning from their experiences with the English Crown that liberty depended upon the existence of laws limiting the authority and discretion of those in charge of the government, the importance of the Magna Carta was that it announced the rule of law.*

The Magna Carta's most important chapter is its thirty-ninth:

> *No free man shall be taken or imprisoned or dispossessed, or outlawed, or banished, or in any way destroyed, nor will we go upon him, nor send upon him, except by the legal judgement of his peers or by the law of the land.*

These principles appear in one form or another in many of our early state declarations of rights, and most prominently in the Fifth and Fourteenth Amendments to the U.S. Constitution, which provide that no person may be deprived of life, liberty, or property without due process of law.

Four hundred years were to pass until the seeds planted by the Magna Carta bore fruit in two English documents, the 1628 Petition of Right and the 1689 Declaration of Rights.

1628 Petition of Right

The Petition of Right was drafted by the Eng-

*lish parliament and was presented to King
Charles I in 1628. It was a revolutionary document, declaring the supremacy of law over the
personal wishes of the king and rejecting the doctrine known as the divine right of kings (the
belief that monarchs obtain their ruling power
directly from God, rather than through the consent of their subjects). Specifically, the petition
demanded important restrictions upon monar-
chal power. Among the provisions were that prisoners committed to jail at the king's command
were to be freed on bail before trial; the quartering of troops in private homes was to be made
illegal; and civilians could not be tried under
martial law. The Petition of Right thus contributed much to the establishment of some of
the essential personal liberties of the English
people. The eminent English historian William
Holdsworth was later to characterize the petition
as "the first of those great constitutional documents since Magna Carta, which safeguard the
liberties of the people by securing the supremacy
of the law."[2]*

*King Charles grudgingly accepted the Peti-
tion of Right, recognizing that he needed the
cooperation of Parliament to raise money to fund
his monarchy. But he had no intention of abiding
by it, and it cost him his head. The struggle for*

---

[2] WILLIAM HOLDSWORTH, A HISTORY OF ENGLISH LAW,
Boston, Little Brown, 1937, 5: 449

power between Charles and Parliament led
to the English Civil War in 1642 and Charles's
conviction for treason and subsequent beheading
in 1649.

In 1689, under a new king and queen
(William and Mary), Parliament adopted the
1689 Decla- English Declaration of Rights (later established
rations of in statutory form as the English Bill of Rights).
Rights This document reaffirmed the principles of the
1628 Petition of Right, denying the divine right
of kings and setting forth thirteen basic rights
and liberties of the English people that Parliament regarded as "true, ancient, and indubitable." In his classic History of England, Lord
Macaulay summed up the significance of the
Declaration of Rights as follows:

> The Declaration of Right[s], though it
> made nothing law which had not been
> law before, contained the germ of the law
> which gave religious freedom to the Dis-
> senter, of the law which secured the inde-
> pendence of the Judges, of the law which
> limited the duration of Parliaments, of the
> law which placed the liberty of the press
> under the protection of juries, of the law
> which prohibited the slave trade, of the law
> which abolished the sacramental test, of
> the law which relieved Roman Catholics
> from civil liabilities, of the law which re-
> formed the representative system, of every

good law which has been passed during more than a century and a half, of every good law which may hereafter, in the course of ages, be found necessary to promote the public weal, and to satisfy the demands of public opinion.[3]

The Magna Carta, the Petition of Right, and the Declaration of Rights provided the historical architecture upon which were created the early English writings on liberty. Included here are three of the most important: two by seventeenth-century writers John Locke and Algernon Sidney, and one by eighteenth-century writer Edmund Burke.

JOHN LOCKE

John Locke (1632–1704) spent the first fifty years of his life in relative obscurity, practicing medicine and occupying several political and administrative positions, primarily in London. In 1683, he moved to Holland, where he became a close friend of Prince William and Princess Mary of Orange — so close, in fact, that he accompanied Princess Mary in February 1689 when she traveled from Holland to England to join her husband for their coronation as the new king and queen of England. Locke, then a relatively un-

[3] THOMAS MACAULAY, THE HISTORY OF ENGLAND, Charles H. Firth, ed., London, J.M. Dent, 1913-1915, 3: 1311

known man, soon became a favorite in the court of William and Mary, a man of political influence with friends in high places, a celebrity in the academic and social circles of late seventeenth-century London.

But John Locke deserves our attention today for much more than fleeting celebrity. His Two Treatises on Government, *published in 1690, is one of the most important works ever written on constitutional law, political theory, and the establishment of democratic government. Locke's immediate purpose in writing the book was to justify the Glorious Revolution of 1688.*[4] *Locke sought, as he said, "to establish the throne of our great restorer, or present King William; to make good his title, in the consent of the people." In achieving this goal, Locke was to formulate a democracy in which government by the consent and with the goodwill of the governed is the ideal.*

Essential reading for all thoughtful Americans

Book II of the work, entitled "Of Civil Government," should be essential reading for all thoughtful Americans who care about their freedoms. It's a powerhouse of a book, loaded with thoughts and words that later resonated throughout all the political debates and documents of the American Revolution — thoughts and words that are as vital and meaningful today as they were more than three hundred years ago.

[4] The Glorious Revolution was a movement that established the supremacy of Parliament over the king.

Locke believed that by nature, people have certain rights and duties. These rights include life, liberty, and the right of property ownership. In exercising these rights, people also have the right to govern themselves in the way they judge to be for the common good. In other words, the people, not the king, are sovereign, a sovereignty based upon a mutual contract among the people to govern themselves. If the terms of the contract need to be changed to accommodate changing circumstances, only the people, not the government, can make such changes.

In Locke's view, civil rulers hold their power not absolutely but conditionally, government being essentially a moral trust. And if in the exercise of its power, the trustee (the government) fails to live up to this trust — that is, fails to protect the life, liberty, and right of property ownership of the people — the people, and only the people, have the right and power to dissolve the government and select a new one.

Civil rulers hold their power not absolutely but conditionally

Another principal point Locke made is that government may be dissolved while society remains intact. In other words, the people themselves constitute a power superior to government. This idea had great weight in Philadelphia in 1787. It's an idea that still has great weight today.

After Locke's time — throughout the mid-eighteenth century, in the period we now refer to as the Age of Reason or the Enlightenment —

the subjects of liberty, human rights, and the relationship between people and their government were examined by a number of European writers, chief among them Montesquieu, in The Spirit of the Laws *(1748), Jean-Jacques Rousseau, in* The Social Contract *(1762), and Voltaire, in* Essay on the Manners and Spirit of Nations *(1756) and* Philosophical Dictionary *(1764).*

A strong influence over the thinking of the Founding Fathers

And although all these works were widely read by and presumably exerted some influence over the Founding Fathers, it was Locke's Two Treatises on Government *that had the greatest effect upon their thinking as they drafted the cornerstone documents of American liberty: the Declaration of Independence, the U.S. Constitution, and the Bill of Rights.*

Here are a few excerpts from Locke's work.

FROM *TWO TREATISES ON GOVERNMENT, BOOK II*
1690

CHAPTER IX

Of the Ends of Political Society and Government.
§. 123. If man in the state of nature be so free, as has been said; if he be absolute lord of his own person and possessions, equal to the greatest, and subject to nobody, why will he part with his free-

dom? Why will he give up this empire, and subject himself to the dominion and control of any other power? To which it is obvious to answer, that though in the state of nature he hath such a right, yet the enjoyment of it is very uncertain, and constantly exposed to the invasion of others: for all being kings as much as he, every man his equal, and the greater part no strict observers of equity and justice, the enjoyment of the property he has in this state is very unsafe, very unsecure. This makes him willing to quit a condition, which, however free, is full of fears and continual dangers: and it is not without reason, that he seeks out, and is willing to join in society with others, who are already united, to have a mind to unite, for the mutual *preservation,* of their lives, liberties and estates, which I call by the general name, property.

§. 124. The great and *chief end*, therefore, of men's uniting into commonwealths, and putting themselves under government, *is the preservation of their property.* . . .

> The chief end of government is the preservation of property

§. 127. It is this makes them so willingly give up every one his single power of punishing, to be exercised by such alone, as shall be appointed to it amongst them; and by such rules as the community, or those authorized by them to that purpose, shall agree on. And in this we have the original *right and rise of both the legislative and executive power,* as well as of the governments and societies themselves.

§. 128. For in the state of nature, to omit the liberty he has of innocent delights, a man has two powers.

The first is to do whatsoever he thinks fit for the preservation of himself, and others within the permission of the *law of nature:* by which law, common to them all, he and all the rest of *mankind are one community,* make up one society, distinct from all other creatures. And were it not for the corruption and viciousness of degenerate men, there would be no need of any other; no necessity that men should separate from this great and natural community, and by positive agreements combine into smaller and divided associations.

The other power a man has in the state of nature, is the *power to punish the crimes* committed against that law. Both these he gives up, when he joins in a private, if I may so call it, or particular politic society, and incorporates into any commonwealth, separate from the rest of mankind. . . .

§. 131. But though men, when they enter into society, give up the equality, liberty, and executive power they had in the state of nature, into the hands of the society, to be so far disposed of by the legislative, as the good of the society shall require; yet it being only with an intention in every one the better to preserve himself, his liberty and property; (for no rational creature can be supposed to change his condition with an intention to be worse) the power of the society, or *legislative* constituted by them, can *never be supposed to extend farther than the common good; . . .* And so whoever has the legislative or supreme power of any commonwealth, is bound to govern by established *standing laws,* promulgated and known to the people, and not by extemporary decrees; by *indifferent* and upright *judges,* who are to decide controversies by those laws; and to employ the force of the community at home, *only in the execution of such laws,* or abroad to prevent or redress foreign injuries, and secure the community from inroads and invasion. And all this to be directed to no other *end,* but the *peace, safety,* and *public good of* the people.

Whoever has the power is bound to govern by standing laws

CHAPTER XIX

Of the Dissolution of Government.

§. 240. Here, it is like, the common question will be made, *Who shall be judge,* whether the prince or legislative act contrary to their trust ? . . . To this I reply. *The people shall be judge;* for who shall be *judge* whether his trustee or deputy acts well, and according to the trust reposed in him, but he who deputes him, and must, by having deputed him, have still a power to discard him, when he fails in his trust? If this be reasonable in particular cases of private men, why should it be otherwise in that of the greatest moment, where the welfare of millions is concerned, and also where the evil, if not prevented, is greater, and the redress very difficult, dear, and dangerous?

§.241. But farther, this question *(Who shall be judge?)* cannot mean, that there is no judge at all: for where there is no judicature on earth, to decide controversies amongst men, God in heaven is *judge*. He alone, it is true, is judge of the right. But *every man* is *judge* for himself, as in all other cases, so in this whether another hath put himself into a state of war with him, and whether he should appeal to the Supreme Judge, as Jephthah did.

§. 242. If a controversy arise betwixt a prince and some of the people, in a matter where the law is silent, or doubtful, and the thing be of great consequence, I should think the proper *umpire,* in such a case, should be the body of the *people:* . . .

The proper umpire of a controversy is the body of the people

§. 243. To conclude, The *power that every individual gave the society,* when he entered into it, can never revert to the individuals again, as long as the society lasts, but will always remain in the community; because without this there can be no community, no commonwealth, which is contrary to the original agreement: so also when the society hath placed the legislative in any assembly of men, to continue in them and their successors, with direction and authority for providing such successors, *the legislative can never revert to the people* whilst that government lasts; because having provided a legislative with power to continue forever, they have given up their political power to the legislative, and cannot resume it. But if they have set limits to the duration of their legislative, and made this supreme power in any person, or assembly, only temporary; or else, when by the miscarriages of those in authority it is forfeited; upon the forfeiture, or at the determination of the time set, *it reverts to the society*, and the people have a right to act as supreme, and continue the legislative in themselves; or erect a new form, or under the old form place it in new hands, as they think good.

ALGERNON SYDNEY

Algernon Sidney (1622–1683), who has been described as "the forgotten Founding Father" of the United States, was an English political philosopher and a leading member of the Whig Party in Parliament in the late seventeenth century. He became a martyr for the cause of liberty when he was tried, convicted, and executed for treason by the Star Chamber [5] *in 1683. (He was posthumously exonerated after the Glorious Revolution in 1688.) His classic work,* Discourses Concerning Government, *was published posthumously in 1698.*

"The forgotten Founding Father"

Discourses *was widely read in the American colonies. It had a profound effect upon a number of American political leaders, including Samuel*

[5] The Court of the Star Chamber was an infamous English court of law from the fifteenth to the seventeenth centuries that tried defendants in secret, juryless proceedings.

Adams, John Adams, Patrick Henry, George
Mason, James Madison, Benjamin Franklin, and
Thomas Jefferson, all of whom acknowledged
Sidney's influence on their thought.

In a letter to Thomas Jefferson in 1823, John
Adams wrote:

> I have lately undertaken to read Algernon
> Sidney on government. . . . As often as I
> have read it . . . it now excites fresh [won-
> der] that this work has excited so little
> interest in the literary world. . . . As splen-
> did an edition of it as the art of printing can
> produce — as well for the intrinsic merit of
> the work, as for the proof it brings of the
> bitter sufferings of the advocates of liberty
> from that time to this, and to show the slow
> progress of moral, philosophical, and polit-
> ical illumination in the world — ought to be
> published in America.

Writings were a leading source for the foundations of liberty and human rights

Jefferson regarded Sidney's writings, along
with those of John Locke, as the leading sources
for the philosophical foundations of liberty and
human rights. As founder of the University of
Virginia, Jefferson issued this statement in 1825:

> Resolved, that it is the opinion of the
> Board that as to the general principles of
> liberty and the rights of man, in nature and

*society, the doctrines of Locke, in his
'Essay Concerning the True Original Extent
and End of Civil Government' and of Sidney, in his 'Discourses on Government,'
may be considered as those generally
approved by our fellow citizens of this, the
United States.*

*Here are a few excerpts from Sidney's influ-
ential work.*

FROM *DISCOURSES
CONCERNING GOVERNMENT*
1698

Chapter One, Section 3
Implicit Faith belongs to Fools, and Truth is com-
prehended by examining Principles. . . . Who will
wear a shoe that hurts him, because the shoe-
maker tells him 'tis well made? or who will live in
a house that yields no defence against the extrem-
ities of weather, because the mason or carpenter
assures him 'tis a very good house? Such as have
reason, understanding, or common sense, will,
and ought to make use of it in those things that
concern themselves and their posterity, and suspect the words of such as are interested in deceiv-
ing or persuading them not to see with their own
eyes, that they may more easily be deceived. This
rule obliges us so far to search into matters of

state, as to examine the original principles of government in general, and of our own in particular. We cannot distinguish truth from falsehood, right from wrong, or know what obedience we owe to the magistrate, or what we may justly expect from him, unless we know what he is, why he is, and by whom he is made to be what he is. . . .

Chapter One, Section 6
God leaves to Man the choice of Forms in Government; and those who constitute one Form, may abrogate it. . . .

Chapter Three, Section 15
A general presumption that Kings will govern well, is not a sufficient security to the People. . . .

'Tis not upon the uncertain will of the prince that the safety of a nation ought to depend

"Tis not therefore upon the uncertain will or understanding of a prince, that the safety of a nation ought to depend. He is sometimes a child, and sometimes overburden'd with years. Some are weak, negligent, slothful, foolish or vicious: others, who may have something of rectitude in their intentions, and naturally are not incapable of doing well, are drawn out of the right way by the subtlety of ill men who gain credit with them. The rule must always be uncertain, and subject to be distorted, which depends upon the fancy of such a man. . . . The good of a people ought to be established upon a more solid foundation. For this reason the law is established, which no passion can disturb. . . .

But if all depended upon the will of a man, the worst would be often the most safe, and the best in the greatest hazard: . . . The most generous nations have above all things sought to avoid this evil: and the virtue, wisdom and generosity of each may be discern'd by the right fixing of the rule that must be the guide of every man's life, and so constituting their magistracy that it may be duly observed. Such as have attained to this perfection, have always flourished in virtue and happiness: They are, as Aristotle says, governed by God, rather than by men, whilst those who subjected themselves to the will of a man were governed by a beast. . . .

Chapter Three, Section 25
Laws and constitutions ought to be weighed, and whilst all due reverence is paid to such as are good, every nation may not only retain in itself a power of changing or abolishing all such as are not so, but ought to exercise that power according to the best of their understanding, and in place of what was either at first mistaken or afterwards corrupted, to constitute that which is most conducing to the establishment of justice and liberty.

But such is the condition of mankind, that nothing can be so perfectly framed as not to give some testimony of human imbecility, and frequently to stand in need of reparations and amendments. Many things are unknown to the wisest, and the best men can never wholly divest themselves of passions and affections. By this means the best and wisest are sometimes led into error, and stand in need of successors like to themselves, who may find remedies for the faults they have committed, and nothing can or ought to be permanent but that which is perfect. . . .

Chapter Three, Section 36

The general revolt of a nation cannot be called a Rebellion

The general revolt of Nation cannot be called a Rebellion. . . . But tho every private man taken singly be subject to the commands of the magistrate, the whole body of the people is not so; for he is by and for the people, and the people is neither by nor for him. The obedience due to him from private men is grounded upon, and measured by the general law; and that law regarding the welfare of the people, cannot set up the interest of one or a few men against the publick. The whole body therefore of a nation cannot be tied to any other obedience than is consistent with the common good, according to their own judgment: and having never been subdued or brought to terms of peace with their magistrates, they cannot be said to revolt or rebel against them to whom they owe no more that seems good to themselves, and who are nothing of or by themselves, than other men. . . .

Chapter Three, Section 45

The difference therefore between good and ill governments is not, that those of one sort have an arbitrary power which the others have not, for they all have it; but that those which are well constituted, place this power so as it may be beneficial to the people, and set such rules as are hardly to be transgressed, whilst those of the other sort fail in one or both of these points. . . .

EDMUND BURKE

The fate of great nations sometimes hinges on relatively minor defaults. If a foolish man, King George III, had listened to the speeches of a wise man, Edmund Burke, there probably wouldn't be a United States of America today.

Edmund Burke (1729–1797) served as a member of the English parliament for twenty-eight years, during which time he became a leading Whig politician and one of Britain's foremost statesmen. Burke considered himself a lineal descendant of the classical republicans, or Whigs, who had brought about the Glorious Revolution.

The series of events that precipitated Burke's criticism of the policies of George III are these. In 1763, Britain defeated France in the French and Indian War. The treaty ending the war gave Britain almost all of France's territory in North America, including most of Canada and lands stretching from the Appalachian Mountains all the way to the Mississippi River. Emboldened by this military success and the acquisition of vast

One of Britain's foremost statesmen

new lands in North America, King George determined to expand his influence and exercise greater authority over the American colonies. Among other things, he issued the Proclamation of 1763, which forbade colonists from settling on Indian lands west of the Appalachians, an extremely unpopular edict among the expansion-minded American colonists. At the same time, and with the approval of the king, Parliament began enacting a number of laws to increase Great Britain's income from the colonies, to help pay for the recent war, and to finance the stationing of British troops on the colonies' western frontiers.[6] Predictably, the colonists were enraged by these actions, which they regarded as "taxation without representation," and began organizing into committees of correspondence to unite against the perceived abuses of power by the English government. King George reacted belligerently, declaring in late 1774: "The die is now cast, the colonies must either submit or triumph."

Edmund Burke viewed the matter differently.

---

[6] Chief among these parliamentary enactments (all of which were greeted with anger and resentment by the colonists) were the Revenue Act of 1764 (also known as the Sugar Act), which taxed molasses being imported into the colonies for their thriving rum industries; in 1765, the Quartering and Stamp Acts, which ordered the colonists to pay for the quartering of British soldiers and to pay a stamp tax on printed items such as newspapers, calling cards, and various legal documents; the Declaratory Act of 1766, which proclaimed that the king and Parliament had full legislative authority over the colonies in all matters; the Townshend Acts of 1767, which placed duties on glass, paint, paper, and tea imported into

"Burke was determined," observed the historian Russell Kirk,

that the King and Parliament should not take away the established rights of those who now lived in the New World. Burke was never in favor of any revolution. Believing as he did that history is "the known march of the ordinary providence of God," he was convinced that violent revolution is impious, a presumptuous interference with providence . . . that [Britain] ought always to seek for peaceable reforms, never taking the sword, except in immediate self-defense. The American Revolution, in Burke's mind, was not really a revolution at all. . . . It was George III who had tried to work a revolution by abrogating the established rights of the colonists; the colonists had not been overthrowing the established order of things, but rather defending the established order of America[7]

Burke opposed the king and Parliament taking away the rights of the colonists

---

of 1773, which the colonials protested at the Boston Tea Party; and finally, and most importantly, the Intolerable Acts of 1774, which closed Boston Harbor until the Crown had been reimbursed for the tea destroyed at the Boston Tea Party, restricted the powers of the Massachusetts legislature, and granted practically dictatorial powers to the new royal governor of Massachusetts, General Thomas Gage, who came to Boston accompanied by additional British redcoats.

[7] EDMUND BURKE, REFLECTIONS ON THE REVOLUTION IN FRANCE, Russell Kirk, ed., New Rochelle, Arlington House, 1965: xii.

In a speech he gave in October 1774 while campaigning for reelection to Parliament, Burke said:

FROM PARLIAMENTARY
CAMPAIGN SPEECH
OCTOBER, 1774

I have held, and ever shall maintain, to the best of my power, unimpaired and undiminished, the just, wise, and necessary constitutional superiority of Great Britain. This is necessary for America as well as for us. . . . But I have ever had a clear opinion, and have ever held a constant correspondent conduct, that this superiority is consistent with all the liberties a sober and spirited American ought to desire. I never mean to put any colonist, or any human creature, in a situation not becoming a free man. To reconcile British superiority with American liberty shall be my great object. . . . I am far from thinking that both, even yet, may not be preserved. . . .

Then on March 22, 1775, Burke rose in Parliament to deliver his celebrated speech on conciliation with the colonies, a brilliantly reasoned criticism of Britain's colonial policy in America.

King George failed to heed Burke's words

Unfortunately for the future of the British Empire, and fortunately for the new American nation, King George failed to heed Burke's words. One month later, the first shots of the

American Revolution were fired at Lexington and Concord. Here are a few excerpts from that speech.

FROM SPEECH ON
CONCILIATION WITH AMERICA
MARCH 22, 1775

Surely it is an awful subject — or there is none so on this side of the grave. When I first had the honor of a seat in this House, the affairs of [America] pressed themselves upon us as the most important and delicate object of parliamentary attention. My little share in this great deliberation oppressed me. I found myself a partaker in a very high trust; and having no sort of reason to rely on the strength of my natural abilities for the proper execution of that trust, I was obliged to take more than common pains to instruct myself in everything which relates to our colonies. I was not less under the necessity of forming some fixed ideas concerning the general policy of the British Empire. . . .

Though I do not hazard anything approaching to a censure on the motives of former Parliaments . . . one fact is undoubted — that under them the state of America has been kept in continual agitation. Everything administered as remedy to the public complaint, if it did not produce, was at least followed by, a heightening of the distemper, until, by a variety of experiments, that important country has been brought into her present situation. . . .

America is an object worth fighting for

America, gentlemen say, is a noble object — it is an object well worth fighting for. Certainly it is, if fighting a people be the best way of gaining them. Gentlemen in this respect will be led to their choice of means by their complexions and their habits. Those who understand the military art will of course have some predilection for it. Those who wield the thunder of the state may have more confidence in the efficacy of arms. But I confess, possibly for want of this knowledge, my opinion is much more in favor of prudent management than of force; considering force not as an odious, but a feeble instrument for preserving a people so numerous, so active, so growing, so spirited as this, in a profitable and subordinate connection with us.

First . . . the use of force alone is but *temporary*. It may subdue for a moment; but it does not remove the necessity of subduing again; and a nation is not governed which is perpetually to be conquered.

My next objection is its *uncertainty*. Terror is not always the effect of force, and an armament is not a victory. If you do not succeed, you are without resource: for, conciliation failing, force remains; but force failing, no further hope of reconciliation is left. Power and authority are sometimes bought by kindness; but they can never be begged as alms by an impoverished and defeated violence.

A further objection to force is that you *impair the object* by your very endeavors to preserve it. The thing you fought for is not the thing which you recover, but depreciated, sunk, wasted, and consumed in the contest. Nothing less will content me than *whole America.* . . .

But there is still [another] consideration concerning this object, which serves to determine my opinion on the sort of policy which ought to be pursued in the management of America . . . I mean its *temper and character.*

In this character of the Americans a love of freedom is the predominating feature which marks and distinguishes the whole. . . . This fierce spirit of liberty is stronger in the English colonies, probably, than in any other people of the earth, and this from a variety of powerful causes. . . .

In America the fierce spirit of liberty is the predominating feature

First, the people of the colonies are descendants of Englishmen. England, Sir, is a nation which still, I hope, respects, and formerly adored, her freedom. The colonists emigrated from you when this part of your character was most predominant; and they took this bias and direction the moment they parted from your hands. They are therefore not only devoted to liberty, but to liberty according to English ideas and on English principles. . . .

The temper and character which prevail in our colonies are, I am afraid, unalterable by any human art. We cannot, I fear, falsify the pedigree of this fierce people, and persuade them that they are not sprung from a nation in whose veins the blood of freedom circulates. The language in which they would hear you tell them this tale would detect the imposition; your speech would betray you. An Englishman is the unfittest person on earth to argue another Englishman into slavery. . . .

My hold of the colonies is in the close affection which grows from common names, from kindred blood, from similar privileges, and equal protection. These are ties which, though light as air, are as strong as links of iron. Let the colonies always keep the idea of their civil rights associated with your government — they will cling and grapple to you, and no force under heaven will be of power to tear them from their allegiance. But let it be once understood that your government may be one thing and their privileges another, that these two things may exist without any mutual relation — the cement is gone, the cohesion is loosened, and everything hastens to decay and dissolution. . . .

Magnanimity in politics is not seldom the truest wisdom; and a great empire and little minds go ill together. . . . We ought to elevate our minds to the greatness of that trust to which the order of Providence has called us. By adverting to the dignity of this high calling, our ancestors have turned a savage wilderness into a glorious empire, and have made the most extensive and the only honorable conquests . . . by promoting the wealth,

A great empire and little minds go ill together

the number, the happiness of the human race. Let us get an American revenue as we have got an American empire. English privileges have made it all that it is; English privileges alone will make it all it can be.

II
WRITINGS FROM THE
COLONIAL AND
REVOLUTIONARY
PERIODS

THE MAYFLOWER
COMPACT
NOVEMBER 11, 1620

In September 1620, the small ship Mayflower sailed from Plymouth, England, bound for the "northern parts of Virginia." On board were 102 passengers — primarily religious pilgrims, along with a few adventurers — who intended to settle under the jurisdiction and laws of the Virginia Company. On November 6, they sighted land far to the north of the region named in their patent, or land grant, that had been bestowed upon them by the Crown. They attempted to sail southward but encountered dangerous waters and finally resolved to enter any safe nearby harbor. On November 21, they cast anchor at Provincetown, Cape Cod, subsequently moving on to Plymouth, Massachusetts.

When the travelers became aware that they would necessarily be settling outside the boundary of Virginia, they also realized that they would have to create a government whose edicts the majority of their members would be willing to enforce. Therefore, before landing at Plymouth, they drew up a compact upon which their community would be based. The signers of the celebrated Mayflower Compact did not intend to create a new kind of constitution; they had no strong democratic inclinations. They were ordinary Englishmen and women, most of them from the lower rungs of society, loyal to their king, materially ambitious, and radical only in their desire to maintain their own unorthodox form of **Circum-** *religious worship. But circumstances forced them* **stances** *to establish a democracy, for the Mayflower Com-* **forced them** *pact was clearly a democratic document, assert-* **to establish** *ing as it did the will of the responsible majority,* **a democracy** *who claimed the right to adopt and administer laws they deemed necessary. Thus, the Mayflower Compact was the first seed of democracy planted on American soil.*

In the name of God, Amen, we whose names are underwritten, the loyal subjects of our dread sovereign lord King James, by the grace of God, of great Britain, France, and Ireland, King, Defender of the Faith, etc.

.   Having undertaken for the glory of God, and advancements of the Christian faith, and honor of our King and country, a voyage to plant the first colony in the northern parts of Virginia, do by these presents, solemnly and mutually in the presence of God, and one another, covenant and combine ourselves together into a civil body politic for our better ordering, and preservation and furtherance of the ends aforesaid; and by virtue hereof to enact, constitute, and frame such just and equal laws, ordinances, acts, constitutions, and offices, from time to time, as shall be thought most meet and convenient for the general good of the colony; unto which we promise all due submission and obedience.

In witness whereof we have hereunto subscribed our names at Cape Cod the eleventh of November, in the reign of our sovereign lord King James of England, France and Ireland, the eighteenth and of Scotland, the fifty-fourth. *Anno Domini*, 1620.

ANDREW HAMILTON

Today when we think about juries at all, many of us think about jury duty, regarding it as a relatively minor but necessary civic responsibility, like stopping for red lights. Others among us look upon it as a boring, unwelcome intrusion into our daily lives. Regrettably, some even go to great lengths to avoid service on a jury panel, concocting creative stories of personal hardship to convince the judge that they should be excused. Not so with colonial Americans, who regarded the jury in quite a different light. They had come to realize that Crown courts without juries, administered by English judges applying English law, were

Crown
courts were
tyrannical
institutions

tyrannical institutions, as was dramatically illustrated in the famous trial of John Peter Zenger.

The Zenger trial is popularly regarded today as one of the building blocks upon which were constructed the freedom of speech and free press clauses of the First Amendment. But less well known, though equally important, is the influence the trial exerted upon the Founding Fathers' vision of the role of the jury in the creation of American freedoms.

Zenger
brought to
trial for the
crime of sedi-
tious libel

Zenger, a relatively unknown printer in New York City, was tried by a jury in 1735 and was acquitted of the crime of seditious libel (meaning the use of language inciting rebellion against the authority of the state). The English law against seditious libel was intended to protect the government from defamation that would threaten public tranquility and security. It was based upon the concept that any publication, whether true or false in its allegations, that contained "written censure upon public men for their conduct as such, or upon the laws, or upon the institutions of the country" and that therefore might bring the government into disrepute, was liable to prosecution.

The English government and its appointed judges in the colonial courts recognized seditious libel as being enforceable in America, and it was under the auspices of this law that Zenger was brought to trial for allegedly defaming the Crown governor of New York, William Cosby, in the pages of Zenger's newspaper, The New York Weekly Journal.

Zenger was represented, brilliantly, by Andrew Hamilton (1676–1741), reputed to be the best lawyer in America. At the trial, when the judge, following the mandate of the English law against seditious libel, refused to allow Hamilton to introduce evidence of the truth of what Zenger had written, Hamilton put the jury, not the judge, at the center of the deliberations. He argued that truth is a defense to libel and that a jury composed of individuals from the neighborhood where the alleged crime occurred was made up of witnesses and was therefore in a better position than the judge to determine the truth of what Zenger had written in his paper.

Hamilton was able to convince a jury of Zenger's peers to disregard governing English law, overrule and nullify the judgment of the Crown-appointed chief justice trying the case, and acquit the defendant — which indeed it did, after deliberating only a few minutes.

Jury nullified the judgment of the Crown

Trial by jury in the manner of the Zenger case was a major departure from English law and custom. And this aspect of the case — the jury as representative of the will of the people — soon became an important theme in national deliberations about the meaning of American freedoms, culminating two generations later in the drafting of our Constitution and Bill of Rights.

When Zenger went before his jury, George

Mason was only ten years old. Madison and Jefferson had not been born. None of the Founding Fathers had yet assessed the central and vital importance of the jury to the establishment and maintenance of American freedoms. No revolution had yet freed the American colonists from England's yoke. But an array of documents published during the years following the trial reveal that Mason, Jefferson, and Madison — in fact, all the Founding Fathers — had Zenger and the importance of a jury very much on their minds.

A leading Antifederalist described jurors as "sentinels and guardians" of "the people." John Adams described the jury as "the voice of the people." The only right guaranteed in all state constitutions written before adoption of the U.S. Constitution was the right of jury trial in all criminal cases. The 1774 Declarations and Resolves of the First Continental Congress[8] stated that "the respective colonies are entitled to . . . the great and inestimable privilege of being tried by their peers of the vicinage [neighborhood]." Our most celebrated document of freedom, the Declaration of Independence[9] condemned George III and Parliament "for depriving us, in many cases, of the benefits of trial by jury."

Today the jury is no longer considered such a major contributor to our civic welfare and the preservation of our freedoms. Times have changed. Laws have changed. Legislatures and

The jury was the representative of the people

8 See page 72.
9 See page 112.

judges have taken away a good deal of the power and majesty that juries in colonial America commanded. But even so, the Zenger case remains an important part of our heritage. It has come to symbolize the idea that personal freedom rests upon the individual's right to criticize his government . . . and that free speech and jury trial are crucial to individual liberty in America.

Freedom rests upon the individual's right to criticize government

FROM ARGUMENT TO THE JURY IN THE TRIAL OF PETER ZENGER AUGUST 4, 1735

Then, gentlemen of the jury, it is to you we must now appeal for witnesses to the truth of the facts we have offered and are denied the liberty to prove; and let it not seem strange that I apply myself to you in this manner, I am warranted to do both by law and reason. The law supposes you to be summoned *out of the neighborhood where the fact is alleged to be committed;* and the reason of your being taken out of the neighborhood is *because you are supposed to have the best knowledge of the fact that is to be tried.* . . . You are citizens of New York; you are really what the law supposes you to be, *honest and lawful men;* and, according to my brief, the facts which we offer to prove were not committed in a corner; they are notoriously known to be true; and therefore in your justice lies our safety. . . .
There is heresy in law as well as in religion,

and both have changed very much; and we well know that it is not two centuries ago that a man would have burned as a heretic for owning such opinions in matters of religion as are publicly written and printed at this day. They were fallible men, it seems, and we take the liberty, not only to differ from them in religious opinion, but to condemn them and their opinions too; and I must presume that in taking these freedoms in thinking and speaking about matters of faith or religion, we are in the right: For, though it is said there are very great liberties of this kind taken in New York, yet I have heard of no information preferred by Mr. Attorney for any offenses of this sort. From which I think it is pretty clear that in New York a man may make very free with his God, but he must take special care what he says of his Governor. It is agreed upon by all men that this is a reign of liberty, and while men keep within the bounds of truth, I hope they may with safety both speak and write their sentiments of the conduct of men of power; I mean of that part of their conduct only which affects the liberty or property of the people under their administration; were this to be denied, then the next step may make them slaves: For what notions can be entertained of slavery beyond that of suffering the greatest injuries and oppressions without the liberty of complaining; or if they do, to be destroyed, body and estate, for so doing?

It is said, and insisted upon by Mr. Attorney,

I hope men may with safety both speak and write the truth

*that government is a sacred thing; that it is to be
supported and reverenced; it is government that
protects our persons and estates; that prevents
treasons, murders, robberies, riots, and all the
train of evils that overturns kingdoms and states
and ruins particular persons; and if those in the
administration, especially the supreme magistrate, must have all their conduct censured by
private men, government cannot subsist.* This is
called *a licentiousness not to be tolerated.* It is
said *that it brings the rulers of the people into
contempt, and their authority not to be regarded,
and so in the end the laws cannot be put in execution.* These, I say, and such as these, are the
general topics insisted upon by men in power and
their advocates. But I wish it might be considered
at the same time how often it has happened that
the abuse of power has been the primary cause
of these evils, and that it was the injustice and
oppression of these great men which has commonly brought them into contempt with the people. The craft and art of such men is great, and
who that is the least acquainted with history or
with law can be ignorant of the specious preten-
ses which have often been made use of by men in
power to introduce arbitrary rule and destroy the
liberties of a free people. . . .

Abuse of power has been the primary cause of these evils

If a libel is understood in the large and unlimited sense urged by Mr. Attorney, there is scarce
a writing I know that may not be called a libel,
or scarce any person safe from being called to

account as a libeler: For Moses, meek as he was, libeled Cain; and who is it that has not libeled the Devil? For according to Mr. Attorney, it is no justification to say one has a bad name. . . . How must a man speak or write, or what must he hear, read, or sing? Or when must he laugh, so as to be secure from being taken up as a libeler? I sincerely believe that were some persons to go through the streets of New York nowadays and read a part of the Bible, if it were not known to be such, Mr. Attorney, with the help of his *innuendo*es, would easily turn it into a libel. As for instance: *Is. IX. 16, The leaders of the people cause them to err, and they that are led by them are destroyed*. But should Mr. Attorney go about to make this a libel, he would read it thus: *The leaders of the people [innuendo,* the Governor and Council of New York] *cause them (innuendo,* the people of this province) *to err, and they* [the people of this Province meaning] *that are led by them* [the Governor and council meaning] *are destroyed [innuendo,* are deceived into the loss of their liberty] which is the worst kind of destruction. . . .

Then if Mr. Attorney is at liberty to come into court, and file an information in the King's name without leave, who is secure whom he is pleased to prosecute as a libeler? And as the Crown law is contended for in bad times, there is no remedy for the greatest oppression of this sort, even though the party prosecuted is acquitted with honor. . . .

There is no remedy for the greatest oppression of this sort

Gentlemen; the danger is great in proportion to the mischief that may happen through our too great credulity. A proper confidence in a court is commendable; but as the verdict (whatever it is) will be yours, you ought to refer no part of your duty to the discretion of other persons. If you should be of opinion that there is no falsehood in Mr. Zenger's papers, you will, nay (pardon me for the expression) you ought to say so; because you don't know whether others (I mean the Court) may be of that opinion. It is your right to do so, and there is much depending upon your resolution as well as upon your integrity.

The loss of liberty to a generous mind is worse than death; and yet we know there have been those in all ages who for the sakes of preferment or some imaginary honor have freely lent a helping hand to oppress, nay, to destroy their country. This brings to my mind that saying of the immortal Brutus, when he looked upon the creatures of Caesar, who were very great men but by no means good men: "You Romans," said Brutus, "if yet I may call you so, consider what you are doing; remember that you are assisting Caesar to forge those very chains which one day he will make yourselves wear." This is what every man (that values freedom) ought to consider: He should act by judgment and not by affection or self-interest; for, where those prevail, no ties of either country or kindred are regarded, as, upon the other hand the man who loves his country prefers its liberty to all other considerations, well

The loss of liberty to a generous mind is worse than death

knowing that without liberty life is a misery. . . .

Power may justly be compared to a great river; while kept within its due bounds, is both beautiful and useful; but when it overflows its banks, it is then too impetuous to be stemmed, it bears down all before it and brings destruction and desolation wherever it comes. If, then this be the nature of power, let us at least do our duty, and like wise men (who value freedom) use our utmost care to support liberty, the only bulwark against lawless power, which in all ages has sacrificed to its wild lust and boundless ambition the blood of the best men that ever lived.

Let us use our utmost care to support liberty; the only bulwark against lawless power

I hope to be pardoned, sir, for my zeal upon this occasion; it is an old and wise caution *that when our neighbor's house is on fire, we ought to take care of our own.* For though blessed be God, I live in a government where liberty is well understood and freely enjoyed; yet experience has shown us all (I'm sure it has to me) that a bad precedent in one government is soon set up for an authority in another; and therefore I cannot but think it mine and every honest man's duty that (while we pay all due obedience to men in authority) we ought at the same time to be upon our guard against power wherever we apprehend that it may affect ourselves or our fellow subjects.

I am truly very unequal to such an undertaking on many accounts. And you see I labor under the weight of many years, and am borne down

with great infirmities of body; yet old and weak as
I am, I should think it my duty, if required, to go
to the utmost part of the land where my service
could be of any use in assisting to quench the
flame of prosecutions upon informations set on
foot by the government to deprive a people of the
right of remonstrating (and complaining too) of
the arbitrary attempts of men in power. Men who
injure and oppress the people under their administration provoke them to cry out and complain;
and then make that very complaint the foundation for new oppressions and prosecutions. I wish
I could say there were no instances of this kind.
But to conclude; the question before the Court
and you gentlemen of the jury is not of small nor
private concern, it is not the cause of a poor printer, nor, of New York alone, which you are now trying: No! It may in its consequence affect every
freeman that lives under a British government on
the main of America. It is the best cause. It is the
cause of liberty; and I make no doubt but your
upright conduct this day will not only entitle you
to the love and esteem of your fellow citizens; but
every man who prefers freedom to a life of slavery
will bless and honor you as men who have baffled
the attempt of tyranny; and by an impartial and
uncorrupt verdict, have laid a noble foundation
for securing to ourselves, our posterity, and our
neighbors that to which nature and the laws of our
country have given us a right — the liberty —

Your conduct this day will have laid a noble foundation

both of exposing and opposing arbitrary power (in these parts of the world, at least) by speaking and writing truth. . . .

JAMES OTIS

James Otis (1725–1783) was a classical scholar, an attorney, and an expert in political theory. In 1754 he was named to the post of king's attorney, and subsequently appointed advocate general of the vice-admiralty court in Boston. Therefore, when in 1760 English customs collectors applied to the superior court for writs of assistance[10] to search homes and shops for smuggled goods, it was Otis's duty to argue for the writs. Instead, he resigned his office and argued for the homeowners and merchants. The basis of his argument was that natural law is superior to acts of Parliament, and this was the doctrine that the political agitators of the period thereafter employed to justify the break with England. The case was decided against Otis, yet he continued to quarrel with the king's governors, becoming increasingly active and vehement in defense of the American colonies and publishing pamphlets that are now regarded as among the best political writings of the colonial period.

[10] Writs of assistance were general search warrants that permitted customs officers to enter premises in the daytime, using force if necessary, to search for goods imported illegally.

The controversy over such writs led to the prohibition of general warrants in the Fourth Amendment to the Constitution.

FROM ARGUMENT AGAINST WRITS OF ASSISTANCE
FEBRUARY 24, 1761

May it please your honors, I was desired by one of the court to look into the books, and consider the question now before them concerning writs of assistance. I have, accordingly, considered it, and now appear not only in obedience to your order, but likewise in behalf of the inhabitants of this town, who have presented another petition, and out of regard to the liberties of the subject. And I take this opportunity to declare that, whether under a fee or not (for in such a cause as this I despise a fee), I will to my dying day oppose with all the powers and faculties God has given me all such instruments of slavery, on the one hand, and villainy, on the other, as this writ of assistance is.

It appears to me the worst instrument of arbitrary power, the most destructive of English liberty and the fundamental principles of law, that ever was found in an English lawbook. . . .

In the first place, may it please your Honors, I will admit that writs of one kind may be legal; that is, special writs, directed to special officers, and to search certain house, etc. especially set forth in the writ, may be granted by the Court of Exchequer at home, upon oath made before the Lord Treasurer by the person who asks it, that he suspects such goods to be concealed in those very places he desires to search. The act of 14 Charles II . . . proves this. And in this light the writ appears like a warrant from a Justice of the Peace to search for stolen goods.

Your honors will find in the old books concerning the office of a justice of the peace precedents of general warrants to search suspected houses. But in more modern books you will find only special warrants to search such and such houses, specially named, in which the complainant has before sworn that he suspects his goods are concealed; and will find it adjudged that special warrants only are legal. In the same manner I rely on it that the writ prayed for in this petition, being general, is illegal. It is a power that places the liberty of every man in the hands of every petty officer. I say I admit that special writs of assistance, to search special places, may be granted to certain persons on oath; but I deny that the writ now prayed for can be granted, for I beg leave to make some observations on the writ itself, before I proceed to other acts of Parliament. In the first place, the writ is universal, being directed "to all and singular Justices, Sheriffs, Constables, and all other officers and subjects"; so that, in short, it is directed to every subject in the King's dominions. **Everyone with this writ** Everyone with this writ may be a tyrant; if this **may be a** commission be legal, a tyrant in a legal manner **tyrant** also may control, imprison, or murder anyone within the realm. In the next place, it is perpetual; there is no return. A man is accountable to no

person for his doings. Every man may reign
secure in his petty tyranny, and spread terror and
desolation around him. In the third place, a person with this writ, in the daytime, may enter all
houses, shops, etc. at will, and command all to
assist him. Fourthly, by this writ, not only
deputies, etc. but even their menial servants, are
allowed to lord it over us. Now, one of the most
essential branches of English liberty is the freedom of one's house. A man's house is his castle; **A man's**
and whilst he is quiet, he is as well guarded as **house is his**
a prince in his castle. This writ, if it should be **castle**
declared legal, would totally annihilate this privilege. Custom-house officers may enter our houses when they please; we are commanded to permit their entry. Their menial servants may enter,
may break locks, bars, and everything in their
way; and whether they break through malice or
revenge, no man, no court, can inquire. Bare suspicion without oath is sufficient. This wanton
exercise of this power is not a chimerical suggestion of a heated brain. I will mention some facts.
Mr. Pew had one of these writs, and when Mr.
Ware succeeded him, he indorsed this writ over to
Mr. Ware; so that these writs are negotiable from
one officer to another; and so your honors have no
opportunity of judging the persons to whom this
vast power is delegated. Another instance is this:
Mr. Justice Walley had called this same Mr. Ware
before him, by a constable, to answer for a breach
of the Sabbath-day Acts, or that of profane swear-

ing. As soon as he had finished, Mr. Ware asked him if he had done. He replied, "Yes." "Well, then," said Mr. Ware, "I will show you a little of my power. I command you to permit me to search your house for uncustomed goods; and went on to search the house from the garret to the cellar, and then served the constable in the same manner. But to show another absurdity in this writ; if it should be established, I insist upon it, every person, by the 14 Charles II, has this power as well as the custom-house officers. The words are, "It shall be lawful for any person or persons authorized," etc. What a scene does this open! Every man, prompted by revenge, ill humor, or wantonness, to inspect the inside of his neighbor's house, may get a writ of assistance. Others will ask it from self-defence; one arbitrary exertion will provoke another, until society be involved in tumult and in blood. . . .

SAMUEL ADAMS

Samuel Adams (1722–1803) was educated at Harvard and for a short time studied law. He entered local politics and was appointed tax collector for the town of Boston. Adams soon became recognized for his writing skills, and in 1764 he was selected to draft the instructions of the town to its representatives in the General Court. It was a startling document: Adams at-

tacked the Stamp Act, suggested the principle of
"no taxation without representation," and hinted
at a union of the colonies. With this writing, he
became famous and a new career was opened to
him. From then on, a steady stream of fiery arti-
cles poured from his pen. In his own day, Adams
was called an "incendiary." He advocated not
only "that the sovereign people have a right to
change their fundamental law . . . whenever they
desire," but also that one should appeal directly
to the people to do the changing. Through his
inflammatory manifestos, articles, letters, and
pamphlets, he likely did more than any other
man to prepare the masses for the Revolution. A
typical Adams manifesto of freedom is his "The
Rights of the Colonists."

*"No taxation
without rep-
resentation"*

FROM "THE RIGHTS OF THE COLONISTS"
1772

Among the natural rights of the colonists are
these: first, a right to *life*; secondly to *liberty*;
thirdly to *property*; together with the right to support and defend them in the best manner they
can. — Those are evident branches of, rather
than deductions from, the duty of self preservation, commonly called the first law of nature.

All men have a right to remain in a state of
nature as long as they please; and in case of intol-

erable oppression, civil or religious, to leave the society they belong to and enter into another.

When men enter into society, it is by voluntary consent; and they have a right to demand and insist upon the performance of such conditions and previous limitations as form an equitable *original compact.*

Every natural right not expressly given up or from the nature of a social compact necessarily ceded remains.

All positive and civil laws should conform to the law of natural reason and equity

All positive and civil laws should conform as far as possible to the law of natural reason and equity.

As neither reason requires nor religion permits the contrary, every man living in or out of a state of civil society has a right peaceably and quietly to worship God according to the dictates of his conscience.

"Just and true liberty, equal and impartial liberty" in matters spiritual and temporal, is a thing that all men are clearly entitled to, by the eternal and immutable laws of God and nature, as well as by the law of nations, and all well-grounded municipal laws, which must have their foundation in the former.

In regard to religion, mutual toleration in the different professions thereof is what all good and candid minds in all ages have ever practiced, and both by precept and example inculcated on mankind; and it is now generally agreed among Christians that this spirit of toleration in the fullest extent consistent with the being of civil society "is the chief characteristical mark of the true church" and in so much that Mr. Locke has asserted, and proved beyond the possibility of contradiction on any solid ground, that such toleration ought to be extended to all whose doctrines are not subversive of society. The only sects which he thinks ought to be and which by all wise laws are excluded from such toleration are those who teach doctrines subversive of the civil government under which they live. . . .

The natural liberty of men by entering into society is abridged or restrained so far only as is necessary for the great end of society, the best good of the whole.

In the state of nature every man is, under God, judge and sole judge of his own rights and the injuries done him. By entering into society he agrees to an arbiter or indifferent judge between him and his neighbors; but he no more renounces his original right than by taking a cause out of the ordinary course of law and leaving the decision to referees or indifferent arbitrations. In the last case he must pay the referees for time and trouble; he should be also willing to pay his just quota for the support of government, the law and constitution, the end of which is to furnish indifferent and impartial judges in all cases that may happen, whether civil, ecclesiastical, marine, or military.

In the state of nature every man is sole judge of his own rights

"The natural liberty of man is to be free from

The natural liberty of man is to be free from any superior power

any superior power on earth, and not to be under the will or legislative authority of man; but only to have the law of nature for his rule."

In the state of nature men may, as the patriarchs did, employ hired servants for the defense of their lives, liberty, and property; and they should pay them reasonable wages. Government was instituted for the purposes of common defense; and those who hold the reins of government have an equitable natural right to an honorable support from the same principle "that the laborer is worthy of his hire"; but then the same community which they serve ought to be assessors of their pay: governors have no right to seek what they please; by this, instead of being content with the station assigned them, that of honorable servants of the society, they would soon become absolute masters, despots, and tyrants. Hence, as a private man has a right to say what wages he will give in his private affairs, so has a community to determine what they will give and grant of their substance for the administration of public affairs. And in both cases more are ready generally to offer their service at the proposed and stipulated price than are able and willing to perform their duty.

In short, it is the greatest absurdity to suppose it is in the power of one or any number of men at the entering into society to renounce their essential natural rights, or the means of preserving

those rights when the great end of civil government from the very nature of its institution is for
the support, protection, and defense of those very
rights, the principal of which, as is before observed, are life, liberty, and property. If men
through fear, fraud, or mistake should *in terms* renounce and give up any essential natural right,
the eternal law of reason and the great end of society would absolutely vacate such renunciation;
the right to freedom being *the gift* of God Almighty, it is not in the power of man to alienate this gift
and voluntarily become a slave.

2nd. *The Rights of the Colonists as Christians.*
These may be best understood by reading, and
carefully studying, the institutes of the great Lawgiver and head of the Christian Church, which are
to be found closely written and promulgated in
the New Testament.

By the act of the British Parliament commonly called the Toleration Act, every subject in England except papists and etc. was restored to, and
re-established in, his natural right to worship God
according to the dictates of his own conscience.
And by the Charter of this province it is granted,
ordained, and established (that it is declared as an
original right) that there shall be liberty of conscience allowed in the worship of God to all Christians except papists inhabiting or which shall
inhabit or be resident within said province or ter-

ritory. Magna Charta itself is in substance but a constrained declaration, or proclamation, and promulgation in the name of King, Lords, and Commons of the sense the latter had of their original inherent, indefeasible natural rights, as also those of free citizens equally perdurable [permanent] with the other. That great author, that great jurist, and even that court writer Mr. Justice Blackstone holds that this recognition was justly obtained of King John sword in hand; and peradventure it must be one day sword in hand again rescued and preserved from total destruction and oblivion.

3rd. *The Rights of the Colonists as Subjects.*
A commonwealth or state is a body politic or civil society of men united together to promote their mutual safety and prosperity by means of their union.

The *absolute rights* of Englishmen, and all freemen in or out of civil society, are principally: *personal security, personal liberty,* and *private property.*

All persons born in the British American colonies are by the laws of God and nature, and by the common law of England, exclusive of all charters from the crown, well entitled, and by the acts of the British Parliament are declared to be entitled to all the natural essential, inherent, and inseparable rights, liberties, and privileges of subjects born in Great Britain or within the

All American colonists are entitled to the rights of persons born in Great Britain realm. Among those rights are the following, which no men or body of men, consistently with their own rights as men and citizens or members of society, can for themselves give up or take away from others:

First, "the first fundamental positive law of all commonwealths or states is the establishing the legislative power; as the first fundamental *natural* law also, which is to govern even the legislative power itself, is the preservation of the society."[11]

Secondly, the legislative has no right to absolute arbitrary power over the lives and fortunes of the people; nor can mortals assume a prerogative, not only too high for men, but for angels, and therefore reserved for the exercise of the Deity alone.

"The legislative cannot justly *assume* to itself a power to rule by extempore arbitrary decrees; but it is bound to see that justice is dispensed, and that the rights of the subjects be decided by promulgated, standing, and known laws and authorized *independent judges"*; that is, independent as far as possible of prince or people. *"There shall be one rule of justice for rich and poor; for the favorite in court and the countryman at the plough."*[12]

There shall be one rule of justice for rich and poor

Thirdly, the supreme power cannot justly take

[11] Locke
[12] id.

from any man any part of his property without his consent, in person or by his representative.

These are some of the first principles of natural law and justice, and the great barriers of all free states, and of the British Constitution in particular. It is utterly irreconcilable to these principles, and to many other fundamental maxims of the common law, common sense, and reason, that a British House of Commons should have a right, at pleasure, to give and grant the property of the colonists. That these colonists are well entitled to all the essential rights, liberties, and privileges of men and freemen born in Britain is manifest, not only from the colony Charter, in general, but acts of the British Parliament. The statute of the 13th of George 2.c.7. naturalizes even foreigners after seven years' residence. The words of the Massachusetts Charter are these: "And further our will and pleasure is, and we do hereby for us, our heirs and successors, grant, establish, and ordain, that all and every of the subjects of us, our heirs and successors which shall go to and inhabit within our said province or territory and every of their children which shall happen to be born there, or on the seas in going thither, or returning from thence shall have and enjoy all liberties and immunities of free and natural subjects within any of the dominions of us, our heirs and successors, to all intents, constructions, and purposes whatsoever as if they and every of them were born within

this our realm of England." Now, what liberty can
there be where property is taken away without
consent? Can it be said with any color of truth and
justice that this continent of three thousand miles
in length, and of a breadth as yet unexplored, in
which, however, it's supposed there are five millions of people, has the least voice, vote, or influence in the decisions of the British Parliament?
Have they, all together, any more right or power
to return a single member to that House of Commons, who have not inadvertently but deliberately assumed a power to dispose of their lives, liberties, and properties, than to choose an emperor
of China! Had the colonists a right to return members to the British Parliament, it would only be
hurtful, as from their local situation and circumstances it is impossible they should be ever truly
and properly represented there. The inhabitants
of this country in all probability in a few years will
be more numerous than those of Great Britain
and Ireland together; yet it is absurdly expected
by the promoters of the present measures that
these, with their posterity to all generations,
should be easy while their property shall be disposed of by a House of Commons at three thousand miles distant from them, and who cannot be
supposed to have the least care or concern for
their real interest; who have not only no natural
care for their interest, but must be in *effect* bribed
against it, as every burden they lay on the

What
liberty
can there
be where
property
is taken
away
without
consent?

colonists is so much saved or gained to themselves. . . . How long such treatment will or ought to be borne is submitted.

JOHN ADAMS

John Adams (1735–1826) — first vice president and second president of the United States, delegate to the First and Second Continental Congresses, co-author with Thomas Jefferson of the Declaration of Independence, father of the sixth president and grandfather of the American minister to England during the Civil War — made the name of Adams one of the most important in American history. After graduating from Harvard in 1755, he studied law for three years and was admitted to the bar. He began to build up a law practice and became interested in Boston affairs, contributing articles on current problems to the local newspapers. Adams was a rigid conservative and an aristocrat. Thus, although he was reluctant to accept a complete break with England and its traditions, and although he was generally opposed to action by masses of the people, when the Revolution came he did not hesitate to join the American cause.

In 1765, he published "A Dissertation on the Canon and Feudal Law." The work was distinguished by superior scholarship and eloquent, forceful prose expressing the advanced, middleclass thought of the day.

FROM *A DISSERTATION ON THE CANON*
AND FEUDAL LAW
AUGUST 12, 1765

"Ignorance and inconsideration are the two great causes of the ruin of mankind." This is an observation of Dr. Tillotson, with relation to the interest of his fellow men in a future and immortal state. But it is of equal truth and importance if applied to the happiness of men in society, on this side of the grave. In the earliest ages of the world, absolute monarchy seems to have been the universal form of government. Kings, and a few of their great counselors and captains, exercised a cruel tyranny over the people, who held a rank in the scale of intelligence, in those days, but little higher than the camels and elephants that carried them and their engines to war.

By what causes it was brought to pass that the people in the Middle Ages became more intelligent in general would not, perhaps, be possible in these days to discover. But the fact is certain; and wherever a general knowledge and sensibility have prevailed among the people, arbitrary government and every kind of oppression have lessened and disappeared in proportion. Man has certainly an exalted soul; and the same principle in human nature — that aspiring, noble principle founded in benevolence, and cherished by knowledge; I mean the love of power, which has been so often the cause of slavery — has, whenever free-

The love of power has often been the cause of slavery

dom has existed, been the cause of freedom. If it is this principle that has always prompted the princes and nobles of the earth by every species of fraud and violence to shake off all the limitations of their power, it is the same that has always stimulated the common people to aspire at independency, and to endeavor at confining the power of the great within the limits of equity and reason.

The poor people, it is true, have been much less successful than the great. They have seldom found either leisure or opportunity to form a union and exert their strength; ignorant as they were of arts and letters, they have seldom been able to frame and support a regular opposition. This, however, has been known by the great to be the temper of mankind; and they have accordingly labored, in all ages, to wrest from the populace, as they are contemptuously called, the knowledge of their rights and wrongs, and the power to assert the former or redress the latter. I say RIGHTS, for such they have, undoubtedly, antecedent to all earthly government — *rights* that cannot be repealed or restrained by human laws — *rights* derived from the great Legislator of the universe.

The two greatest systems of tyranny are the canon and the feudal law

Since the promulgation of Christianity, the two greatest systems of tyranny that have sprung from this original are the canon and the feudal law. The desire of dominion, that great principle by which we have attempted to account for so much good and so much evil, is, when properly restrained, a very useful and noble movement in the human mind. But when such restraints are taken off, it becomes an encroaching, grasping, restless, and ungovernable power. Numberless have been the systems of iniquity contrived by the great for the gratification of this passion in themselves; but in none of them were they ever more successful than in the invention and establishment of the canon and the feudal law.

By the former of these [the canon law], the most refined, sublime, extensive, and astonishing constitution of policy that ever was conceived by the mind of man was framed by the Romish clergy for the aggrandizement of their own order. All the epithets I have here given to the Romish policy are just, and will be allowed to be so when it is considered that they even persuaded mankind to believe, faithfully and undoubtingly, that God Almighty had entrusted them with the keys of heaven, whose gates they might open and close at pleasure; with a power of dispensation over all the rules and obligations of morality; with authority to license all sorts of sins and crimes; with a power of deposing princes and absolving subjects from allegiance; with a power of procuring or withholding the rain of heaven and the beams of the sun; with the management of earthquakes, pestilence, and famine; nay, with the mysterious, awful, incomprehensible power of creating out of bread and wine the flesh and blood of God himself. All these opinions they were enabled to spread and rivet among the people by reducing their minds to a state of sordid ignorance and staring timidity, and by infusing into them a religious horror of letters

Human nature was chained fast for ages in servitude

and knowledge. Thus was human nature chained fast for ages in a cruel, shameful, and deplorable servitude to him and his subordinate tyrants, who, it was foretold, would exalt himself above all that was called God and that was worshipped.

In the latter [the feudal law] we find another system, similar in many respects to the former; which, although it was originally formed, perhaps, for the necessary defense of a barbarous people against the inroads and invasions of her neighboring nations, yet for the same purposes of tyranny, cruelty, and lust which had dictated the canon law, it was soon adopted by almost all the princes of Europe and wrought into the constitutions of their government. It was originally a code of laws for a vast army in a perpetual encampment. The general was invested with the sovereign propriety of all the lands within the territory. Of him, as his servants and vassals, the first rank of his great officers held the lands; and in the same manner the other subordinate officers held of them; and all ranks and degrees held their lands by a variety of duties and services, all tending to bind the chains the faster on every order of mankind. In this manner the common people were held together in herds and clans in a state of servile dependence on their lords, bound, even by the tenure of their lands, to follow them, whenever they commanded, to their wars, and in a state of total ignorance of everything divine and human excepting the use of arms and the culture of their lands.

But another event still more calamitous to human liberty was a wicked confederacy between the two systems of tyranny above described. It seems to have been even stipulated between them that the temporal grandees should contribute everything in their power to maintain the ascendancy of the priesthood, and that the spiritual grandees in their turn should employ their ascendancy over the consciences of the people, in impressing on their minds a blind, implicit obedience to civil magistracy.

A wicked confederacy between two systems of tyranny

Thus, as long as this confederacy lasted and the people were held in ignorance, liberty, and, with her, knowledge and virtue too, seem to have deserted the earth, and one age of darkness succeeded another, till God in his benign providence raised up the champions who began and conducted the Reformation. From the time of the Reformation to the first settlement of America, knowledge gradually spread in Europe, but especially in England; and in proportion as that increased and spread among the people, ecclesiastical and civil tyranny, which I use as synonymous expressions for the canon and feudal laws, seem to have lost their strength and weight. The people grew more and more sensible of the wrong that was done them by these systems, more and more impatient under it, and determined at all hazards to rid themselves of it; till at last, under the execrable race of the Stuarts, the struggle between the people and the confederacy aforesaid of temporal and spiritual tyranny became formidable, violent, and bloody.

It was this great struggle that peopled America. It was not religion alone, as is commonly supposed; but it was a love of universal liberty, and a hatred, a dread, a horror, of the infernal confederacy before described, that projected, conducted, and accomplished the settlement of America.

It was a resolution formed by a sensible people — I mean the Puritans — almost in despair. They had become intelligent in general, and many of them learned. . . . They saw clearly that of all the nonsense and delusion which had ever passed through the mind of man, none had ever been more extravagant than the notions of absolutions, indelible characters, uninterrupted successions, and the rest of those fantastical ideas, derived from the canon law, which had thrown such a glare of mystery, sanctity, reverence, and right reverend eminence and holiness around the idea of a priest as no mortal could deserve, and as always must, from the constitution of human nature, be dangerous in society. For this reason they demolished the whole system of diocesan episcopacy; and, deriding, as all reasonable and impartial men must do, the ridiculous fancies of sanctified effluvia from episcopal fingers, they

The Puritans saw clearly that non- sense and delusion derived from the canon law

established sacerdotal ordination on the foundation of the Bible and common sense. This conduct at once imposed an obligation on the whole body of the clergy to industry, virtue, piety, and learning, and rendered that whole body infinitely more independent of the civil powers, in all respects, than they could be where they were formed into a scale of subordination, from a pope down to priests and friars and confessors — necessarily and essentially a sordid, stupid, and wretched herd — or than they could be in any other country where an archbishop held the place of a universal bishop, and the vicars and curates that of the ignorant, dependent, miserable rabble aforesaid — and infinitely more sensible and learned than they could be in either. . . . They knew that government was a plain, simple, intelligible thing, founded in nature and reason, and quite comprehensible by common sense. They detested all the base services and servile dependencies of the feudal system. They knew that no such unworthy dependencies took place in the ancient seats of liberty, the republics of Greece and Rome; and they thought all such slavish subordinations were equally inconsistent with the constitution of human nature and that religious liberty with which Jesus had made them free. This was certainly the opinion they had formed; and they were far from being singular or extravagant in thinking so. . . .

They knew that government was a plain and simple thing

They were convinced, by their knowledge of human nature, derived from history and their own experience, that nothing could preserve their posterity from the encroachments of the two systems of tyranny, in opposition to which, as has been observed already, they erected their government in church and state, but knowledge diffused generally through the whole body of the people. Their civil and religious principles, therefore, conspired to prompt them to use every measure and take every precaution in their power to propagate and perpetuate knowledge. For this purpose they laid very early the foundations of colleges and invested them with ample privileges and emoluments; and it is remarkable that they have left among their posterity so universal an affection and veneration for those seminaries, and for liberal education, that the meanest of the people contribute cheerfully to the support and maintenance of them every year, and that nothing is more generally popular than projections for the honor, reputation, and advantage of those seats of learning. But the wisdom and benevolence of our fathers rested not here. They made an early provision by law that every town consisting of so many families should be always furnished with a grammar school. They made it a crime for such a town to be destitute of a grammar schoolmaster for a few months, and subjected it to a heavy penalty. So that the education of all ranks of people was made the care and expense of the public, in a manner that I believe has been unknown to any other people ancient or modern. . . .

[For] liberty cannot be preserved without a

general knowledge among the people, who have a right, from the frame of their nature, to knowledge, as their great Creator, who does nothing in vain, has given them understandings, and a desire to know; but besides this, they have a right, an indisputable unalienable, indefeasible, divine right to that most dreaded and envied kind of knowledge; I mean, of the characters and conduct of their rulers. Rulers are no more than attorneys, agents, and trustees, for the people; and if the cause, the interest and trust, is insidiously betrayed, or wantonly trifled away, the people have a right to revoke the authority that they themselves have deputed, and to constitute abler and better agents, attorneys, and trustees. And the preservation of the means of knowledge among the lowest ranks is of more importance to the public than all the property of all the rich men in the country. It is even of more consequence to the rich themselves, and to their posterity. . . . But none of the means of information are more sacred, or have been cherished with more tenderness and care by the settlers of America, than the press. Care has been taken that the art of printing should be encouraged, and that it should be easy and cheap and safe for any person to communicate his thoughts to the public. . . .

Let us dare to read, think, speak, and write. Let every order and degree among the people rouse their attention and animate their resolution. Let them all become attentive to the grounds and principles of government, ecclesiastical and civil.

Let us dare to read, think, speak, and write

Let us study the law of nature; search into the spirit of the British Constitution; read the histories of ancient ages; contemplate the great examples of Greece and Rome; set before us the conduct of our own British ancestors, who have defended for us the inherent rights of mankind against foreign and domestic tyrants and usurpers, against arbitrary kings and cruel priests; in short, against the gates of earth and hell. Let us read and recollect and impress upon our souls the views and ends of our own more immediate forefathers in exchanging their native country for a dreary, inhospitable wilderness. Let us examine into the nature of that power, and the cruelty of that oppression, which drove them from their homes. Recollect their amazing fortitude, their bitter sufferings — the hunger, the nakedness, the cold, which they patiently endured — the severe labors of clearing their grounds, building their houses, raising their provisions, amidst dangers from wild beasts and savage men, before they had time or money or materials for commerce. Recollect the civil and religious principles and hopes and expectations which constantly supported and carried them through all hardships with patience and resignation. Let us recollect it was liberty, the hope of liberty for themselves and us and ours, which conquered all discouragements, dangers, and trials. In such researches as these let us all in our several

Liberty conquered all discouragements, dangers, and trials

departments cheerfully engage — but especially the proper patrons and supporters of law, learning, and religion!

Let the pulpit resound with the doctrines and sentiments of religious liberty. . . .

Let the bar proclaim "the laws, the rights, the generous plan of power" delivered down from remote antiquity — inform the world of the mighty struggles and numberless sacrifices made by our ancestors in defense of freedom. . . .

Let the colleges join their harmony in the same delightful concert. . . .

In a word, let every sluice of knowledge be opened and set a-flowing, The encroachments upon liberty in the reigns of the first James and the first Charles, by turning the general attention of learned men to government, are said to have produced the greatest number of consummate statesmen which has ever been seen in any age or nation. The Brookes, Hampdens, Vanes, Seldens, Miltons, Nedhams, Harringtons, Nevilles, Sidneys, Lockes, are all said to have owed their eminence in political knowledge to the tyrannies of those reigns. The prospect now before us in America ought in the same manner to engage the attention of every man of learning to matters of power and of right, that we may be neither led nor driven blindfold to irretrievable destruction. . . .

DECLARATIONS AND RESOLVES OF THE FIRST CONTINENTAL CONGRESS OCTOBER 14, 1774

In September 1774, in response to growing British oppression throughout the colonies, delegates from all the states gathered in Philadelphia and convened the First Continental Congress. On October 14, they approved and adopted the Declarations and Resolves of the First Continental Congress. This document based the rights of the colonists not only upon the principles of English constitutional law and the colonial charters, but also upon the law of nature. It cited a number of acts instituted by Parliament over the previous ten years that had violated these principles. It condemned standing armies. It reiterated that Americans were entitled to all English liberties, including no taxation without representation, the right of trial by jury, and the freedom to petition the king and Parliament for the redress of grievances. It was one of the most important forerunners of the Declaration of Independence and the revolutionary declarations (or bills of rights) and constitutions that the states adopted in the period 1776 to 1787.

An important forerunner of the Declaration of Independence

Whereas, since the close of the last war, the British parliament, claiming a power, of right, to bind the people of America by statutes in all cases whatsoever, hath, in some acts, expressly imposed taxes on them, and in others, under various pretences, but in fact for the purpose of raising a revenue, hath imposed rates and duties payable in these colonies, established a board of commissioners, with unconstitutional powers, and extended the jurisdiction of courts of admiralty, not only for collecting the said duties, but for the trial of causes merely arising within the body of a county.

And whereas, in consequence of other statutes, judges, who before held only estates at will in their offices, have been made dependant on the crown alone for their salaries, and standing armies kept in times of peace: And whereas it has lately been resolved in parliament, that by force of a statute, made in the thirty-fifth year of the reign of King Henry the Eighth, colonists may be transported to England, and tried there upon accusations for treasons and misprisions, or concealments of treasons committed in the colonies, and by a late statute, such trials have been directed in cases therein mentioned:

And whereas, in the last session of parliament, three statutes were made; one entitled, "An act to discontinue, in such manner and for such time as are therein mentioned, the landing and discharging, lading, or shipping of goods, wares and merchandise, at the town, and within the harbour of Boston, in the province of Massachusetts-Bay in North-America;" another entitled, "An act for the better regulating the government of the province

of Massachusetts-Bay in New England;" and
another entitled, "An act for the impartial administration of justice, in the cases of persons questioned for any act done by them in the execution
of the law, or for the suppression of riots and
tumults, in the province of the Massachusetts-
Bay in New England;" and another statute was
then made, "for making more effectual provision
for the government of the province of Quebec,
etc." All which statutes are impolitic, unjust, and
cruel, as well as unconstitutional, and most dangerous and destructive of American rights:

Parliament's
statutes are
impolitic,
unjust, and
cruel

And whereas, assemblies have been frequently dissolved, contrary to the rights of the people,
when they attempted to deliberate on grievances;
and their dutiful, humble, loyal, and reasonable
petitions to the crown for redress, have been
repeatedly treated with contempt, by his Majesty's ministers of state:

The good people of the several colonies of
New-Hampshire, Massachusetts-Bay, Rhode-
Island and Providence Plantations, Connecticut,
New-York, New-Jersey, Pennsylvania, Newcas-
tle, Kent, and Sussex on Delaware, Maryland,
Virginia, North-Carolina, and South-Carolina,
justly alarmed at these arbitrary proceedings of
parliament and administration, have severally
elected, constituted, and appointed deputies to
meet, and sit in general Congress, in the city of
Philadelphia, in order to obtain such establishment, as that their religion, laws, and liberties,

may not be subverted: Whereupon the deputies
so appointed being now assembled, in a full and
free representation of these colonies, taking into
their most serious consideration, the best means
of attaining the ends aforesaid, do, in the first
place, as Englishmen, their ancestors in like cases
have usually done, for asserting and vindicating
their rights and liberties, DECLARE,

That the inhabitants of the English colonies in
North-America, by the immutable laws of nature,
the principles of the English constitution, and the
several charters or compacts, have the following
RIGHTS:

The inhabitants of the English colonies have the following rights

Resolved . . . That they are entitled to life, liberty and property: and they have never ceded to
any foreign power whatever, a right to dispose of
either without their consent.

Resolved . . . That our ancestors, who first settled these colonies, were at the time of their emigration from the mother country, entitled to all
the rights, liberties, and immunities of free and
natural-born subjects, within the realm of England.

Resolved . . . That by such emigration they by
no means forfeited, surrendered, or lost any of
those rights, but that they were, and their descendants now are, entitled to the exercise and enjoyment of all such of them, as their local and other
circumstances enable them to exercise and enjoy.

Resolved . . . That the foundation of English
liberty, and of all free government, is a right in the

people to participate in their legislative council: and as the English colonists are not represented, and from their local and other circumstances, cannot properly be represented in the British parliament, they are entitled to a free and exclusive power of legislation in their several provincial legislatures, where their right of representation can alone be preserved, in all cases of taxation and internal polity, subject only to the negative of their sovereign, in such manner as has been heretofore used and accustomed: But, from the necessity of the case, and a regard to the mutual interest of both countries, we cheerfully consent to the operation of such acts of the British parliament, as are bona fide, restrained to the regulation of our external commerce, for the purpose of securing the commercial advantages of the whole empire to the mother country, and the commercial benefits of its respective members; excluding every idea of taxation internal or external, for raising a revenue on the subjects, in America, without their consent.

Resolved . . . That the respective colonies are entitled to the common law of England, and more especially to the great and inestimable privilege of being tried by their peers of the vicinage [neighborhood], according to the course of that law.

Resolved . . . That they are entitled to the benefit of such of the English statutes, as existed at the time of their colonization; and which they have, by experience, respectively found to be applicable to their several local and other circumstances.

Resolved . . . That these, his majesty's colonies, are likewise entitled to all the immunities and privileges granted and confirmed to them by royal charters, or secured by their several codes of provincial laws.

Resolved . . . That they have a right peaceably to assemble, consider of their grievances, and petition the king; and that all prosecutions, prohibitory proclamations and commitments for the same, are illegal.

Resolved . . . That the keeping a standing army in these colonies, in times of peace, without the consent of the legislature of that colony, in which such army is kept, is against law.

Resolved . . . It is indispensably necesary to good government, and rendered essential by the English constitution, that the constituent branches of the legislature be independent of each other; that, therefore, the exercise of legislative power in several colonies, by a council appointed, during pleasure, by the crown, is unconstitutional, dangerous and destructive to the freedom of American legislation.

All and each of which the aforesaid deputies, in behalf of themselves, and their constituents, do claim, demand, and insist on, as their indubitable rights and liberties; which cannot be legally taken from them, altered or abridged by any power whatever, without their own consent, by their representatives in their several provincial legislatures.

In the course of our inquiry, we find many infringements and violations of the foregoing rights, which, from an ardent desire, that harmony and mutual intercourse of affection and interest may be restored, we pass over for the present, and proceed to state such acts and measures as have been adopted since the last war, which demonstrate a system formed to enslave America.

Resolved . . . That the following acts of parliament are infringements and violations of the rights of the colonists; and that the repeal of them is essentially necessary, in order to restore harmony between Great-Britain and the American colonies, viz.

The several acts of 4 Geo. III. ch. 15, and ch. 34.— 5 Geo. III. ch. 25.—6 Geo. III. ch. 52.—7 Geo. III. ch. 41. and ch. 46.—8 Geo. III. ch. 22. which impose duties for the purpose of raising a revenue in America, extend the power of the admiralty courts beyond their ancient limits, deprive the American subject of trial by jury, authorise the judges certificate to indemnify the prosecutor from damages, that he might otherwise be liable to, requiring oppressive security from a claimant of ships and goods seized, before he shall be allowed to defend his property, and are subversive of American rights.

Also 12 Geo. III. ch. 24. intituled, "An act for the better securing his majesty's dockyards, magazines, ships, ammunition, and stores," which declares a new offence in America, and deprives the American subject of a constitutional trial by jury of the vicinage, by authorising the trial of any person, charged with the committing any offence described in the said act, out of the realm, to be indicted and tried for the same in any shire or county within the realm.

Also the three acts passed in the last session of parliament, for stopping the port and blocking up the harbour of Boston, for altering the charter and government of Massachusetts-Bay, and that which is entitled, "An act for the better administration of justice, etc."

Also the act passed in the same session for establishing the Roman Catholic religion, in the province of Quebec, abolishing the equitable system of English laws, and erecting a tyranny there, to the great danger (from so total a dissimilarity of religion, law and government) of the neighbouring British colonies, by the assistance of whose blood and treasure the said country was conquered from France.

Also the act passed in the same session . . . providing suitable quarters for officers and soldiers in his majesty's service, in North-America.

Also, that the keeping a standing army in several of these colonies, in time of peace, without the consent of the legislature of that colony, in which such army is kept, is against law.

To these grievous acts and measures, Ameri-

To these grievous acts and measures, Americans cannot submit

cans cannot submit, but in hopes their fellow subjects in Great-Britain will, on a revision of them, restore us to that state, in which both countries found happiness and prosperity, we have for the present, only resolved to pursue the following peaceable measures: 1. To enter into a non-importation, non-consumption, and non-exportation agreement or association. 2. To prepare an address to the people of Great-Britain, and a memorial to the inhabitants of British America: and 3. To prepare a loyal address to his majesty, agreeable to resolutions already entered into.

PATRICK HENRY

Patrick Henry (1736–1799) was one of the most influential of our Founding Fathers and the most celebrated orator of the American Revolution. Henry was elected to membership in Virginia's House of Burgesses in 1765 and thereafter served in the Virginia Convention, in the Continental Congress, and as his state's first governor. After

A leading Antifederalist

the Revolution, as leader of the Antifederalist faction in the Continental Congress, he fought against the Federalists, whose numbers initially included his erstwhile allies James Madison, Alexander Hamilton, John Jay, and George Washington. The Federalists believed that the new Constitution that the Congress had adopted was sufficient, in and of itself, to guarantee individual freedoms. Patrick Henry and the other

Antifederalists disagreed. They were suspicious of the extraordinary powers that were to be granted to the federal government by the Constitution, and they were militant advocates of inclusion of a bill of rights in that document. Given the stature of such adversaries as Hamilton, Madison, and Washington, it is a wonder the Antifederalists prevailed in their position. It is safe to say, I think, that much of the credit for the existence in our Constitution of a great bill of rights should be accorded to Patrick Henry.

For most Americans, Patrick Henry is remembered for the memorable words of his speech to the Virginia Convention on the eve of the Revolutionary War: "I know not what course others may take; but as for me, give me liberty or give me death!" His passionate advocacy of enactment of resolutions to arm his fellow Virginians against British aggression permanently thrust him into the historical memory of all Americans. There is little in modern oratory to compare to this stirring speech. Here is its full text.

"Give me liberty or give me death!"

SPEECH TO THE VIRGINIA PROVINCIAL CONVENTION MARCH 23, 1775

Mr. President, It is natural for man to indulge in the illusions of hope. We are apt to shut our eyes against a painful truth, and listen to the song of that siren, till she transforms us into beasts. Is this the part of wise men, engaged in a great and arduous struggle for liberty? Are we disposed to be of the number of those who, having eyes, see not, and having ears, hear not, the things which so nearly concern their temporal salvation? For my part, whatever anguish of spirit it may cost, I am willing to know the whole truth; to know the worst and provide for it.

I have but one lamp by which my feet are guided

I have but one lamp by which my feet are guided; and that is the lamp of experience. I know of no way of judging of the future but by the past. And judging by the past, I wish to know what there has been in the conduct of the British ministry for the last ten years to justify those hopes with which gentlemen have been pleased to solace themselves and the house? Is it that insidious smile with which our petition has been lately received? Trust it not, sir; it will prove a snare to your feet. Suffer not yourselves to be betrayed with a kiss. Ask yourselves how this gracious reception of our petition comports with these warlike preparations which cover our waters and darken our land. Are fleets and armies necessary to a work of love and reconciliation? Have we shown ourselves so unwilling to be reconciled that force must be called in to win back our love? Let us not deceive ourselves, sir. These are the implements of war and subjugation — the last arguments to which kings resort. I ask gentlemen, sir, what means this martial array if its purpose be not to force us to submission? Can gentlemen assign any

other possible motive for it? Has Great Britain
any enemy in this quarter of the world, to call for
all this accumulation of navies and armies? No,
sir, she has none. They are meant for us: they can
be meant for no other. They are sent over to bind
and rivet upon us those chains which the British
ministry have been so long forging. And what
have we to oppose to them? Shall we try argument? Sir, we have been trying that for the last
ten years. Have we anything new to offer on the
subject? Nothing. We have held the subject up in
every light of which it is capable; but it has been
all in vain. Shall we resort to entreaty and humble supplication? What terms shall we find which
have not been already exhausted? Let us not, I
beseech you, sir, deceive ourselves longer. Sir, we
have done everything that could be done to avert
the storm which is now coming on. We have petitioned — we have remonstrated — we have sup-
plicated — we have prostrated ourselves before
the throne, and have implored its imposition to
arrest the tyrannical hands of the ministry and
Parliament. Our petitions have been slighted; our
remonstrances have produced additional violence
and insult; our supplications have been disregarded; and we have been spurned with contempt
from the foot of the throne. In vain, after these
things, may we indulge the fond hope of peace
and reconciliation. There is no longer any room
for hope. If we wish to be free — if we mean to
preserve inviolate those inestimable privileges for

*Let us not, I
beseech you,
deceive our-
selves longer*

which we have been so long contending — if we mean not basely to abandon the noble struggle in which we have been so long engaged, and which we have pledged ourselves never to abandon until the glorious object of our contest shall be obtained — we must fight! — I repeat it, sir, we must fight; an appeal to arms and to the God of Hosts is all that is left us!

They tell us, sir, that we are weak — unable to cope with so formidable an adversary. But when shall we be stronger? Will it be the next week, or the next year? Will it be when we are totally disarmed, and when a British guard shall be stationed in every house? Shall we gather strength by irresolution and inaction? Shall we acquire the means of effectual resistance by lying supinely on our backs and hugging the delusive phantom of hope, until our enemies shall have bound us hand and foot? Sir, we are not weak, if we make a proper use of those forces which the God of nature hath placed in our power. Three millions of people, armed in the holy cause of liberty, and in such a country as that which we possess, are invincible by any force which our enemy can send against us. Besides, sir, we shall not fight our battles alone. There is a just God who presides over the destinies of nations, and who will raise up friends to fight our battles for us. The battle, sir, is not to the strong alone; it is to the vigilant, the active, the brave. Besides, sir, we have no election. If we were base enough to

An appeal to arms and to the God of Hosts is all that is left us!

There is a just God who presides over the destinies of nations

desire it, it is now too late to retire from the contest. There is no retreat but in submission and slavery! Our chains are forged. Their clanking may be heard on the plains of Boston! The war is inevitable — and let it come! I repeat it, sir, let it come!!!

It is vain, sir, to extenuate the matter. Gentlemen may cry peace, Peace, peace, peace — but there is no peace. The war is actually begun! The next gale that sweeps from the north will bring to our ears the clash of resounding arms! Our brethren are already in the field! Why stand we here idle? What is it that gentlemen wish? What would they have? Is life so dear, or peace so sweet, as to be purchased at the price of chains and slavery? Forbid it, Almighty God! I know not what course others may take; but as for me, give me liberty, or give me death!

Give me liberty, or give me death!

GEORGE WASHINGTON

When reflecting upon the illustrious career of George Washington (1732–1799), an interesting question to consider is this: when, on June 14, 1775, the Second Continental Congress asked Washington to assume command of the provincial army that had been assembled in the Boston area, what if he had chosen to stay home? Would there be a United States of America?

Washington didn't have to go to war, you know. In these days, when too many of our pub-

What if Washington had stayed home?

lic figures seem to be engaged only in promoting their self-interest, it is well to remember how public-spirited was this extraordinary man. By the age of twenty-six, he had served in the military with high distinction, first as an officer in the Virginia militia and later as an aide to British general Braddock in the French and Indian War, rising to the rank of colonel. At the time of his release from military service in 1759, Washington was our most famous American-born soldier.

His military service apparently behind him, Washington retired to his home at Mount Vernon to lead the comfortable life of a wealthy Virginia squire, which indeed he did for the next sixteen years. He occupied himself with business matters as well as service as a legislator, a warden of the Church of England, and a county court judge. He possessed great wealth, large land holdings, and an enviable reputation. He led a pleasurable life, surrounded by a loving family and a wide circle of interesting friends. Moreover, Washington's ancestors, like those of many colonists of his time, had been Royalists, and during his early

A loyal and devoted admirer of England

years he too had been a loyal and devoted admirer of England and all things English. That this man, in these circumstances, at this time, would volunteer to lead an armed insurrection against the mighty British Empire, forsaking his comfort and risking his wealth, and indeed his life, for an ideal called American freedom, is extraordinary.

Look at the awesome challenge Washington

faced. His country was asking him to train, inspire, and lead a ragtag bunch of poorly equipped, undisciplined, untested troops of the newly formed Continental army, plus various state militia units, against a large force of seasoned British redcoats. Washington described them as "raw militia, badly officered, and with no government."

As an experienced military commander, Washington recognized the huge odds against victory. He told the Congress, "I beg it may be remembered by every gentleman in this room, that I this day declare with the utmost sincerity, I do not think myself equal to the command I am honored with."

And then later, this letter:

LETTER TO HIS WIFE
JUNE 18, 1775

You may believe me, my dear Patsy, when I assure you in the most solemn manner, that, so far from seeking this appointment, I have used every endeavor in my power to avoid it, not only from my unwillingness to part with you and the family, but from a consciousness of its being a trust too great for my capacity. . . . But as it has been a kind of destiny that has thrown me upon this service, I shall hope that my undertaking it is designed to answer some good purpose. . . . It was utterly out of my power to refuse this appoint-

"I do not think myself equal to the command I am honored with"

It has been a kind of destiny that has thrown me upon this service

ment, without exposing my character to such censures as would have reflected dishonor upon myself, and given pain to my friends.

Nonetheless, Washington accepted the commission from Congress on June 19 and two days later was on the road to Boston. The rest of the story is history, with our greatest patriot as its hero. In fact, no one can come away from a study of the Revolutionary War without concluding that but for George Washington, the cause of the colonies most likely would have failed. In 1777, the Marquis de Lafayette wrote to Washington: "If you were lost for America, there is nobody who could keep the army and the Revolution for six months." In his later years, Washington continued in service to the nation, completing two terms as our first president. Upon the conclusion of his second term in office, he delivered his celebrated Farewell Address, offering his thoughts about America's future, principally advising that the new republic avoid sectionalism and political infighting, preserve its moral and religious standards, and remain neutral in its relationships with foreign powers.

FROM FAREWELL ADDRESS
SEPTEMBER 17, 1796

Friends and Fellow Citizens:
The period for a new election of a Citizen, to administer the Executive government of the United

States, being not far distant, and the time actually arrived, when your thoughts must be employed in designating the person, who is to be cloathed with that important trust, it appears to me proper, especially as it may conduce to a more distinct expression of the public voice, that I should now apprise you of the resolution I have formed, to decline being considered among the number of those, out of whom a choice is to be made. . . .

[A] solicitude for your welfare, which cannot end but with my life, and the apprehension of danger, natural to that solicitude, urge me on an occasion like the present, to offer to your solemn contemplation, and to recommend to your frequent review, some sentiments; which are the result of much reflection, of no inconsiderable observation, and which appear to me all important to the permanency of your felicity as a People. These will be offered to you with the more freedom, as you can only see in them the disinterested warnings of a parting friend, who can possibly have no personal motive to bias his counsel. . . .

The Unity of Government, which constitutes you one people is also now dear to you. It is justly so, for it is a main Pillar in the Edifice of your real independence, the support of your tranquility at home; your peace abroad; of your safety; of your prosperity; of that very Liberty which you so highly prize. But as it is easy to foresee, that from different causes and from different quarters, much pains will be taken, many artifices em-

ployed, to weaken in your minds the conviction of
this truth; as this is the point in your political
fortress against which the batteries of internal and
external enemies will be most constantly and
actively (though often covertly and insidiously)
directed, it is of infinite moment, that you should
properly estimate the immense value of your
national Union to your collective and individual
happiness; that you should cherish a cordial,
habitual, and immovable attachment to it; accus-
toming yourselves to think and speak of it as of
the Palladium [safeguard] of your political safety
and prosperity; watching for its preservation with
jealous anxiety; discountenancing whatever may
suggest even a suspicion, that it can in any event
be abandoned, and indignantly frowning upon the
first dawning of every attempt to alienate any
portion of our Country from the rest, or to enfee-
ble the sacred ties which now link together the
various parts.

**Your nation-
al Union is
the
Palladium
[safeguard]
of your polit-
ical safety
and
prosperity**

For this you have every inducement of sympathy and interest; Citizens by birth or choice, of a
common country, that country has a right to con-
centrate your affections. The name of AMERICAN,
which belongs to you, in your national capacity,
must always exalt the just pride of Patriotism,
more than any appellation derived from local discriminations. With slight shades of difference, you
have the same Religion, Manners, Habits, and
Political Principles. You have in a common cause
fought and triumphed together. The Indepen-

dence and Liberty you possess are the work of joint counsels, and joint efforts; of common dangers, sufferings, and successes. . . .

In contemplating the causes which may disturb our Union, it occurs as matter of serious concern, that any ground should have been furnished for characterizing parties by *geographical discriminations — Northern* and *Southern, Atlantic* and *Western;* whence designing men may endeavor to excite a belief, that there is a real difference of local interests and views. One of the expedients of Party to acquire influence, within particular districts, is to misrepresent the opinions and aims of other districts. You cannot shield yourselves too much against the jealousies and heartburnings, which spring from these misrepresentations; they tend to render alien to each other those, who ought to be bound together by fraternal affection. . . .

You have in a common cause fought and triumphed together

To the efficacy and permanency of your Union, a Government for the whole is indispensable. No alliances, however strict between the parts can be an adequate substitute. They must inevitably experience the infractions and interruptions which all alliances in all times have experienced. Sensible of this momentous truth, you have improved upon your first essay, by the adoption of a Constitution of Government better calculated than your former for an intimate Union, and for the efficacious management of your common concerns. . . . The basis of our political systems is the

The basis of our political systems is the right of the people to alter their Constitution

right of the people to make and to alter their Constitutions of Government. But the Constitution which at any time exists, 'till changed by an explicit and authentic act of the whole People, is sacredly obligatory upon all. The very idea of the power and the right of the People to establish government presupposes the duty of every individual to obey the established Government. . . .

Towards the preservation of your Government and the permanency of your present happy state, it is requisite, not only that you steadily discountenance irregular oppositions to its acknowledged authority, but also that you resist with care the spirit of innovation upon its principles however specious the pretexts. One method of assault may be to effect, in the forms of the Constitution, alterations which will impair the energy of the system, and thus to undermine what can not be directly overthrown. In all the changes to which you may be invited, remember that time and habit are at least as necessary to fix the true character of Governments, as of other human institutions; that experience is the surest standard, by which to test the real tendency of the existing Constitution of a country; that facility in changes upon the credit of mere hypotheses and opinion exposes to perpetual change, from the endless variety of hypotheses and opinion: and remember, especially, that for the efficient management of your common interests, in a country so extensive as ours, a Government of as much vigour as is consistent with the perfect security of Liberty is indispensable. . . .

Of all the dispositions and habits which lead to political prosperity, Religion and Morality are indispensable supports. In vain would that man claim the tribute of Patriotism, who should labour to subvert these great Pillars of human happiness, these firmest props of the duties of Men and Citizens. The mere Politician, equally with the pious man ought to respect and to cherish them. A volume could not trace all their connections with private and public felicity. Let it simply be asked where is the security for property, for reputation, for life, if the sense of religious obligation *desert* the oaths, which are the instruments of investigation in Courts of Justice? And let us with caution indulge the supposition that morality can be maintained without religion. Whatever may be conceded to the influence of refined education on minds of peculiar structure, reason and experience both forbid us to expect that national morality can prevail in exclusion of religious principle.

'Tis substantially true that virtue or morality is a necessary spring of popular government. The rule indeed extends with more or less force to every species of free Government. Who that is a sincere friend to it, can look with indifference upon attempts to shake the foundation of the fabric.

Morality is a necessary spring of popular government

Promote then, as an object of primary importance, institutions for the general diffusion of knowledge. In proportion as the structure of a government gives force to public opinion, it is essential that public opinion should be enlightened. . . .

Against the insidious wiles of foreign influence, (I conjure you to believe me, fellow citizens) the jealousy of a free people ought to be *constantly* awake, since history and experience prove that foreign influence is one of the most baneful foes of Republican Government. But that jealousy to be useful must be impartial; else it becomes the instrument of the very influence to be avoided, instead of a defence against it. Excessive partiality for one foreign nation and excessive dislike of another, cause those whom they actuate to see danger only on one side, and serve to veil and even second the arts of influence on the other. Real Patriots, who may resist the intrigues of the favourite, are liable to become suspected and odious; while its tools and dupes usurp the applause and confidence of the people, to surrender their interests.

> **Foreign influence is the baneful foe of Republican Government**

The Great rule of conduct for us in regard to foreign Nations is in extending our commercial relations to have with them as little *political* connection as possible. So far as we have already formed engagements let them be fulfilled, with perfect good faith. Here let us stop. . . .

Our detached and distant situation invites and enables us to pursue a different course. If we remain one People, under an efficient government, the period is not far off, when we may defy material injury from external annoyance; when we may take such an attitude as will cause the neutrality we may at any time resolve upon to be scrupulously respected; when belligerent nations, under the impossibility of making acquisitions upon us, will not lightly hazard the giving us provocation; when we may choose peace or war, as our interest, guided by justice shall Counsel.

Why forego the advantages of so peculiar a situation? Why quit our own to stand upon foreign ground? Why, by interweaving our destiny with that of any part of Europe, entangle our peace and prosperity in the toils of European Ambition, Rivalship, Interest, Humor, or Caprice?. . .

Why quit our own land to stand upon foreign ground?

Though in reviewing the incidents of my Administration, I am unconscious of intentional error, I am nevertheless too sensible of my defects not to think it probable that I may have committed many errors. Whatever they may be I fervently beseech the Almighty to avert or mitigate the evils to which they may tend. I shall also carry with me the hope that my Country will never cease to view them with indulgence; and that after forty five years of my life dedicated to its Service, with an upright zeal, the faults of incompetent abilities will be consigned to oblivion, as myself must soon be to the Mansions of rest.

Relying on its kindness in this as in other things, and actuated by that fervent love towards it, which is so natural to a Man, who views in it the native soil of himself and his progenitors for several Generations; I anticipate with pleasing expectation that retreat, in which I promise myself to realize, without alloy, the sweet enjoyment of partaking, in the midst of my fellow Citizens, the benign influence of good Laws under a free Government, the ever-favourite object of my heart, and the happy reward, as I trust, of our mutual cares, labours and dangers.

THOMAS PAINE

In 1775, as the struggle between the American colonies and Great Britain accelerated and war broke out at Lexington and Concord, Thomas Paine (1737–1809), then living in Philadelphia, joined a group of advocates of the American cause, including two individuals who would come to be recognized as Founding Fathers of our republic, John Adams and Benjamin Rush. This group believed that American independence was inevitable and, recognizing Paine's writing talents, urged him to write a pamphlet supporting the idea. The pamphlet, entitled Common Sense, *first appeared in print in January 1776. It immediately became one of the most successful and influential pamphlets in the history of political writing, selling (by Paine's estimate) some 150,000 copies. (Paine directed that his share of the profits be used to buy supplies for the Continental army.)*

Common Sense *presents a strong argument* *for American independence. It is also a vigorous attack on the English monarchy and the principle of hereditary rule. Paine later wrote that the aim of his work was "to bring forward and establish the representative system of government."*

The language of Common Sense *is powerful stuff. "Of more worth is one honest man to society, and in the sight of God," Paine wrote, "than all the crowned ruffians that ever lived." George III is "the royal brute of England." On the issue of independence, he wrote: "There is something absurd in supposing a continent to be perpetually governed by an island." Toward the end of the pamphlet, he offered an awesome view of the significance of the American Revolution: "We have it in our power to begin the world over again." In a world "overrun with oppression," America alone would be the home of freedom, "an asylum for mankind."*

However, Common Sense *was important to its readers in the colonies (and survived as one of the most important documents in American history) not because of the ideas that Paine advocated — they were the common currency among a number of American patriots — but because of the way in which he presented them. Here was a new style of political writing directed not merely to the educated elite. Paine assumed knowledge of no authority but the Bible, with which all citizens were familiar, and avoided the florid lan-*

A strong argument for American independence

Here was a new style of political writing

guage common to political pamphlets of the era. His style was the equal of his argument: anyone can grasp the nature of politics and government; all that is required is common sense.

And as we now know, although some of the ideas he came to champion in his later years were quite radical, many of Paine's truths did prevail. No less a personage than John Adams observed in 1806: "I know not whether any man in the world has had more influence on its inhabitants or its affairs in the last thirty years than Thomas Paine."

FROM *COMMON SENSE* FEBRUARY 14, 1776

Volumes have been written on the subject of the struggle between England and America. Men of all ranks have embarked in the controversy, from different motives, and with various designs: but all have been ineffectual, and the period of debate is closed. . . .

I have heard it asserted by some, that as America hath flourished under her former connection with Great Britain, the same connection is necessary towards her future happiness, and will always have the same effect. Nothing can be more fallacious than this kind of argument. We may as well assert that because a child has thriven upon milk, that it is never to have meat, or that the first twenty years of our lives is to become a precedent for the next twenty. But even this is admitting more than is true; for I answer roundly, that America would have flourished as much, and probably much more, had no European power taken any notice of her. The commerce by which she hath enriched herself are the necessaries of life, and will always have a market while eating is the custom of Europe.

But she has protected us, say some. That she hath engrossed us is true, and defended the continent at our expense as well as her own is admitted; and she would have defended Turkey from the same motive, viz., for the sake of trade and dominion.

Alas! we have been long led away by ancient prejudices, and made large sacrifices to superstition. We have boasted the protection of Great Britain without considering that her motive was *interest,* not *attachment-,* and that she did not protect us from *our enemies* on *our account,* but from her enemies on her own account, from those who had no quarrel with us on any *other account,* but who will always be our enemies on the *same account.* Let Britain waive her pretensions to the continent, or the continent throw off the dependence, and we should be at peace with France and Spain were they at war with Britain. . . .

But Britain is the parent country, say some. Then the more shame upon her conduct. Even brutes do not devour their young, nor savages make war upon their families; wherefore, the assertion, if true, turns to her reproach; but it happens not to be true, or only partly so, and the

We have been led away by ancient prejudices

phrase *parent or mother country* hath been . . .
adopted by the king and his parasites, with a low,
papistical design of gaining an unfair bias on the
credulous weakness of our minds. Europe, and
not England, is the parent country of America.
This new world hath been the asylum for the per-
secuted lovers of civil and religious liberty from
every part of Europe. Hither have they fled, not
from the tender embraces of a mother, but from
the cruelty of the monster; and it is so far true of
England, that the same tyranny which drove the
first emigrants from home, pursues their descendants still. . . .

The same tyranny which drove the first emigrants from home, pursues their descendants still

I challenge the warmest advocate for reconciliation to show a single advantage that this continent can reap, by being connected with Great
Britain. I repeat the challenge, not a single
advantage is derived. Our corn will fetch its price
in any market in Europe, and our imported goods
must be paid for, buy them where we will.

But the injuries and disadvantages we sustain
by that connection are without number; and our
duty to mankind at large, as well as to ourselves,
instructs us to renounce the alliance: because any
submission to, or dependence on, Great Britain,
tends directly to involve this continent in European wars and quarrels, and sets us at variance
with nations, who would otherwise seek our
friendship, and against whom we have neither
anger nor complaint. As Europe is our market for
trade, we ought to form no partial connection with

any part of it. It is the true interest of America to steer clear of European contentions, which she never can do, while, by her dependence on Britain, she is made the make-weight in the scale of British politics.

Europe is too thickly planted with kingdoms to be long at peace, and whenever a war breaks out between England and any foreign power, the trade of America goes to ruin, *because of her connection with Britain*. The next war may not turn out like the last, and should it not, the advocates for reconciliation now will be wishing for separation then, because neutrality in that case would be a safer convoy than a man of war. Everything that is right or natural pleads for separation. The blood of the slain, the weeping voice of nature cries, *'tis time to part*. Even the distance at which the Almighty hath placed England and America is a strong and natural proof that the authority of the one over the other, was never the design of heaven. . . .

It is the good fortune of many to live distant from the scene of present sorrow; the evil is not sufficiently brought to *their* doors to make *them* feel the precariousness with which all American property is possessed. But let our imaginations transport us for a few moments to Boston; that seat of wretchedness will teach us wisdom, and instruct us forever to renounce a power in whom we can have no trust. The inhabitants of that unfortunate city, who but a few months ago were in ease and affluence, have now no other alternative than to stay and starve, or turn out to beg. Endangered by the fire of their friends if they continue within the city, and plundered by the soldiery if they leave it, in their present situation they are prisoners without the hope of redemption, and in a general attack for their relief they would be exposed to the fury of both armies. . . .

But if you say, you can still pass the violations over, then I ask, hath your house been burnt? Hath your property been destroyed before your face? Are your wife and children destitute of a bed to lie on, or bread to live on? Have you lost a parent or a child by their hands, and yourself the ruined and wretched survivor? If you have not, then you are not a judge of those who have. But if you have, and can still shake hands with the murderers, then you are unworthy the name of husband, father, friend, or lover; and whatever may be your rank or title in life, you have the heart of a coward, and the spirit of a sycophant . . .

Every quiet method for peace has been ineffective

Every quiet method for peace hath been ineffectual. Our prayers have been rejected with disdain; and have tended to convince us that nothing flatters vanity or confirms obstinacy in kings more than repeated petitioning — and nothing hath contributed more than that very measure to make the kings of Europe absolute. Witness Denmark and Sweden. Wherefore, since nothing but blows will do, for God's sake let us come to a final separation, and not leave the next generation to be cutting throats under the violated unmeaning names of parent and child.

To say, they will never attempt it again, is idle and visionary; we thought so as the repeal of the stamp act, yet a year or two undeceived us; as well may we suppose that nations which have been once defeated will never renew the quarrel.

As to government matters, it is not in the power of Britain to do this continent justice: the business of it will soon be too weighty and intricate to be managed with any tolerable degree of convenience, by a power so distant from us, and so very ignorant of us; for if they cannot conquer us, they cannot govern us. To be always running three or four thousand miles with a tale or a petition, waiting four or five months for an answer, which, when obtained, requires five or six more to explain it in, will in a few years be looked upon as folly and childishness. There was a time when it was proper, and there is a proper time for it to cease.

Small islands not capable of protecting themselves are the proper objects for kingdoms to take under their care; but there is something very absurd in supposing a continent to be perpetually governed by an island. In no instance hath nature made the satellite larger than its primary planet; and as England and America, with respect to each other, reverse the common order of nature, it is evident that they belong to different systems. England to Europe: America to itself. . . .

But where, say some, is the king of America?

There is something very absurd in supposing a continent to be governed by an island

I'll tell you, friend, he reigns above, and doth not make havoc of mankind like the royal brute of Great Britain. Yet that we may not appear to be defective even in earthly honors, let a day be solemnly set apart for proclaiming the charter; let it be brought forth placed on the divine law, the Word of God; let a crown be placed thereon, by which the world may know, that so far as we **In America the law is king** approve of monarchy, that in America *the law is king*. For as in absolute governments the king is law, so in free countries the law ought to be king, and there ought to be no other. But lest any ill use should afterwards arise, let the crown at the conclusion of the ceremony be demolished, and scattered among the people whose right it is.

A government of our own is our natural right; and when a man seriously reflects on the precariousness of human affairs, he will become convinced, that it is infinitely wiser and safer to form a constitution of our own in a cool deliberate manner, while we have it in our power, than to trust such an interesting event to time and chance. . . .

Ye that tell us of harmony and reconciliation, can ye restore to us the time that is passed? Can ye give to prostitution its former innocence? Neither can ye reconcile Britain and America. The last cord now is broken; the people of England are presenting addresses against us. There are injuries which nature cannot forgive; she would cease to be nature if she did. As well can the lover forgive the ravisher of his mistress, as the continent forgive the murders of Britain. The Almighty hath implanted in us these unextinguishable feelings for good and wise purposes. They are the guardians of his image in our hearts. They distinguish us from the herd of common animals. The social compact would dissolve, and justice be extirpated [rooted out] from the earth, or have only a casual existence, were we callous to the touches of affection. The robber and the murderer would often escape unpunished, did not the injuries which our tempers sustain, provoke us into justice.

0! ye that love mankind! Ye that dare oppose not only the tyranny but the tyrant, stand forth! Every spot of the old world is overrun with oppression. Freedom hath been hunted round the globe. Asia and Africa have long expelled her. Europe regards her like a stranger, and England hath given her warning to depart. 0! receive the fugitive, and prepare in time an asylum for mankind.

Most Americans probably recall only one statement by Thomas Paine: "These are the times that try men's souls." These words were first set forth as the lead sentence of Paine's pamphlet The American Crisis.

Paine published The American Crisis *on December 23, 1776, while he was serving in General George Washington's Continental army at its winter headquarters in Morristown, New Jersey. Several days later, Washington was to*

"*These are the times that try men's souls*"

achieve two great strategic victories over General Howe's British forces: first, the capture of a Hessian brigade at Trenton on December 26, 1776, after Washington's famous crossing of the Delaware River; and second, the January 3, 1777, victory over Howe's subordinate, General Lord Cornwallis, at Princeton. In a campaign lasting only three weeks, in the dead of winter, when traditionally gentleman soldiers were not supposed to fight, the military genius of America's greatest gentleman, combined with the fortitude of his five thousand men, had driven the British from New Jersey and saved the American cause.

However, even with these victories, Washington's army was by no means in a comfortable situation. Cornwallis' forces were still on his trail, and his men were cold, malnourished, and dogtired, frequently falling asleep on the march. In an effort to boost morale, Washington, who had been particularly impressed by Paine's pamphlet, ordered that it be read to his troops.

Washington ordered that the pamphlet be read to his troops

Not only the celebrated first sentence but the entire pamphlet remains a classic statement of the American Revolutionary cause.

FROM *THE AMERICAN CRISIS* DECEMBER 23, 1776

These are the times that try men's souls. The summer soldier and the sunshine patriot will, in this crisis, shrink from the service of his country;

but he that stands it NOW, deserves the love and thanks of man and woman. Tyranny, like hell, is not easily conquered; yet we have this consolation with us, that the harder the conflict, the more glorious the triumph. What we obtain too cheap, we esteem too lightly; 'tis dearness only that gives everything its value. Heaven knows how to put a proper price upon its goods; and it would be strange indeed, if so celestial an article as FREE-DOM should not be highly rated. Britain, with an army to enforce her tyranny, has declared that she has a right (not only to TAX) but "to BIND us in ALL CASES WHATSOEVER," and if being bound in that manner, is not slavery, then is there no such a thing as slavery upon earth. Even the expression is impious, for so unlimited a power can belong only to God. . . .

I have as little superstition in me as any man living, but my secret opinion has ever been, and still is, that God Almighty will not give up a people to military destruction, or leave them unsupportedly to perish, who have so earnestly and so repeatedly sought to avoid the calamities of war, by every decent method which wisdom could invent. Neither have I so much of the infidel in me, as to suppose that He has relinquished the government of the world, and given us up to the care of devils; and as I do not, I cannot see on what grounds the king of Britain can look up to Heaven for help against us: a common murderer, a highwayman, or a housebreaker, has as good a pretence as he.

'Tis surprising to see how rapidly a panic will sometimes run through a country. All nations and ages have been subject to them: Britain has trembled like an ague at the report of a French fleet of flat bottomed boats; and in the fourteenth century the whole English army, after ravaging the kingdom of France, was driven back like men petrified with fear; and this brave exploit was performed by a few broken forces collected and headed by a woman, Joan of Arc. Would that heaven might inspire some Jersey maid to spirit up her countrymen, and save her fair fellow sufferers from ravage and ravishment!. . .

I call not upon a few, but upon all: not on this state or that state, but on every state; up and help us; lay your shoulders to the wheel; better have too much force than too little, when so great an object is at stake. Let it be told to the future world, that in the depth of winter, when nothing but hope and virtue could survive, that the city and the country, alarmed at one common danger, came forth to meet and to repulse it. Say not that thousands are gone, turn out your tens of thousands; throw not the burden of the day upon Providence, but "show your faith by your works," that God may bless you. It matters not where you live, or what rank of life you hold, the evil or the blessing will reach you all. The far and the near, the home counties and the back, the rich and poor, will suffer or rejoice alike. The heart that feels not now, is dead: the blood of his children will curse his cowardice, who shrinks back at a time when a little might have saved the whole, and made them happy. I love the man that can smile in trouble, that can gather strength from distress, and grow brave by reflection. 'Tis the business of little minds to shrink; but he whose heart is firm, and whose conscience approves his conduct, will pursue his principles unto death. My own line of reasoning is to myself as straight and clear as a ray of light. Not all the treasure of the world, so far as I believe, could have induced me to support an offensive war, for I think it murder; but if a thief breaks into my house, burns and destroys my property, and kills or threatens to kill me, or those that are in it, and to "bind me in all cases whatsoever," to his absolute will, am I to suffer it? What signifies it to me, whether he who does it is a king or a common man; my country-man or not my countryman: whether it be done by an individual villain, or an army of them? If we reason to the root of things we shall find no differ-ence; neither can any just cause be assigned why we should punish in the one case and pardon in the other. Let them call me rebel, and welcome, I feel no concern from it; but I should suffer the misery of devils, were I to make a whore of my soul by swearing allegiance to one whose charac-ter is that of a sottish, stupid, stubborn, worthless, brutish man. I conceive likewise a horrid idea in receiving mercy from a being, who at the last day shall be shrieking to the rocks and mountains to

I love the man that can smile in trouble

If a thief breaks into my house and kills or threatens to kill me, am I to suffer it?

cover him, and fleeing with terror from the orphan, the widow, and the slain of America.

There are cases which cannot be overdone by language, and this is one. There are persons too who see not the full extent of the evil which threatens them, they solace themselves with hopes that the enemy, if they succeed, will be merciful. It is the madness of folly, to expect mercy from those who have refused to do justice; and even mercy, where conquest is the object, is only a trick of war; the cunning of the fox is as murderous as the violence of the wolf; and we ought to guard equally against both. . . .

I thank God that I fear not. I see no real cause for fear. I know our situation well, and can see the way out of it. . . . By perseverance and fortitude we have the prospect of a glorious issue; by cowardice and submission, the sad choice of a variety of evils — a ravaged country — a depopulated city — habitations without safety, and slavery without hope — our homes turned into barracks and bawdy-houses for Hessians, and a future race to provide for, whose fathers we shall doubt of. Look on this picture and weep over it! And if there yet remains one thoughtless wretch who believes it not, let him suffer it unlamented. . . .

I know our situation well, and can see the way out of it

THOMAS JEFFERSON

You may recall what President John F. Kennedy once said about Thomas Jefferson. At a dinner honoring Nobel Prize recipients, Kennedy said that his guests were "the most extraordinary collection of talent, of human knowledge, that has ever been gathered together at the White House, with the possible exception of when Thomas Jefferson dined alone." Indeed, Thomas Jefferson (1743–1826) is one of the most extraordinary figures in American history. He was co-author with John Adams of the Declaration of Independence, third president of the United States, a brilliant statesman, and an architect, scientist, inventor, naturalist, educator, and public servant. Of the handful of political leaders who were the primary architects of the American republic — among them George Washington, James Madison, John Adams, and Alexander Hamilton — as a thinker and philosopher Jefferson ranks first. He was, undoubtedly, a genius.

One of the most extraordinary figures in American history

And nowhere is that genius captured so well as in his writings. The historians Adrienne Koch and William Peden observed:

> *The writings of Thomas Jefferson are today more meaningful than ever before in America's history. No better record of the social principles which are the heart of the American democratic "experiment" exists than these letters and documents. Those who are eager to know the varied and subtle character of the man will find in them another, not inconsiderable, reward. No leader in the period of the American Enlightenment was as articulate, as wise, as*

conscious of the implications and consequences of a free society as he. To Jefferson, therefore, we must go for fresh contacts with the commanding personalities and events of those days, and for the fullest expression of governments through consent, through reason, through law, and through energetic and progressive change. [13]

A vast literary legacy

Jefferson left a vast literary legacy in the form of books, journal entries, notes, addresses, and letters. During his lifetime, he wrote a staggering number of letters, estimated at between fifty and seventy-five thousand! From such a huge literary reservoir, it is obviously difficult to fashion a selection of Jefferson's writings that would satisfy all readers. Nevertheless, on the topic of American freedoms, here are three of my favorites:

THE DECLARATION OF INDEPENDENCE
JULY 4, 1776

A DECLARATION BY THE REPRESENTATIVES OF THE UNITED STATES OF AMERICA, IN *GENERAL* CONGRESS ASSEMBLED

When, in the course of human events, it becomes necessary for one people to dissolve the political bands which have connected them with another,

[13] THE LIFE AND SELECTED WRITINGS OF THOMAS JEFFERSON, Adrienne Koch and William Peden, eds., The Modern Library, New York, 1944, xv.

and to assume among the powers of the earth the separate and equal station to which the laws of nature and of nature's God entitle them, a decent respect to the opinions of mankind requires that they should declare the causes which impel them to the separation.

We hold these truths to be self-evident: that all men are created equal; that they are endowed, by their Creator with certain unalienable rights; that among these are life, liberty, and the pursuit of happiness; that to secure these rights, governments are instituted among men, deriving their just powers from the consent of the governed; that whenever any form of government becomes destructive of these ends, it is the right of the people to alter or to abolish it, and to institute new government, laying its foundation on such principles, and organizing its powers in such form, as to them shall seem most likely to effect their safety and happiness. Prudence, indeed, will dictate that governments long established, should not be changed for light and transient causes; and accordingly all experience hath shown that mankind are more disposed to suffer while evils are sufferable, than to right themselves by abolishing the forms to which they are accustomed. But when a long train of abuses and usurpations, pursuing invariably the same object, evinces a design to reduce them under absolute despotism, it is their right, it is their duty to throw off such government, and to provide new guards for their future security. Such has been the patient suffer-

All men are created equal

ance of these colonies; and such is now the necessity which constrains them to alter their former systems of government. The history of the present king of Great Britain is a history of repeated injuries and usurpations, all having in direct object the establishment of an absolute tyranny over these states. To prove this, let facts be submitted to a candid world.

He has refused his assent to laws the most wholesome and necessary for the public good.

He has forbidden his governors to pass laws of immediate and pressing importance, unless suspended in their operation till his assent should be obtained; and, when so suspended, he has utterly neglected to attend to them.

He has refused to pass other laws for the accommodation of large districts of people, unless those people would relinquish the right of representation in the legislature, a right inestimable to them, and formidable to tyrants only.

He has called together legislative bodies at places unusual, uncomfortable, and distant from the depository of their public records, for the sole purpose of fatiguing them into compliance with his measures.

He has dissolved representative houses repeatedly for opposing with manly firmness his invasions on the right of the people.

He has refused for a long time after such dissolutions to cause others to be elected, whereby the legislative powers, incapable of annihilation, have returned to the people at large for their exercise, the state remaining, in the meantime, exposed to all the dangers of invasion from without and convulsions within.

He has endeavored to prevent the population of these states; for that purpose obstructing the laws for naturalization of foreigners, refusing to pass others to encourage their migrations hither, and raising the conditions of new appropriations of lands.

He has obstructed the administration of justice by refusing his assent to laws for establishing judiciary powers.

He has made judges dependent on his will alone for the tenure of their offices, and the amount and payment of their salaries.

He has erected a multitude of new offices, and sent hither swarms of new officers to harass our people, and eat out their substance.

He has kept among us in times of peace standing armies without the consent of our legislatures. He has affected to render the military independent of, and superior to, the civil power.

He has combined with others to subject us to a jurisdiction foreign to our constitutions, and unacknowledged by our laws, giving his assent to their acts of pretended legislation for quartering large bodies of armed troops among us; for protecting them by a mock trial from punishment for any murders which they should commit on the inhabitants of these states; for cutting off our trade with all parts of the world; for imposing taxes on us without our consent; for depriving us in many cases of the benefits of trial by jury; for transporting us beyond seas to be tried for pretended offences; for abolishing the free system of English laws in a neighboring province, establishing therein an arbitrary government, and enlarging its boundaries, so as to render it at once an example and fit instrument for introducing the same absolute rule into these colonies; for taking away our charters, abolishing our most valuable laws, and altering fundamentally the forms of our governments; for suspending our own legislatures, and declaring themselves invested with power to legislate for us in all cases whatsoever.

He has abdicated government here by declaring us out of his protection, and waging war against us.

He has plundered our seas, ravaged our coasts, burnt our towns, and destroyed the lives of our people.

He is at this time transporting large armies of foreign mercenaries to complete the works of death, desolation and tyranny already begun with circumstances of cruelty and perfidy scarcely paralleled in the most barbarous ages, and totally unworthy the head of a civilized nation.

He has constrained our fellow-citizens, taken captive on the high seas, to bear arms against their country, to become the executioners of their friends and brethren, or to fall themselves by their hands.

He has excited domestic insurrection among us, and has endeavoured to bring on the inhabitants of our frontiers, the merciless Indian savages, whose known rule of warfare is an undistinguished destruction of all ages, sexes and conditions.

In every stage of these oppressions we have petitioned for redress in the most humble terms: our repeated petitions have been answered only by repeated injuries.

A prince whose character is thus marked is unfit to be the ruler of a free people.

Nor have we been wanting in attentions to our British brethren. We have warned them from time to time of attempts by their legislature to extend an unwarrantable jurisdiction over us. We have reminded them of the circumstances of our emigration and settlement here, we have appealed to their native justice and magnanimity and we have conjured them by the ties of our common kindred to disavow these usurpations which would inevitably interrupt our connection and correspondence. They too have been deaf to the voice of justice and of consanguinity. We must therefore acquiesce in the necessity which denounces our separation and hold them as we hold the rest of mankind, enemies in war, in peace friends!

They have been deaf to the voice of justice

We, therefore, the representatives of the United States of America in General Congress assembled, appealing to the supreme judge of the world for the rectitude of our intentions, do in the name, and by the authority of the good people of these colonies, solemnly publish and declare, that these **These united** united colonies are, and of right ought to be free **colonies are,** and independent states; that they are absolved **and of right** from all allegiance to the British crown, and that **ought to be** all political connection between them and the **free** state of Great Britain is, and ought to be, totally dissolved; and that, as free and independent states, they have full power to levy war, conclude peace, contract alliances, establish commerce, and to do all other acts and things which independent states may of right do.

And for the support of this declaration, with a firm reliance on the protection of divine providence, we mutually pledge to each other our lives, our fortunes, and our sacred honor.

AN ACT FOR ESTABLISHING RELIGIOUS FREEDOM 1786

God hath Well aware that Almighty God hath created the **created the** mind free; that all attempts to influence it by tem- **mind free** poral punishments or burdens, or by civil incapacitations, tend only to beget habits of hypocrisy and meanness, and are a departure from the plan of the Holy Author of our religion, who being Lord both of body and mind, yet chose not to propagate it by coercions on either, as was in his

Almighty power to do; that the impious presumption of legislators and rulers, civil as well as ecclesiastical, who, being themselves but fallible and uninspired men have assumed dominion over the faith of others, setting up their own opinions and modes of thinking as the only true and infallible, and as such endeavoring to impose them on others, hath established and maintained false religions over the greatest part of the world, and through all time; that to compel a man to furnish contributions of money for the propagation of opinions which he disbelieves, is sinful and tyrannical; that even the forcing him to support this or that teacher of his own religious persuasion, is depriving him of the comfortable liberty of giving his contributions to the particular pastor whose morals he would make his pattern, and whose powers he feels most persuasive to righteousness, and is withdrawing from the ministry those temporary rewards, which proceeding from an approbation of their personal conduct, are an additional incitement to earnest and unremitting labors for the instruction of mankind; that our civil rights have no dependence on our religious opinions, more than our opinions in physics or geometry; that, therefore, the proscribing any citizen as unworthy the public confidence by laying upon him an incapacity of being called to the offices of trust and emolument, unless he profess or renounce this or that religious opinion, is depriv-

Civil rights have no dependence on our religious opinions

ing him injuriously of those privileges and advantages to which in common with his fellow citizens he has a natural right; that it tends also to corrupt the principles of that very religion it is meant to encourage, by bribing, with a monopoly of worldly honors and emoluments, those who will externally profess and conform to it: that though indeed these are criminal who do not withstand such temptation, yet neither are those innocent who lay the bait in their way; that to suffer the civil magistrate to intrude his powers into the field of opinion and to restrain the profession or propagation of principles, on the supposition of their ill tendency, is a dangerous fallacy, which at once destroys all religious liberty, because he being of course judge of that tendency, will make his opinions the rule of judgment, and approve or condemn the sentiments of others only as they shall square with or suffer from his own; that it is time enough for the rightful purposes of civil government, for its offices to interfere when principles break out into overt acts against peace and good order; and finally, that truth is great and will prevail if left to herself, that she is the proper and sufficient antagonist to error, and has nothing to fear from the conflict, unless by human interposition disarmed of her natural weapons, free argument and debate, errors ceasing to be dangerous when it is permitted freely to contradict them.

Truth is great and will prevail if left to herself

Be it therefore enacted by the General Assembly, That no man shall be compelled to frequent or support any religious worship, place or ministry whatsoever, nor shall be enforced, restrained, molested, or burdened in his body or goods, or shall otherwise suffer on account of his religious opinions or belief; but that all men shall be free to profess, and by argument to maintain, their opinions in matters of religion, and that the same shall in nowise diminish, enlarge, or affect their civil capacities.

And though we well know this Assembly, elected by the people for the ordinary purposes of legislation only, have no power to restrain the acts of succeeding assemblies, constituted with powers equal to our own, and that therefore to declare this act irrevocable, would be of no effect in law, yet we are free to declare, and do declare, that the rights hereby asserted are of the natural rights of mankind, and that if any act shall be hereafter passed to repeal the present or to narrow its operation, such act will be an infringement of natural right.

FROM FIRST INAUGURAL ADDRESS
MARCH 4, 1801

Friends and Fellow Citizens: — ...

During the contest of opinion through which we have passed, the animation of discussions and of exertions has sometimes worn an aspect which might impose on strangers unused to think freely and to speak and to write what they think; but this being now decided by the voice of the nation, announced according to the rules of the constitution, all will, of course, arrange themselves under the will of the law, and unite in common efforts for the common good. All, too, will bear in mind this sacred principle, that though the will of the majority is in all cases to prevail, that will, to be rightful, must be reasonable; that the minority possesses their equal rights, which equal laws must protect, and to violate which would be oppression. Let us, then, fellow citizens, unite with one heart and one mind. Let us restore to social intercourse that harmony and affection without which liberty and even life itself are but dreary things. And let us reflect that having banished from our land that religious intolerance under which mankind so long bled and suffered, we have yet gained little if we countenance a political intolerance as despotic, as wicked, and capable of as bitter and bloody persecutions. During the throes and convulsions of the ancient world, during the agonizing spasms of infuriated man, seeking through blood and slaughter his long-lost liberty, it was not wonderful that the agitation of the billows should reach even this distant and peaceful shore; that this should be more felt and feared by some and less by others; that this should divide

Let us unite with one heart and one mind

opinions as to measures of safety. But every difference of opinion is not a difference of principle. We have called by different names brethren of the same principle. We are all republicans — we are federalists. If there be any among us who would wish to dissolve this Union or to change its republican form, let them stand undisturbed as monuments of the safety with which error of opinion may be tolerated where reason is left free to combat it. I know, indeed, that some honest men fear that a republican government cannot be strong; that this government is not strong enough. But would the honest patriot, in the full tide of successful experiment, abandon a government which has so far kept us free and firm, on the theoretic and visionary fear that this government, the world's best hope, may by possibility want energy to preserve itself? I trust not. I believe this, on the contrary, the strongest government on earth. I believe it the only one where every man, at the call of the laws, would fly to the standard of the law, and would meet invasions of the public order as his own personal concern. Sometimes it is said that man cannot be trusted with the government of himself. Can he, then, be trusted with the government of others? Or have we found angels in the forms of kings to govern him? Let history answer this question.

Have we found angels in the form of kings to govern man?

Let us, then, with courage and confidence pursue our own federal and republican principles, our attachment to union and representative government. Kindly separated by nature and a wide ocean from the exterminating havoc of one quarter of the globe; too high-minded to endure the degradations of the others; possessing a chosen country, with room enough for our descendants to the hundredth and thousandth generation; entertaining a due sense of our equal right to the use of our own faculties, to the acquisitions of our industry, to honor and confidence from our fellow citizens, resulting not from birth but from our actions and their sense of them; enlightened by a benign religion, professed, indeed, and practiced in various forms, yet all of them including honesty, truth, temperance, gratitude, and the love of man; acknowledging and adoring an overruling Providence, which by all its dispensations proves that it delights in the happiness of man here and his greater happiness hereafter; with all these blessings, what more is necessary to make us a happy and a prosperous people? Still one thing more, fellow citizens — a wise and frugal government, which shall restrain men from injuring one another, which shall leave them otherwise free to regulate their own pursuits of industry and improvement, and shall not take from the mouth of labor the bread it has earned. This is the sum of good government, and this is necessary to close the circle of our felicities.

A wise and frugal government shall restrain men from injuring one another

About to enter, fellow citizens, on the exercise of duties which comprehend everything dear and valuable to you, it is proper you should understand what I deem the essential principles of our government, and consequently those which ought to shape its administration. I will compress them within the narrowest compass they will bear, stating the general principle, but not all its limitations. Equal and exact justice to all men, of whatever state or persuasion, religious or political; peace, commerce, and honest friendship, with all nations — entangling alliances with none; the support of the state governments in all their rights, as the most competent administrations for our domestic concerns and the surest bulwarks against anti-republican tendencies; the preservation of the general government in its whole constitutional vigor, as the sheet anchor of our peace at home and safety abroad; a jealous care of the right of election by the people — a mild and safe corrective of abuses which are lopped by the sword of revolution where peaceable remedies are unprovided; absolute acquiescence in the decisions of the majority — the vital principle of republics, from which is no appeal but to force, the vital principle and immediate parent of despotism; a well-disciplined militia — our best reliance in peace and for the first moments of war, till regulars may relieve them; the supremacy of the civil over the military authority; economy in the public expense, that labor may be lightly burdened; the honest payment of our debts and sacred preservation of the public faith; encouragement of agriculture, and of commerce as its handmaid; the diffusion of information and the arraignment of all abuses at the bar of the public reason; freedom of religion; freedom of the press; freedom of person under the protection of the habeas corpus; and trial by juries impartially selected — these principles form the bright constellation which has gone before us, and guided our steps through an age of revolution and reformation. The wisdom of our sages and blood of our heroes have been devoted to their attainment. They should be the creed of our political faith — the text of civic instruction — the touchstone by which to try the services of those we trust; and should we wander from them in moments of error or alarm, let us hasten to retrace our steps and to regain the road which alone leads to peace, liberty, and safety. . . .

These principles form the bright constellation which has gone before us

Jefferson's letters demonstrate his extraordinary range of interest. They recreate not only the personality and thought of the most versatile American of his time, but also the age in which he lived. Here are two of the most popular of Jefferson's letters. First, an incisive statement of the need for the separation of political powers in a republican government:

His letters demonstrate his extraordinary range of interest

FROM LETTER TO JOSEPH C. CABELL
FEBRUARY 2, 1816

No, my friend, the way to have good and safe government, is not to trust it all to one, but to divide it among the many, distributing to every one exactly the functions he is competent to. Let the national government be entrusted with the defence of the nation, and its foreign and federal relations; the State governments with the civil rights, laws, police, and administration of what concerns the State generally; the counties with the local concerns of the counties, and each ward direct the interests within itself. It is by dividing and subdividing these republics from the great national one down through all its subordinations, until it ends in the administration of every man's farm by himself; by placing under every one what his own eye may superintend, that all will be done for the best. What has destroyed liberty and the rights of man in every government which has ever existed under the sun? The generalizing and concentrating all cares and powers into one body, no matter whether of the autocrats of Russia or France, or of the aristocrats of a Venetian senate. . . .

Next, this brilliant exposition of the power of the people in the governance of their republic to adapt and change their laws to meet new needs:

The way to have good and safe government is to divide it among the many

FROM LETTER TO MAJOR JOHN CARTWRIGHT
JUNE 5, 1824

Can one generation bind another, and all others, in succession forever? I think not. The Creator has made the earth for the living, not the dead. Rights and powers can only belong to persons, not to things, not to mere matter, unendowed with will. The dead are not even things. The particles of matter which composed their bodies, make part now of the bodies of other animals, vegetables, or minerals, of a thousand forms. To what then are attached the rights and powers they held while in the form of men? A generation may bind itself as long as its majority continues in life; when that has disappeared, another

Nothing is unchangeable but the inherent and unalienable rights of man

majority is in place, holds all the rights and powers their predecessors once held, and may change their laws and institutions to suit themselves. Nothing then is unchangeable but the inherent and unalienable rights of man. . . .

FROM THE NORTHWEST ORDINANCE
JULY 13, 1787

Although not as well known as America's other seminal declarations of freedom, the Northwest Ordinance deserves our attention. This law, which applied to the great territory west of the Appalachian Mountains, contains the first bill of rights enacted by the federal government of the United

States, establishing as part of the colonial policy the principle that settlers of uninhabited territories should enjoy the same personal liberties as the citizens of the parent country. Congress passed the ordinance in July 1787, just two months before the U.S. Constitution was adopted.

Probably the most famous clause in the Northwest Ordinance is Article VI, which prohibited slavery in the territory. No comparable provision appears in either the U.S. Constitution or the Bill of Rights. The language of the Thirteenth Amendment to the Constitution, which abolished slavery throughout the United States, is similar to that found in Article VI of the Northwest Ordinance.

Its Article VI prohibited slavery in the territory

AN ORDINANCE FOR THE GOVERNMENT OF THE TERRITORY OF THE UNITED STATES NORTHWEST OF THE RIVER OHIO

Section 14. It is hereby ordained and declared by the authority aforesaid, that the following articles shall be considered as articles of compact, between the original States and the people and States in the said territory, and forever remain unalterable, unless by common consent, to wit:

ARTICLE 1

No person, demeaning himself in a peaceable and orderly manner, shall ever be molested on account of his mode of worship or religious sentiments, in the said territory.

ARTICLE 2

The inhabitants of the said territory shall always be entitled to the benefits of the writ *of habeas corpus,* and of the trial by jury; of a proportionate representation of the people in the legislature, and of judicial proceedings according to the course of the common law. All persons shall be bailable, unless for capital offences, where the proof shall be evident, or the presumption great. All fines shall be moderate; and no cruel or unusual punishments shall be inflicted. No man shall be deprived of his liberty or property, but by the judgment of his peers or the law of the land, and, should the public exigencies make it necessary, for the common preservation, to take any person's property, or to demand his particular services, full compensation shall be made for the same. And, in the just preservation of rights and property, it is understood and declared, that no law ought ever to be made, or have force in the said territory, that shall, in any manner whatever, interfere with or affect private contracts or en-gagements, *bonafide,* and without fraud previously formed. . . .

There shall be no slavery or involuntary servitude in the said territory

ARTICLE 6

There shall be neither slavery nor involuntary servitude in the said territory, otherwise than in the punishment of crimes whereof the party shall have been duly convicted: *Provided, always,* That any person escaping into the same, from whom labor or service is lawfully claimed in any one of the original States, such fugitive may be lawfully reclaimed, and conveyed to the person claiming his or her labor or service as aforesaid. . . .

BENJAMIN FRANKLIN

By any measure, Benjamin Franklin (1706–1794) was one of the most remarkable figures in the history of the world. And certainly no American who has ever lived, except possibly Thomas Jefferson, did so many important things as well as Franklin. We are all familiar with his scientific discoveries, his inventions, his writings. But many historians believe that as significant as these accomplishments are, they are not the equal of the great works Franklin performed for the cause of American freedom as a statesman and diplomat.

His greatest accomplishments were as a diplomat

During the two decades before the Revolutionary War, Franklin principally served his country as a representative of the Pennsylvania legislature to the English government, arguing for more equitable tax treatment of the American colonies. Franklin came home from London on May 5, 1775, about two weeks after the Revolutionary War had begun. The people of Philadelphia immediately elected him to serve in the Second Continental Congress. During that time, he helped Jefferson draft the Declaration of Independence and was one of its signers. At the signing ceremony, John Hancock is said to have warned his fellow delegates, "We must be unanimous; there must be no pulling different ways; we must all hang together." "Yes," Franklin replied, "we must all hang together, or assuredly we shall all hang separately."

"we must all hang together, or assuredly we shall all hang separately."

In 1787, Franklin served as a delegate — the oldest, for he was then eighty-one years of age — to the Continental Congress that met in Independence Hall in Philadelphia to draft the U.S. Constitution. When he set his name to that document, Franklin became the only Founding Father to sign all four documents that were instrumental in the establishment of American freedom: the Constitution, the Declaration of Independence, the Treaty of Alliance with France, and the Treaty of Peace with Great Britain. Franklin was at his best in this exquisitely reasoned address to his fellow members of the Continental Congress.

FROM SPEECH RECOMMENDING THE ADOPTION OF THE CONSTITUTION SEPTEMBER 17, 1787

MR. PRESIDENT,

I confess that there are several parts of this Constitution which I do not at present approve, but I am not sure I shall never approve them; for, having lived long, I have experienced many instances of being obliged by better information or fuller consideration to change opinions, even on important subjects, which I once thought right but found to be otherwise. It is therefore that the older I grow the more apt I am to doubt my own judgment and to pay attention to the judgment of others. Most men, indeed, as well as most sects in religion think themselves in possession of all truth. . . . But though many private persons think almost as highly of their own infallibility as of that of their sect, few express it so naturally as a certain French lady who in a little dispute with her sister said: "I don't know how it happens, sister, but I meet with nobody but myself that is always in the right."

I meet with nobody but myself that is always in the right

In these sentiments, Sir, I agree to this Constitution with all its faults, if they are such; because I think a general government necessary for us, and there is no form of government but what may be a blessing to the people if well administered; and believe farther that this is likely to be well administered for a course of years and can only end in despotism, as other forms have done before it, when the people shall become so corrupt as to need despotic government, being incapable of any other. I doubt too whether any other convention we can obtain may be able to make a better Constitution. For when you assemble a number of men to have the advantage of their joint wisdom, you inevitably assemble with those men all their prejudices, their passions, their errors of opinion, their local interests, and their selfish views. From such an assembly can a perfect production be expected? It therefore astonishes me, Sir, to find this system approaching so near to perfection as it does. . . . Thus I consent, Sir, to this Constitution because I expect no better, and because I am not sure that it is not the best. The opinions I have had of its errors I sacrifice to the public good. I have never whispered a syllable of them abroad. Within these walls they were born, and here they shall die. . . .

It astonishes me to find this system approaching so near to perfection

On the whole, Sir, 1 cannot help expressing a wish that every member of the Convention who may still have objections to it would, with me, on this occasion doubt a little of his infallibility, and, to make manifest our unanimity, put his name to this instrument.

JAMES MADISON

James Madison (1751–1836), the fourth president of the United States, is often called the Father of the Constitution. Madison was born into a Virginia landowning family. He matriculated at the College of New Jersey (now Princeton University), where he made an excellent record as a student of history and government. After graduation in 1771, he became interest-

ed in the colonies' struggle for religious tolerance and their conflict with England. In 1776, he was elected to the Virginia Convention, becoming a member of the committee formed to write a state constitution. From then on, he was almost consistently prominent in the affairs of the young nation — as a member of the Continental Congress, a member of the Virginia House of Delegates, a congressman from Virginia, secretary of state under Jefferson, and president of the United States.

He served as the principal draftsman of the Constitution, whose provisions he brilliantly defended in The Federalist, a series of essays written in collaboration with Alexander Hamilton and John Jay to persuade Americans to accept the newly formulated federal Constitution. In the famous The Federalist No. 10, he argued strongly for the protection of property interests against the attacks of the majority.

The principal draftsman of the Constitution

THE FEDERALIST, NO. 10
MARCH 22, 1788

To the People of the State of New York:
Among the numerous advantages promised by a well-constructed Union, none deserves to be more accurately developed than its tendency to break and control the violence of faction. The friend of popular governments never finds himself so much alarmed for their character and fate, as when he

contemplates their propensity to this dangerous vice. He will not fail, therefore, to set a due value on any plan which, without violating the principles to which he is attached, provides a proper cure for it. The instability, injustice, and confusion introduced into the public councils, have, in truth, been the mortal diseases under which popular governments have everywhere perished; as they continue to be the favorite and fruitful topics from which the adversaries to liberty derive their most specious declamations. The valuable improvements made by the American constitutions on the popular models, both ancient and modern, cannot certainly be too much admired; but it would be an unwarrantable partiality, to contend that they have as effectually obviated the danger on this side, as was wished and expected. Complaints are everywhere heard from our most considerate and virtuous citizens, equally the friends of public and private faith, and of public and personal liberty, that our governments are too unstable, that the public good is disregarded in the conflicts of rival parties, and that measures are too often decided, not according to the rules of justice and the rights of the minor party, but by the superior force of an interested and overbearing majority. However anxiously we may wish that these complaints had no foundation, the evidence of known facts will not permit us to deny that they are in some degree true. It will be found, indeed, on a candid review of our situation, that some of the distress-es under which we labor have been erroneously charged on the operation of our governments; but it will be found, at the same time, that other causes will not alone account for many of our heaviest misfortunes; and, particularly, for that prevailing and increasing distrust of public engagements and alarm for private rights, which are echoed from one end of the continent to the other. These must be chiefly, if not wholly, effects of the unsteadiness and injustice with which a factious spirit has tainted our public administrations.

By a faction, I understand a number of citizens, whether amounting to a majority or minority of the whole, who are united and actuated by some common impulse of passion, or of interest, adverse to the rights of other citizens, or to the permanent and aggregate interests of the community.

> A faction is a group of citizens who are united by impulses adverse to the rights of other citizens

There are two methods of curing the mischiefs of faction: the one, by removing its cause; the other, by controlling its effects.

There are again two methods of removing the causes of faction: the one, by destroying the liberty which is essential to its existence; the other, by giving to every citizen the same opinions, the same passions, and the same interests.

> There are two methods of curing the mischiefs of faction

It could never be more truly said than of the first remedy, that it was worse than the disease. Liberty is to faction what air is to fire, an aliment without which it instantly expires. But it could not be less folly to abolish liberty, which is essential to political life, because it nourishes faction, than it would be to wish the annihilation of air, which is essential to animal life, because it imparts to fire its destructive agency.

The second expedient is as impracticable as the first would be unwise. As long as the reason of man continues fallible, and he is at liberty to exercise it, different opinions will be formed. As long as the connection subsists between his reason and his self-love, his opinions and his passions will have a reciprocal influence on each other; and the former will be objects to which the latter will attach themselves. The diversity in the faculties of men, from which the rights of property originate, is not less an insuperable obstacle to a uniformity of interests.

The protection of these faculties is the first object of government. From the protection of different and unequal faculties of acquiring property, the possession of different degrees and kinds of property immediately results; and from the influence of these on the sentiments and views of the respective proprietors, ensues a division of the society into different interests and parties.

The latent causes of faction are thus sown in the nature of man; and we see them everywhere brought into different degrees of activity, according to the different circumstances of civil society. A zeal for different opinions concerning religion, concerning government, and many other points, as well of speculation as of practice; an attachment to different leaders ambitiously contending

for pre-eminence and power; or to persons of
other descriptions whose fortunes have been
interesting to the human passions, have, in turn,
divided mankind into parties, inflamed them with
mutual animosity, and rendered them much more
disposed to vex and oppress each other than to cooperate for their common good. So strong is this
propensity of mankind to fall into mutual ani-
mosities, that where no substantial occasion presents itself, the most frivolous and fanciful distinctions have been sufficient to kindle their
unfriendly passions and excite their most violent
conflicts. But the most common and durable
source of factions has been the various and
unequal distribution of property. Those who hold
and those who are without property have ever
formed distinct interests in society. Those who are
creditors, and those who are debtors, fall under a
like discrimination. A landed interest, a manufacturing interest, a mercantile interest, a moneyed
interest, with many lesser interests, grow up of
necessity in civilized nations, and divide them into
different classes, actuated by different sentiments
and views. The regulation of these various and
interfering interests forms the principal task of
modern legislation, and involves the spirit of party
and faction in the necessary and ordinary opera-
tions of the government.

No man is allowed to be a judge in his own
cause, because his interest would certainly bias
his judgment, and, not improbably, corrupt his

The most common source of factions has been the unequal distribution of property

integrity. With equal, nay with greater reason, a
body of men are unfit to be both judges and parties at the same time; yet what are many of the
most important acts of legislation, but so many
judicial determinations, not indeed concerning
the rights of single persons, but concerning the
rights of large bodies of citizens? And what are
the different classes of legislators but advocates
and parties to the causes which they determine?
Is a law proposed concerning private debts? It is
a question to which the creditors are parties on
one side and the debtors on the other. Justice
ought to hold the balance between them. Yet the
parties are, and must be, themselves the judges;
and the most numerous party, or, in other words,
the most powerful faction must be expected to
prevail. Shall domestic manufactures be encouraged, and in what degree, by restrictions on foreign manufactures? are questions which would be
differently decided by the landed and the manufacturing classes, and probably by neither with a
sole regard to justice and the public good. The
apportionment of taxes on the various descriptions of property is an act which seems to require
the most exact impartiality; yet there is, perhaps;
no legislative act in which greater opportunity
and temptation are given to a predominant party
to trample on the rules of justice. Every shilling
with which they overburden the inferior number,
is a shilling saved to their own pockets.

It is in vain to say that enlightened statesmen

will be able to adjust these clashing interests, and render them all subservient to the public good. Enlightened statesmen will not always be at the helm. Nor, in many cases, can such an adjustment be made at all without taking into view indirect and remote considerations, which will rarely prevail over the immediate interest which one party may find in disregarding the rights of another or the good of the whole.

Enlightened statesmen will not always be at the helm

The inference to which we are brought is, that the *causes* of faction cannot be removed, and that relief is only to be sought in the means of controlling its *effects*.

If a faction consists of less than a majority, relief is supplied by the republican principle, which enables the majority to defeat its sinister views by regular vote. It may clog the administration, it may convulse the society; but it will be unable to execute and mask its violence under the forms of the Constitution. When a majority is included in a faction, the form of popular government, on the other hand, enables it to sacrifice to its ruling passion or interest both the public good and the rights of other citizens. To secure the public good and private rights against the danger of such a faction, and at the same time to preserve the spirit and the form of popular government, is then the great object to which our inquiries are directed. Let me add that it is the great desideratum [something needed] by which this form of government can be rescued from the opprobrium [disgrace or scorn] under which it has so long labored, and be recommended to the esteem and adoption of mankind.

By what means is this object attainable? Evidently by one of two only. Either the existence of the same passion or interest in a majority at the same time must be prevented, or the majority, having such coexistent passion or interest, must be rendered, by their number and local situation, unable to concert and carry into effect schemes of oppression. If the impulse and the opportunity be suffered to coincide, we well know that neither moral nor religious motives can be relied on as an adequate control. They are not found to be such on the injustice and violence of individuals, and lose their efficacy in proportion to the number combined together, that is, in proportion as their efficacy becomes needful.

From this view of the subject it may be concluded that a pure democracy, by which I mean a society consisting of a small number of citizens, who assemble and administer the government in person, can admit of no cure for the mischiefs of faction. A common passion or interest will, in almost every case, be felt by a majority of the whole; a communication and concert result from the form of government itself; and there is nothing to check the inducements to sacrifice the weaker party or an obnoxious individual. Hence it is that such democracies have ever been spectacles of turbulence and contention; have ever been found incompatible with personal security or the rights of property; and have in general been as short in their lives as they have been violent in their deaths. Theoretic politicians, who have patronized this species of government, have erroneously supposed that by reducing mankind to a perfect equality in their political rights, they would, at the same time, be perfectly equalized and assimilated in their possessions, their opinions, and their passions.

A republic, by which I mean a government in which the scheme of representation takes place, opens a different prospect, and promises the cure for which we are seeking. Let us examine the points in which it varies from pure democracy, and we shall comprehend both the nature of the cure and the efficacy which it must derive from the Union.

The two great points of difference between a democracy and a republic are: first, the delegation of the government, in the latter, to a small number of citizens elected by the rest; secondly, the greater number of citizens, and greater sphere of country, over which the latter may be extended.

The two great points of difference between a democracy and a republic

The effect of the first difference is, on the one hand, to refine and enlarge the public views, by passing them through the medium of a chosen body of citizens, whose wisdom may best discern the true interest of their country, and whose patriotism and love of justice will be least likely to sacrifice it to temporary or partial considerations. Under such a regulation, it may well happen that the public voice, pronounced by the representa-

tives of the people, will be more consonant to the
public good than if pronounced by the people
themselves, convened for the purpose. On the
other hand, the effect may be inverted. Men of
factious tempers, of local prejudices, or of sinister
designs, may, by intrigue, by corruption, or by
other means, first obtain the suffrages [votes],
and then betray the interests, of the people. The
question resulting is, whether small or extensive
republics are more favorable to the election of
proper guardians of the public weal; and it is
clearly decided in favor of the latter by two obvious considerations;

In the first place, it is to be remarked that,
however small the republic may be, the representatives must be raised to a certain number, in
order to guard against the cabals [plots] of a few;
and that, however large it may be, they must be
limited to a certain number, in order to guard
against the confusion of a multitude. Hence, the
number of representatives in the two cases not
being in proportion to that of the two constituents,
and being proportionally greater in the small
republic, it follows that, if the proportion of fit
characters be not less in the large than in the
small republic, the former will present a greater
option, and consequently a greater probability of
a fit choice.

In the next place, as each representative will
be chosen by a greater number of citizens in the
large than in the small republic, it will be more

difficult for unworthy candidates to practise with success the vicious arts by which elections are too often carried; and the suffrages of the people being more free, will be more likely to centre in men who possess the most attractive merit and the most diffusive and established characters.

It must be confessed that in this, as in most other cases, there is a mean, on both sides of which inconveniences will be found to lie. By enlarging too much the number of electors, you render the representative too little acquainted with all their local circumstances and lesser interests; as by reducing it too much, you render him unduly attached to these, and too little fit to comprehend and pursue great and national objects. The federal Constitution forms a happy combination in this respect; the great and aggregate interests being referred to the national, the local and particular to the State legislatures.

The federal Constitution forms a happy combination

The other point of difference is, the greater number of citizens and extent of territory which may be brought within the compass of republican than of democratic government; and it is this circumstance principally which renders factious combinations less to be dreaded in the former than in the latter. The smaller the society, the fewer probably will be the distinct parties and interests composing it; the fewer the distinct parties and interests, the more frequently will a majority be found of the same party; and the smaller the number of individuals composing a majority, and the smaller the compass within which they are placed, the more easily will they concert and execute their plans of oppression. Extend the sphere and you take in a greater variety of parties and interests; you make it less probable that a majority of the whole will have a common motive to invade the rights of other citizens; or if such a common motive exists, it will be more difficult for all who feel it to discover their own strength, and to act in unison with each other. Besides other impediments, it may be remarked that, where there is a consciousness of unjust or dishonorable purposes, communication is always checked by distrust in proportion to the number whose concurrence is necessary.

Hence, it clearly appears, that the same advantage which a republic has over a democracy, in controlling the effects of faction, is enjoyed by a large over a small republic, — is enjoyed by the Union over the States composing it. Does the advantage consist in the substitution of representatives whose enlightened views and virtuous sentiments render them superior to local prejudices and to schemes of injustice"? It will not be denied that the representation of the Union will be most likely to possess these requisite endowments. Does it consist in the greater security afforded by a greater variety of parties, against the event of any one party being able to outnumber and oppress the rest? In an equal degree does the increased variety of parties comprised within the Union, increase this security. Does it, in fine, consist in the greater obstacles opposed to the concert and accomplishment of the secret wishes of an unjust and interested majority? Here, again, the extent of the Union gives it the most palpable advantage.

The extent of the Union gives it the most palpable advantage

The influence of factious leaders may kindle a flame within their particular States, but will be unable to spread a general conflagration through the other States. A religious sect may degenerate into a political faction in a part of the Confederacy; but the variety of sects dispersed over the entire face of it must secure the national councils against any danger from that source. A rage for paper money, for an abolition of debts, for an equal division of property, or for any other improper or wicked project, will be less apt to pervade the whole body of the Union than a particular member of it; in the same proportion as such a malady is more likely to taint a particular county or district, than an entire State.

In the extent and proper structure of the Union, therefore, we behold a republican remedy for the diseases most incident to republican government. And according to the degree of pleasure and pride we feel in being republicans, ought to be our zeal in cherishing the spirit and supporting the character of Federalists.   PUBLIUS

III
WRITINGS FROM
THE
ANTEBELLUM PERIOD

The seventy years between the ratification of the Bill of Rights and the commencement of the Civil War — the era commonly referred to as the antebellum period of our history — was for the young republic a time of economic growth, territorial expansion, and political maturation, highlighted by such events as the presidency of Thomas Jefferson, the Louisiana Purchase, the War of 1812, the Missouri Compromise, the Monroe Doctrine, the Age of Jackson, and the Dred Scott decision. Overshadowing all matters during the entire antebellum period, however, was the issue of slavery and its abolition. By the early 1800s, all the northern states had outlawed slavery, but the plantation system had spread throughout the southern states, creating an economic system based upon slavery that Southerners had no intention of changing.

To one degree or another, almost all the leading political leaders of the time — John Quincy Adams, John Marshall, Henry Clay, Andrew Jackson, James Monroe, Zachary Taylor, Stephen A. Douglas, Martin Van Buren, and John C.

Overshadowing all was the issue of slavery

Calhoun, for example — were confronted with the slavery issue. And the question presents itself as to how competent and wise were they to deal with it. Surely they had to have been regarded as lesser figures compared to such towering heroes of the Revolutionary era as George Washington, Thomas Jefferson, and James Madison. But one most influential figure in American history did appear on the scene at this time, the statesman and orator Daniel Webster.

DANIEL WEBSTER

Daniel Webster (1782–1852) was a major player in American politics from the time of the War of 1812 until the beginning of the Civil War. During that eventful fifty-year period, he was involved with every significant issue confronting the new nation. He was one of our greatest senators, an excellent secretary of state, an outstanding lawyer, and an important contributor to the constitutional development of the United States. And unquestionably, Webster had no equal as an orator. Whether in the Senate, before the Supreme Court, or on the political stump, he was a golden-tongued spellbinder, often holding audiences in thrall for hours. Here first is his memorable address at the dedication of the Bunker Hill Monument.

A golden-tongued orator

FROM SPEECH AT THE LAYING OF THE CORNER-STONE OF THE BUNKER HILL MONUMENT JUNE 17, 1825

We are among the sepulchers of our fathers. We are on ground distinguished by their valor, their constancy, and the shedding of their blood. We are here, not to fix an uncertain date in our annals, nor to draw into notice an obscure and unknown spot. If our humble purpose had never been conceived, if we ourselves had never been born, the 17th of June, 1775, would have been a day on which all subsequent history would have poured its light, and the eminence where we stand a point of attraction to the eyes of successive generations. But we are Americans. We live in what may be called the early age of this great continent; and we know that our posterity, through all time, are here to suffer and enjoy the allotments of humanity. We see before us a probable train of great events; we know that our own fortunes have been happily cast; and it is natural, therefore, that we should be moved by the contemplation of occurrences which have guided our destiny before many of us were born, and settled the condition in which we should pass that portion of our existence which God allows to men on earth.

We know that our own fortunes have been happily cast

We do not read even of the discovery of this continent, without feeling something of a personal interest in the event; without being reminded how much it has affected our own fortunes and our own existence. . . .

Nearer to our times, more closely connected to our fates, and therefore still more interesting to our feelings and our affections, is the settlement of our own country by colonists from England. . . .

But the great event in the history of the continent which we are now met here to commemorate, that prodigy of modern times, at once the **The blessing** wonder and the blessing of the world, is the **of the world** American Revolution. In a day of extraordinary **is the** prosperity and happiness, of high national honor, **American** distinction, and power, we are brought together, **Revolution** in this place, by our love of country, by our admiration of exalted character, by our gratitude for signal services and patriotic devotion. . . .

The great wheel of political revolution began to move in America. Here its rotation was guarded, regular, and safe. Transferred to the other continent, from unfortunate but natural causes, it received an irregular and violent impulse; it whirled along with a fearful celerity, till at length, like the chariot-wheels in the races of antiquity, it took fire from the rapidity of its own motion and blazed onward, spreading conflagration and terror around.

We learn from the result of this experiment, how fortunate was our own condition, and how admirably the character of our people was calculated for setting great example of popular governments. . . . In the American Revolution, no man sought or wished for more than to defend and enjoy his own. None hoped for plunder or for spoil. Rapacity was unknown to it; the axe was not among the instruments of its accomplishment; and we all know that it could not have lived a single day under any well-founded imputation of possessing a tendency adverse to the Christian religion . . . .

When Louis the Fourteenth said, "I am the state," he expressed the essence of the doctrine of unlimited power. By the rules of that system, the people are disconnected from the state; they are its subjects; it is their lord. These ideas, founded in the love of power, and long supported by the excess and the abuse of it, are yielding in our age to other opinions; and the civilized world seems at last to be proceeding to the conviction of that fundamental and manifest truth, that the powers of government are but a trust, and that they cannot be lawfully exercised but for the good of the community. . . .

The powers of government are but a trust

We may hope that the growing influence of enlightened sentiment will promote the permanent peace of the world. Wars to maintain family alliances, to uphold or to cast down dynasties, to regulate successions to thrones, which have occupied so much room in the history of modern times, if not less likely to happen at all, will be less likely to become general and involve many nations, as the great principle shall be more and more established, that the interest of the world is peace, and its first great statute, that every nation possesses the power of establishing a government for itself. But public opinion has attained also an influence over governments which do not admit the popular principle into their organization. A necessary respect for the judgment of the world operates, in some measure, as a control over the most unlimited forms of authority. . . . Let us thank God that we live in an age when something has influence besides the bayonet, and when the sternest authority does not venture to encounter the scorching power of public reproach. . . .

And, now, let us indulge an honest exultation in the conviction of the benefit which the example of our country has produced, and is likely to produce, on human freedom and human happiness. And let us endeavor to comprehend in all its magnitude and to feel in all its importance, the part assigned to us in the great drama of human affairs. We are placed at the head of the system of representative and popular governments. Thus far our example shows that such governments are compatible, not only with respectability and power, but with repose, with peace, with security of personal rights, with good laws and in just administration.

We are not propagandists. Wherever other systems are preferred, either as being thought better in themselves, or as better suited to existing condition, we leave the preference to be

Marginal note: Let us thank God we live in an age when something has influence besides the bayonet

enjoyed. Our history hitherto proves, however, that the popular form is practicable, and that with wisdom and knowledge men may govern themselves; and the duty incumbent on us is, to preserve the consistency of this cheering example, and take care that nothing may weaken its authority with the world. If, in our case, the representative system ultimately fail, popular governments must be pronounced impossible. No combination of circumstances more favorable to the experiment can ever be expected to occur. The last hopes of mankind, therefore, rest with us; and if it should be proclaimed, that our example had become an argument against the experiment, the knell of popular liberty would be sounded throughout the earth.

The last hopes of mankind rest with us

These are incitements to duty; but they are not suggestions of doubt. Our history and our condition, all that is gone before us, and all that surrounds us, authorize the belief, that popular governments, though subject to occasional variations, in form perhaps not always for the better, may yet, in their general character, be as durable and permanent as other systems. We know, indeed, that in our country any other is impossible. The *principle* of free governments adheres to the American soil. It is bedded in it, immovable as its mountains.

And let the sacred obligations which have devolved on this generation, and on us, sink deep into our hearts. Those who established our liberty and our government are daily dropping from among us. The great trust now descends to new hands. Let us apply ourselves to that which is presented to us, as our appropriate object. We can win no laurels in a war for independence. Earlier and worthier hands have gathered them all. Nor are there places for us by the side of Solon, and Alfred, and other founders of states. Our fathers have filled them. But there remains to us a great duty of defense and preservation; and there is opened to us also a noble pursuit, to which the spirit of the times strongly invites us.

Let our age be the age of improvement

Our proper business is improvement. Let our age be the age of improvement. In a day of peace, let us advance the arts of peace and the works of peace. Let us develop the resources of our land, call forth its powers, build up its institutions, promote all its great interests, and see whether we also, in our day and generation, may not perform something worthy to be remembered. Let us cultivate a true spirit of union and harmony. In pursuing the great objects which our condition points out to us, let us act under a settled conviction, and an habitual feeling, that these twenty-four States are one country. Let our conceptions be enlarged to the circle of our duties. Let us extend our ideas over the whole of the vast field in which we are called to act. Let our object be, OUR COUNTRY, OUR WHOLE COUNTRY, AND NOTHING BUT OUR COUNTRY. And, by the blessing of God, may that country itself become a vast and splendid monument, not of oppression and terror, but of Wisdom, of Peace, and of Liberty, upon which the world may gaze with admiration forever!

Webster delivered one of his greatest orations in Boston's Faneuil Hall on August 2, 1826. A month earlier, the American public had been shocked and saddened by the simultaneous deaths, on July 4, 1826 — the fiftieth anniversary of the Declaration of Independence — of the two most prominent survivors of the American Revolution. This extraordinary coincidence, and the historical associations suggested by it, stirred the whole country, and the thoughts and emotions of a whole country were never more adequately voiced than in Webster's eulogy. Here is an excerpt from that masterful speech.

Webster's famous eulogy

FROM SPEECH IN COMMEMORATION OF THE LIVES AND SERVICES OF JOHN ADAMS AND THOMAS JEFFERSON AUGUST 2, 1826

ADAMS and JEFFERSON are no more. On our fiftieth anniversary, the great day of national jubilee, in the very hour of public rejoicing, in the midst of echoing and reechoing voices of thanksgiving, while their own names were on all tongues, they took their flight together to the world of spirits.

If it be true that no one can safely be pronounced happy while he lives, if that event which terminates life can alone crown its honors and its glory, what felicity is here! The great epic of their lives, how happily concluded! Poetry itself has hardly terminated illustrious lives, and finished the career of earthly renown, by such a consummation. If we had the power, we could not wish to reverse this dispensation of the Divine Providence. The great objects of life were accomplished, the drama was ready to be closed. It has closed: our patriots have fallen: but so fallen, at such age, with such coincidence, on such a day, that we cannot rationally lament that that end has come, which we knew could not be long deferred.

Neither of these great men could have died without leaving an immense void in our American society

Neither of these great men, fellow-citizens, could have died, at any time, without leaving an immense void in our American society. They have been so intimately, and for so long a time, blended with the history of the country, and especially so united, in our thoughts and recollections, with the events of the Revolution, that the death of either would have touched the chords of public sympathy. We should have felt that one great link, connecting us with former times, was broken; that we had lost something more, as it were, of the presence of the Revolution itself, and of the act of independence, and were driven on, by another great remove from the days of our country's early distinction, to meet posterity, and to mix with the future. Like the mariner, whom the currents of the ocean and the winds carry along, till he sees the stars which have directed his course and lighted his pathless way descend, one by one, beneath the rising horizon, we should have felt that the stream of time had borne us onward till another great luminary, whose light had cheered us and whose guidance we had followed, had sunk away from our sight.

But the concurrence of their death on the anniversary of Independence has naturally awakened stronger emotions. Both had been Presidents, both had lived to great age, both were early patriots, and both were distinguished and ever honored by their immediate agency in the act of independence. It cannot but seem striking and extraordinary, that these two should live to see the fiftieth year from the date of that act; that they should complete that year; and that then, on the day which had fast linked for ever their own fame with their country's glory, the heavens should open to receive them both at once. As their lives themselves were the gifts of Providence, who is not willing to recognize in their happy termination, as well as in their long continuance, proofs that our country and its benefactors are objects of His care?

ADAMS and JEFFERSON, I have said, are no more. As human beings, indeed, they are no more. They are no more, as in 1776, bold and fearless advocates of independence; no more, as at subsequent periods, the head of the government: no more, as we have recently seen them, aged and venerable objects of admiration and regard. They are no more. They are dead. But how little is there of the great and good which can die! To their country they yet live, and live for ever. They live in all that perpetuates the remembrance of men on earth; in the recorded proofs of their own great actions, in the offspring of their intellect in the deep-engraved lines of public gratitude, and in the respect and homage of mankind. They live in their example; and they live, emphatically, and will live, in the influence which their lives and efforts, their principles and opinions, now exercise, and will continue to exercise, on the affairs of men, not only in their own country, but throughout the civilized world. A superior and commanding human intellect, a truly great man, when Heaven vouchsafes so rare a gift, is not a temporary flame, burning brightly for a while, and then giving place to returning darkness. It is rather a spark of fervent heat, as well as radiant light, with power to enkindle the common mass of human mind; so that when it glimmers in its own decay, and finally goes out in death, no night follows, but it leaves the world all light, all on fire, from the potent contact of its own spirit. Bacon died; but the human understanding, roused by the touch of his miraculous wand to a perception of the true philosophy and the just mode of inquiring after truth, has kept on its course successfully and gloriously. Newton died; yet the courses of the spheres are still known, and

How little is there of the great and good which can die!

they yet move on by the laws which he discovered, and in the orbits which he saw, and
described for them, in the infinity of space.

No two men now live, fellow-citizens, perhaps
it may be doubted whether any two men have
ever lived in one age, who, more than those we
now commemorate, have impressed on mankind
their own sentiments in regard to politics and government, infused their own opinions more deeply
into the opinions of others, or given a more lasting
direction to the current of human thought. Their
work doth not perish with them. The tree which
they assisted to plant will flourish, although they
water it and protect it no longer; for it has struck
its roots deep, it has sent them to the very centre;
no storm, not of force to burst the orb, can over-
turn it; its branches spread wide: they stretch
their protecting arms broader and broader, and its
top is destined to reach the heavens. We are not
deceived. There is no delusion here. No age will
come in which the American Revolution will
appear less than it is, one of the greatest events in
human history. No age will come in which it shall
cease to be seen and felt, on either continent, that
a mighty step, a great advance, not only in American affairs, but in human affairs, was made on
the 4th of July, 1776. And no age will come, we
trust, so ignorant and so unjust as not to see and
acknowledge the efficient agency of those we now
honor in producing that momentous event. . . .

*Their work
doth not
perish with
them*

On January 25, 1830, Senator Robert Y. Hayne of South Carolina concluded his remarks to the Senate on a tariff bill under consideration. He had set forth a number of pro-slavery and states' rights arguments, chief among them the ideas that states could nullify a federal law they believed to be unconstitutional and that states could even secede from the Union. Webster immediately arose and in a long — more than one hundred manuscript pages — extemporaneous rebuttal delivered the speech that many scholars regard as the most significant of his entire career.

The most significant speech of his career

FROM SPEECH IN
THE SENATE OF THE UNITED STATES
("THE REPLY TO HAYNE")
JANUARY 26 AND 27, 1830

The Constitution of the United States is not unalterable

Let it be remembered, that the Constitution of the United States is not unalterable. It is to continue in its present form no longer than the people who established it shall choose to continue it. If they shall become convinced that they have made an injudicious or inexpedient partition and distribution of power between the State governments and the general government, they can alter that distribution at will.

If any thing be found in the national Constitution, either by original provision or subsequent interpretation, which ought not to be in it, the people know how to get rid of it. If any construc-

tion, unacceptable to them, be established, so as
to become practically a part of the Constitution,
they will amend it, at their own sovereign pleasure. But while the people choose to maintain it
as it is, while they are satisfied with it, and refuse
to change it, who has given, or who can give, to
the State legislatures a right to alter it, either by
interference, construction, or otherwise? Gentlemen do not seem to recollect that the people have
any power to do any thing for themselves. They
imagine there is no safety for them, any longer
than they are under the close guardianship of the
State legislatures. Sir, the people have not trusted
their safety, in regard to the general Constitution,
to these hands. They have required other security, and taken other bonds. They have chosen to
trust themselves, first, to the plain words of the
instrument, and to such construction as the government themselves, in doubtful cases, should put
on their own powers, under their oaths of office,
and subject to their responsibility to them; just as
the people of a State trust their own State governments with a similar power. Secondly, they
have reposed their trust in the efficacy of frequent
elections, and in their own power to remove their
own servants and agents whenever they see
cause. Thirdly, they have reposed trust in the
judicial power, which, in order that it might be
trustworthy, they have made as respectable, as
disinterested, and as independent as was practicable. Fourthly, they have seen fit to rely, in case

The people have the power to do any thing for themselves

of necessity, or high expediency, on their known and admitted power to alter or amend the Constitution, peaceably and quietly, whenever experience shall point out defects or imperfections. And, finally, the people of the United States have at no time, in no way, directly or indirectly, authorized any State legislature to construe or interpret *their* high instrument of government; much less, to interfere, by their own power, to arrest its course and operation.

The people have not authorized any State legislature to arrest the course and operation of the Constitution

If, Sir, the people in these respects had done otherwise than they have done, their Constitution could neither have been preserved, nor would it have been worth preserving. And if its plain provisions shall now be disregarded, and these new doctrines interpolated in it, it will become as feeble and helpless a being as its enemies, whether early or more recent, could possibly desire. It will exist in every State but as a poor dependent on State permission. It must borrow leave to be; and will be, no longer than State pleasure, or State discretion, sees fit to grant the indulgence, and to prolong its poor existence.

But, Sir, although there are fears, there are hopes also. The people have preserved this, their own chosen Constitution, for forty years, and have seen their happiness, prosperity, and renown grow with its growth, and strengthen with its strength. They are now, generally, strongly attached to it. Overthrown by direct assault, it cannot be evaded, undermined, NULLIFIED, it will not be, if we and those who shall succeed us here, as agents and representatives of the people, shall conscientiously and vigilantly discharge the two great branches of our public trust, faithfully to preserve, and wisely to administer it.

Mr. President, I have thus stated the reasons of my dissent to the doctrines which have been advanced and maintained. I am conscious of having detained you and the Senate much too long. I was drawn into the debate with no previous deliberation, such as is suited to the discussion of so grave and important a subject. But it is a subject of which my heart is full, and I have not been willing to suppress the utterance of its spontaneous sentiments. I cannot, even now, persuade myself to relinquish it, without expressing once more my deep conviction, that, since it respects nothing less than the Union of the States, it is of most vital and essential importance to the public happiness. I profess, Sir, in my career hitherto, to have kept steadily in view the prosperity and honor of the whole country, and the preservation of our Federal Union. It is to that Union we owe our safety at home, and our consideration and dignity abroad. It is to that Union that we are chiefly indebted for whatever makes us most proud of our country. That Union we reached only by the discipline of our virtues in the severe school of adversity. It had its origin in the necessities of disordered finance, prostrate commerce, and ruined credit. Under its benign influences, these great interests immedi-

It is a subject of which my heart is full

ately awoke, as from the dead, and sprang forth with newness of life. Every year of its duration has teemed with fresh proofs of its utility and its blessings; and although our territory has stretched out wider and wider, and our population spread farther and farther, they have not outrun its protection or its benefits. It has been to us all a copious fountain of national, social, and personal happiness.

The Union of the States has been a copious fountain of national, social, and personal happiness

I have not allowed myself, Sir, to look beyond the Union, to see what might lie hidden in the dark recess behind. I have not cooly weighted the chances of preserving liberty when the bonds that unite us together shall be broken asunder. I have not accustomed myself to hang over the precipice of disunion, to see whether, with my short sight, I can fathom the depth of the abyss below; nor could I regard him as a safe counsellor in the affairs of this government, whose thoughts should be mainly bent on considering, not how the Union may be best preserved, but how tolerable might be the condition of the people when it should be broken up and destroyed. While the Union lasts, we have high, exciting, gratifying prospects spread out before us, for us and our children. Beyond that I seek not to penetrate the veil. God grant that, in my day, at least, that curtain may not rise! God grant that on my vision never may be opened what lies behind! When my eyes shall be turned to behold for the last time the sun in heaven, may I not see him shining on the broken

While the Union lasts, we have high prospects before us

and dishonored fragments of a once glorious Union;
on States dissevered, discordant, belligerent; on a
land rent with civil feuds, or drenched, it may be,
in fraternal blood! Let their last feeble and linger-
ing glance rather behold the gorgeous ensign of
the republic, now known and honored throughout
the earth, still full high advanced, its arms and
trophies streaming in their original lustre, not a
stripe erased or polluted, nor a single star ob-
scured, bearing for its motto, no such miserable
interrogatory as "What is all this worth?" nor
those other words of delusion and folly, "Liberty
first and Union afterwards"; but everywhere,
spread all over in characters of living light, blazing
on all its ample folds, as they float over the sea
and over the land, and in every wind under the
whole heavens, that other sentiment, dear to every
true American heart, — Liberty *and* Union, now
and for ever, one and inseparable!. . .

Liberty *and* Union, now and for ever, one and inseparable

JAMES FENIMORE COOPER

*Born into a wealthy, landed family and raised on
the great Cooper estate in western New York,
American novelist and social critic James Feni-
more Cooper (1789–1851) was trained to live the
enviable life of a Tory squire. However, he developed great skill as a writer, and he is best known
today as the creator of* The Leatherstocking
Tales, *a series of novels about frontiersman Natty*

Bumppo that includes such classics as The Last
of the Mohicans *and* The Deerslayer.

*He went abroad in 1826, traveled throughout
the Continent, and did not return to America until
1833. During his absence, he lost touch with the
American people and wrote about them more ro-
mantically than ever. Yet he allowed his upper-
class conservative bias against the common man
to be strengthened by his cosmopolitan contacts
in Europe. Returning to America, Cooper became a
vehement critic of almost everything his neighbors cherished. Although he was concerned
about the freedom of individuals and the rights of*
Cooper dis- *property owners, he feared that majority rule*
trusted *would bring disorder and injustice. He believed*
majority rule *instead that the United States should be ruled by
a small aristocracy of public-spirited landowners
like himself. But no matter how critical Cooper
was of democracy, he believed in it. His essay
"The American Democrat" was a complete statement of his views.*

FROM "THE AMERICAN DEMOCRAT"
1838

On Liberty

Liberty, like equality, is a word more used than
understood. Perfect and absolute liberty is as incompatible with the existence of society, as equality of condition. It is impracticable in a state of
nature even, since, without the protection of the

law, the strong would oppress and enslave the weak. We are then to understand by liberty, merely such a state of the social compact as permits the members of a community to lay no more restraints on themselves, than are required by their real necessities, and obvious interests. To this definition may be added, that it is a requisite of liberty, that the body of a nation should retain the power to modify its institutions, as circumstances shall require.

The nation should retain the power to modify its institutions

The natural disposition of all men being to enjoy a perfect freedom of action, it is a common error to suppose that the nation which possesses the mildest laws, or laws that impose the least personal restraints, is the freest. This opinion is untenable, since the power that concedes this freedom of action, can recall it. Unless it is lodged in the body of the community itself, there is, therefore, no pledge for the continuance of such a liberty. A familiar, supposititious case will render this truth more obvious.

A slave holder in Virginia is the master of two slaves: to one he grants his liberty, with the means to go to a town in a free state. The other accompanies his old associate clandestinely. In this town, they engage their services voluntarily, to a common master, who assigns to them equal shares in the same labor, paying them the same wages. In time, the master learns their situation, but, being an indulgent man, he allows the slave to retain his present situation. In all material things, these brothers are equal; they labor together, receive the same wages, and eat of the same food. Yet one is bond, and the other free, since it is in the power of the master, or of his heir, or of his assignee, at any time, to reclaim the services of the one who was not legally manumitted [freed], and reduce him again to the condition of slavery. One of these brothers is the master of his own acts, while the other, though temporarily enjoying the same privileges, holds them subject to the will of a superior.

This is an all important distinction in the consideration of political liberty, since the circumstances of no two countries are precisely the same, and all municipal regulations ought to have direct reference to the actual condition of a community. It follows that no country can properly be deemed free, unless the body of the nation possess, in the last resort, the legal power to frame its laws according to its wants. This power must also abide in the nation, or it becomes merely an historical fact, for he that was once free is not necessarily free always, any more than he that was once happy, is to consider himself happy in perpetuity.

This definition of liberty is new to the world, for a government founded on such principles is a novelty. Hitherto, a nation has been deemed free, whose people were possessed of a certain amount of franchises, without any reference to the general repository of power. Such a nation may not be absolutely enslaved, but it can scarcely be consid-

This definition of liberty is new to the world

ered in possession of an affirmative political liberty, since it is not the master of its own fortunes.

Having settled what is the foundation of liberty, it remains to be seen by what process a people can exercise this authority over themselves. The usual course is to refer all matters of choice to the decision of majorities. The common axiom of democracies, however, which says that "the majority must rule," is to be received with many limitations. Were the majority of a country to rule without restraint, it is probable as much injustice and oppression would follow, as are found under the dominion of one. It belongs to the nature of men to arrange themselves in parties, to lose sight of truth and justice in partisanship and prejudice, to mistake their own impulses for that which is proper, and to do wrong because they are indisposed to seek the right. Were it wise to trust power, unreservedly, to majorities, all fundamental and controlling laws would be unnecessary, since they might, as occasion required, emanate from the will of numbers. Constitutions would be useless.

The axiom that democracies must rule is to be received with many limitations

The majority rules in prescribed cases, and in no other. It elects to office, it enacts ordinary laws, subject however to the restrictions of the constitution, and it decides most of the questions that arise in the primitive meetings of the people; questions that do not usually effect any of the principal interests of life.

The majority does not rule in settling fundamental laws, under the constitution; or when it does rule in such cases, it is with particular checks produced by time and new combinations; it does not pass judgment in trials at law, or under impeachment, and it is impotent in many matters touching vested rights. . . .

Though majorities often decide wrong, it is believed that they are less liable to do so than minorities. There can be no question that the educated and affluent classes of a country, are more capable of coming to wise and intelligent decisions in affairs of state than the mass of a population. Their wealth and leisure afford them opportunities for observation and comparison, while their general information and greater knowledge of character, enable them to judge more accurately of men and measures. That these opportunities are not properly used, is owing to the unceasing desire of men to turn their advantages to their own particular benefit, and to their passions. All history proves, when power is the sole possession of a few, that it is perverted to their sole advantage, the public suffering in order that their rulers may prosper. The same nature which imposes the necessity of governments at all, seems to point out the expediency of confiding its control, in the last resort, to the body of the nation, as the only lasting protection against gross abuses.

When power is in the sole possession of a few, it is perverted to their sole advantage

We do not adopt the popular polity because it is perfect, but because it is less imperfect than any other. As man, by his nature, is liable to err, it is vain to expect an infallible whole that is com-

posed of fallible parts. The government that ema-
nates from a single will, supposing that will to be
pure, enlightened, impartial, just and consistent,
would be the best in the world, were it attainable
for men. Such is the government of the universe,
the result of which is perfect harmony. As no man
is without spot in his justice, as no man has infinite wisdom, or infinite mercy, we are driven to
take refuge in the opposite extreme, or in a government of many.

It is common for the advocates of monarchy
and aristocracy to deride the opinion of the mass,
as no more than the impulses of ignorance and
prejudices. While experience unhappily shows
that this charge has too much truth, it also shows
that the educated and few form no exemption to
the common rule of humanity. The most intelligent men of every country in which there is liberty of thought and action, yielding to their interests
or their passions, are always found taking the
opposite extremes of contested questions, thus tri-
umphantly refuting an arrogant proposition, that
of the exclusive fitness of the few to govern, by an
unanswerable fact. The minority of a country is
never known to agree, except in its efforts to
reduce and oppress the majority. Were this not so,
parties would be unknown in all countries but
democracies, whereas the factions of aristocracies
have been among the fiercest and least govern-
able of any recorded in history.

Although real political liberty can have but one

Real political
liberty can
have but one
character,
that of a
popular base

character, that of a popular base, the world contains many modifications of governments that
are, more or less, worthy to be termed free. In
most of these states however, the liberties of the
mass, are of the negative character of franchises,
which franchises are not power of themselves, but
merely an exemption from the abuses of power.
Perhaps no state exists, in which the people,
either by usage, or by direct concessions from the
source of authority, do not possess some of these
franchises; for, if there is no such thing, in practice, as perfect and absolute liberty, neither is
there any such thing, in practice, as total and
unmitigated slavery. In the one case, nature has
rendered man incapable of enjoying freedom
without restraint, and in the other, incapable of
submitting, entirely without resistance, to oppression. The harshest despots are compelled to
acknowledge the immutable principles of their
eternal justice, affecting necessity and the love of
right, for their most ruthless deeds. . . .

Although it is true, that no genuine liberty can
exist without being based on popular authority in
the last resort, it is equally true that it can not
exist when thus based, without many restraints
on the power of the mass. These restraints are
necessarily various and numerous. A familiar
example will show their action. The majority of
the people of a state might be in debt to its minority. Were the power of the former unrestrained,
circumstances might arise in which they would

declare depreciated bank notes a legal tender, and thus clear themselves of their liabilities, at the expense of their creditors. To prevent this, the constitution orders that nothing shall be made a legal tender but the precious metals, thus limiting the power of majorities in a way that government is not limited in absolute monarchies, in which paper in often made to possess the value of gold and silver.

Liberty therefore may be defined to be a controlling authority that resides in the body of a nation, but so restrained as only to be exercised on certain general principles that shall do as little violence to natural justice, as is compatible with the peace and security of society.

Liberty may be defined to be a controlling authority in the body of a nation

Advantages of a Democracy

The principal advantage of a democracy, is a general elevation in the character of the people. If few are raised to a very great height, few are depressed very low. As a consequence, the average of society is much more respectable than under any other form of government. The vulgar charge that the tendency of democracies is to levelling, meaning to drag all down to the level of the lowest, is singularly untrue, its real tendency being to elevate the depressed to a condition not unworthy of their manhood. In the absence of privileged orders . . . and distinctions, devised permanently to separate men into social castes, it is true none are great but those who become so by

The average democratic society is much more respectable than any other form of government

their acts, but, confining the remark to the upper classes of society, it would be much more true to say that democracy refuses to lend itself to unnatural and arbitrary distinctions, than to accuse it of a tendency to level those who have a just claim to be elevated. A denial of a favor is not an invasion of a right.

Democracies are exempt from the military charges, both pecuniary and personal, that become necessary in governments in which the majority are subjects, since no force is required to repress those who, under other systems, are dangerous to the state, by their greater physical power.

The success of democracies is mainly dependant on the intelligence of the people

As the success of democracies is mainly dependant on the intelligence of the people, the means of preserving the government are precisely those which most conduce to the happiness and social progress of man. Hence we find the state endeavoring to raise its citizens in the scale of being, the certain means of laying the broadest foundation of national prosperity. If the arts are advanced in aristocracies, through the taste of patrons, in democracies, though of slower growth, they will prosper as a consequence of general information; or as a superstructure reared on a wider and more solid foundation.

Democracies being, as nearly as possible, founded in natural justice, little violence is done to the sense of right by the institutions, and men have less occasion than usual, to resort to fallacies and false principles in cultivating the faculties.

As a consequence, common sense is more encouraged, and the community is apt to entertain juster notions of all moral truths, than under systems that are necessarily sophisticated. Society is thus a gainer in the greatest element of happiness, or in the right perception of the different relations between men and things.

Democracies being established for the common interests, and the publick agents being held in constant check by the people, their general tendency is to serve the whole community, and not small portions of it, as is the case in narrow governments. It is as rational to suppose that a hungry man will first help his neighbor to bread, when master of his own acts, as to suppose that any but those who feel themselves to be truly public servants, will first bethink themselves of the publick, when in situations of public trust. In a government of one, that one and his parasites will be the first and best served; in a government of a few, the few; and in a government of many, the many. Thus the general tendency of democratical institutions is to equalize advantages, and to spread its blessings over the entire surface of society.

Democracies, other things being equal, are the cheapest form of government, since little money is lavished in representation, and they who have to pay the taxes, have also, directly or indirectly, a voice in imposing them.

Democracies are the cheapest form of government

Democracies are less liable to popular tumults than any other polities, because the people, having legal means in their power to redress wrongs,

The man who can right himself by a vote, will seldom resort to a musket

have little inducement to employ any other. The man who can right himself by a vote, will seldom resort to a musket. Grievances, moreover, are less frequent, the most corrupt representatives of a democratick constituency generally standing in awe of its censure.

As men in bodies usually defer to the right, unless acting under erroneous impressions, or excited by sudden resentments, democracies pay more respect to abstract justice, in the management of their foreign concerns, than either aristocracies or monarchies, an appeal always lying against abuses, or violations of principle, to a popular sentiment, that, in the end, seldom fails to decide in favor of truth.

In democracies, with a due allowance for the workings of personal selfishness, it is usually a motive with those in places of trust to consult the interests of the mass, there being little doubt that in this system, the entire community has more regard paid to its wants and wishes than in either of the two others.

ALEXIS DE TOCQUEVILLE

In 1831, forty-four years after the Constitution had been drafted, the young French nobleman Alexis de Tocqueville (1805–1859) traveled to the United States to investigate the world's new republican society. Tocqueville undertook the trip ostensibly to study the penal system of the new American republic. But his focus quickly broad-

ened *to include far more significant matters than
penal reform. The trip turned into an intense
nine-month investigation of all aspects of American life. This investigation gave rise four years
later to Part I of* Democracy in America.

*Tocqueville first traveled the eastern sea-
board of the United States, spending a good
deal of time in New York City, Philadelphia, and
Boston, where he became acquainted with the
most prominent and influential thinkers of early
nineteenth-century America. He then headed
westward, traveling through an unspoiled and
inhospitable wilderness, across the Great Lakes
to the frontier fort that would later become Green
Bay, Wisconsin, then south down the Ohio and
Mississippi Valleys to New Orleans, then north
through the Old South to Washington, D.C.*

*Tocqueville had none of the apparatus of the
modern social scientist — no computers, no focus
groups, no opinion polls, no team of interviewers.
But he was a first-rate observer, a meticulous
reporter, and an avid reader, both of popular literature and of historical and legal treatises. He
interviewed more than two hundred people, with
the goal of answering the following questions:
"Who are these nomad people, the Americans?"
"How does this democracy of theirs work?" The
information he obtained and his insightful com-
mentary upon it were entered into fourteen note-
books which were to become the structural blue-
print for his book.*

Tocqueville wrote that the purpose of his book

**"How does
this Ameri-
can democ-
racy work?"**

was "to show what a democratic people really was in our day . . . by a rigorously accurate picture." And indeed, there is no question that the work is an accurate, rigorous, thorough examination of early nineteenth-century America — our legislative, executive, and judicial systems; our manners, customs, and morals; the nature of our freedoms; and our uncommon vision of the equality of man.

Over the years, Democracy in America *has exerted a profound influence on political thought in Europe and in this country. It has been translated and published in numerous editions in England, America, Belgium, Denmark, Germany, Hungary, Italy, Russia, Serbia, Spain, and Sweden, and it continues to be studied in political science and history courses at numerous American colleges.*

FROM *DEMOCRACY IN AMERICA*
1838

In the United States, the inhabitants were thrown but as yesterday upon the soil which they now occupy, and they brought neither customs nor traditions with them there; they meet one another for the first time with no previous acquaintance; in short, the instinctive love of their country can scarcely exist in their minds; but every one takes as zealous an interest in the affairs of his township, his county, and the whole State, as if they were his own, because every one, in his sphere, takes an active part in the government of society.

The lower orders in the United States are alive to the perception of the influence exercised by the general prosperity upon their own welfare; and simple as this observation is, it is one which is but too rarely made by the people. But in America the people regards this prosperity as the result of its own exertions; the citizen looks upon the fortune of the public as his private interest, and he co-operates in its success, not so much from a sense of pride or of duty, as from, what I shall venture to term, cupidity [greed].

It is unnecessary to study the institutions and the history of the Americans in order to know the truth of this remark, for their manners render it sufficiently evident. As the American participates in all that is done in his country, he thinks himself obliged to defend whatever may be censured; for it is not only his country that is then attacked upon these occasions, but it is himself. The consequence is, that his national pride resorts to a thousand artifices, and descends to all the petty tricks of personal vanity.

Nothing is more embarrassing in the ordinary intercourse of life, than this irritable patriotism of the Americans. . . .

It is not impossible to conceive the surprising liberty that the Americans enjoy; some idea may

Nothing is more embarrassing than this irritable patriotism of the Americans

likewise be formed of the extreme equality which subsists amongst them, but the political activity that pervades the United States must be seen in order to be understood. No sooner do you set foot upon American ground than you are stunned by a kind of tumult; a confused clamor is heard on every side; and a thousand simultaneous voices demand the satisfaction of their social wants. Everything is in motion around you; here, the people of one quarter of a town are met to decide upon the building of a church; there, the election of a representative is going on; a little further, the delegates of a district are posting to the town in order to consult upon some local improvements; or in another place the laborers of a village quit their plows to deliberate upon the project of a road or a public school. Meetings are called for the sole purpose of declaring their disapprobation of the line of conduct pursued by the Government; whilst in other assemblies the citizens salute the authorities of the day as the fathers of their country. Societies are formed which regard drunkenness as the principal cause of the evils under which the State labors, and solemnly bind themselves to give an example of temperance.

The great political agitation of American legislative bodies, which is the only one that attracts the attention of foreign countries, is a mere episode or a sort of continuation of that universal movement which originates in the lowest classes of the people and extends successively to all the

No sooner do you set foot upon American ground than you are stunned by a kind of tumult

ranks of society. It is impossible to spend more effort in the pursuit of happiness.

The cares of the political life engross a most prominent place in the occupation of a citizen of the United States; and almost the only pleasure of which as American has any idea, is to take a part in the Government, and to discuss the part he has taken. This feeling pervades the most trifling habits of life; even the women frequently attend public meetings, and listen to political harangues as a recreation from their household labors. Debating clubs are to a certain extent a substitute for theatrical entertainments: an American cannot converse, but he can discuss, and when he attempts talk he falls into a dissertation. He speaks to you as if he was addressing a meeting; and if he should warm in the course of the discussion, he will say "Gentlemen" to the person with whom he is conversing.

In some countries the inhabitants display a certain repugnance to avail themselves of the political privileges which the law invests them; it would seem that they set too high a value upon their time to spend it on the interests of the community; and they prefer to withdraw within the exact limits of a wholesome egotism, marked out by four sunkfences and quickset hedge. But if an American were condemned to confine his activity to his own affairs, he would be robbed of one half of his existence; he would feel an immense void in the life which he is accustomed to lead, and his

If an American were condemned to confine his activity to his own affairs, he would be robbed of one half of his existence

wretchedness would be unbearable. I am persuaded that if ever a despotic government is
established in America, it will find it more difficult
to surmount the habits which free institutions
have engendered, than to conquer the love of
freedom itself.

HENRY DAVID THOREAU

*Those in opposition to slavery, the abolitionists,
counted among their number a young writer of
exceptional talent, Henry David Thoreau (1817–
1862). His classic essay, "On the Duty of Civil
Disobedience," was written to protest the government's war with Mexico, a military action
Thoreau believed was being waged to benefit the
slave states and extend their territory.*

*The essay was delivered as a lecture. As pub-
lisher David Godine wrote in his edition of the
Thoreau classic, the essay*

> *was originally delivered as a lecture to the
> Concord Lyceum on January 26, 1848. In
> a small sense, Thoreau tried to explain to
> his curious and somewhat bewildered fel-
> low-townsmen why on a July night in 1846
> he had chosen to go to jail rather than pay
> a trifling poll tax. In a larger and deeper
> sense, he was probing a far more delicate
> and critical problem, as relevant in his day*

as our own, 'the relation of the individual to the state.'[14]

"Civil Disobedience" famously begins with the words "That government is best which governs least" and goes on to summarize Thoreau's political philosophy.

Although little noticed at the time, "Civil Disobedience" was to become one of the most famous essays ever written. Such leading historical figures as Leo Tolstoy, Mohandas K. Gandhi, and Martin Luther King, Jr., acknowledged the impact of Thoreau's writing on their thought. King said that when he read "Civil Disobedience" in college, he was deeply moved. No one, he wrote, "has been more eloquent and passionate in getting this idea across than Henry David Thoreau. As a result of his [Thoreau's] writings . . . we are the heirs of a legacy of creative protest. It goes without saying that the teachings of Thoreau are alive today; indeed, they are more alive today than ever before."

Henry David Thoreau unquestionably, as he himself put it, marched to a different drummer. Regarded as an extraordinary individual in his day, in modern society he would more likely be characterized as off the wall, eccentric, or weird. Nevertheless, the man had something important to say, and he said it well.

"That government is best which governs least"

Thoreau's teachings are alive today

[14] HENRY DAVID THOREAU, CIVIL DISOBEDIENCE, David R. Godine, Boston, 1969, v.

FROM *CIVIL DISOBEDIENCE*
1849

**That govern-
ment is best
which gov-
erns least**

I heartily accept the motto, "That government is best which governs least;" and I should like to see it acted up to more rapidly and systematically. Carried out, it finally amounts to this, which also I believe, — "That government is best which governs not at all;" and when men are prepared for it, that will be the kind of government which they will have. Government is at best but an expedient; but most governments are usually, and all governments are sometimes, inexpedient. The objections which have been brought against a standing army, and they are many and weighty, and deserve to prevail, may also at last be brought against a standing government. The standing army is only an arm of the standing government. The government itself, which is only the mode which the people have chosen to execute their will, is equally liable to be abused and perverted before the people can act through it. Witness the present Mexican war, the work of comparatively a few individuals using the standing government as their tool; for, in the outset, the people would not have consented to this measure.

This American government — what is it but a tradition, though a recent one, endeavoring to transmit itself unimpaired to posterity, but each instant losing some of its integrity? It has not the vitality and force of a single living man; for a single man can bend it to his will. It is a sort of wooden gun to the people themselves. But it is not the less necessary for this; for the people must have some complicated machinery or other, and hear its din, to satisfy that idea of government which they have. Governments show thus how successfully men can be imposed on, even impose on themselves, for their own advantage. It is excellent, we must all allow. Yet this government never of itself furthered any enterprise, but by the alacrity with which it got out of its way. *It* does not keep the country free. *It* does not settle the West. *It* does not educate. The character inherent in the American people has done all that has been accomplished; and it would have done somewhat more, if the government had not sometimes got in its way. For government is an expedient by which men would fain succeed in letting one another alone; and, as has been said, when it is most expedient, the governed are most let alone by it. Trade and commerce, if they were not made of india-rubber, would never manage to bounce over the obstacles which legislators are continually putting in their way; and, if one were to judge these men wholly by the effects of their actions and not partly by their intentions, they would deserve to be classed and punished with those mischievous persons who put obstructions on the railroads.

But, to speak practically and as a citizen,

unlike those who call themselves no-government men, I ask for, not at once no government, but *at once* a better government. Let every man make known what kind of government would command his respect, and that will be one step toward obtaining it.

I ask for, not at once no government, but *at once* a better government

After all, the practical reason why, when the power is once in the hands of the people, a majority are permitted, and for a long period continue, to rule is not because they are most likely to be in the right, nor because this seems fairest to the minority, but because they are physically the strongest. But a government in which the majority rule in all cases cannot be based on justice, even as far as men understand it. Can there not be a government in which majorities do not virtually decide right and wrong, but conscience? — in which majorities decide only those questions to which the rule of expediency is applicable? Must the citizen ever for a moment, or in the least degree, resign his conscience to the legislator? Why has every man a conscience, then? I think that we should be men first, and subjects afterward. It is not desirable to cultivate a respect for the law, so much as for the right. The only obligation which I have a right to assume is to do at any time what I think right. . . .

I think we should be men first, and subjects after

How does it become a man to behave toward this American government to-day? I answer that he cannot without disgrace be associated with it. I cannot for an instant recognize that political organization as *my* government which is the *slave's* government also.

All men recognize the right of revolution; that is, the right to refuse allegiance to and to resist the government, when its tyranny or its inefficiency are great and unendurable. But almost all say that such is not the case now. But such was the case, they think, in the Revolution of '75. If one were to tell me that this was a bad government because it taxed certain foreign commodities brought to its ports, it is most probable that I should not make an ado about it, for I can do without them. All machines have their friction; and possibly this does enough good to counterbalance the evil. At any rate, it is a great evil to make a stir about it. But when the friction comes to have its machine, and oppression and robbery are organized, I say, let us not have such a machine any longer. In other words, when a sixth of the population of a nation which has undertaken to be the refuge of liberty are slaves, and a whole country is unjustly overrun and conquered by a foreign army, and subject to military law, I think that it is not too soon for honest men to rebel and revolutionize. What makes this duty the more urgent is the fact, that the country so overrun is not our own, but ours is the invading army. . . .

Practically speaking, the opponents to a reform in Massachusetts are not a hundred thousand politicians at the South, but a hundred thousand merchants and farmers here, who are more interested in commerce and agriculture than they are in humanity, and are not prepared to do justice to the slave and to Mexico, *cost what it may.* I quarrel not with far-off foes, but with those who, near at home, cooperate with, and do the bidding of, those far away, and without whom the latter would be harmless. We are accustomed to say, that the mass of men are unprepared; but improvement is slow, because the few are not materially wiser or better than the many. It is not so important that many should be as good as you, as that there be some absolute goodness somewhere; for that will leaven the whole lump. There are thousands who are *in opinion* opposed to slavery and to the war, who yet in effect do nothing to put an end to them; who, esteeming themselves children of Washington and Franklin, sit down with their hands in their pockets, and say that they know not what to do, and do nothing; who even postpone the question of freedom to the question of free trade, and quietly read the prices-current along with the latest advices from Mexico, after dinner, and, it may be, fall asleep over them both. What is the price-current of an honest man and patriot today? They hesitate, and they regret, and sometimes they petition; but they do nothing in earnest and with effect. They will wait, well disposed, for others to remedy the evil, that they may no longer have it to regret. At most, they give only a cheap vote, and a feeble countenance and Godspeed, to the right, as it goes by

There are thousands who sit down with their hands in their pockets and do nothing about slavery

them. There are nine hundred and ninety-nine patrons of virtue to one virtuous man. But it is easier to deal with the possessor of a thing than with the temporary guardian of it. . . .

It is not a man's duty, as a matter of course, to devote himself to the eradication of any, even the most enormous, wrong; he may still properly have other concerns to engage him; but it is his duty, at least, to wash his hands of it, and, if he give it no thought longer, not to give it practically his support. . . .

Unjust laws exist: shall we be content to obey them, or shall we endeavor to amend them, and obey them until we have succeeded, or shall we transgress them at once? Men generally, under such a government as this, think that they ought to wait until they have persuaded the majority to alter them. They think that, if they should resist, the remedy would be worse than the evil. But it is the fault of the government itself that the remedy *is* worse than the evil. *It* makes it worse. Why is it not more apt to anticipate and provide for reform? Why does it not cherish its wise minority? Why does it cry and resist before it is hurt? Why does it not encourage its citizens to be on the alert to point out its faults, and *do* better than it would have them? Why does it always crucify Christ, and excommunicate Copernicus and Luther, and pronounce Washington and Franklin rebels?. . .

If the injustice is part of the necessary friction

Unjust laws exist: shall we be content to obey them?

of the machine of government, let it go: perchance it will wear smooth — certainly the machine will wear out. If the injustice has a spring, or a pulley, or a rope, or a crank, exclusively for itself, then perhaps you may consider whether the remedy will not be worse than the evil; but if it is of such a nature that it requires you to be the agent of injustice to another, then, I say, break the law. Let your life be a counter friction to stop the machine. What I have to do is to see, at any rate, that I do not lend myself to the wrong which I condemn.

As for adopting the ways which the State has provided for remedying the evil, I know not of such ways. They take too much time, and a man's life will be gone. I have other affairs to attend to.

I came into this world, not chiefly to make this a good place to live, but to live in it, be it good or bad

I came into this world, not chiefly to make this a good place to live, but to live in it, be it good or bad. A man has not everything to do, but something; and because he cannot do *everything*, it is not necessary that he should do *something* wrong. It is not my business to be petitioning the Governor or the Legislature any more than it is theirs to petition me; and if they should not hear my petition, what should I do then? But in this case the State has provided no way: its very Constitution is the evil. This may seem to be harsh and stubborn and unconciliatory; but it is to treat with the utmost kindness and consideration the only spirit that can appreciate or deserves it. So is all change for the better, like birth and death, which convulse the body.

I do not hesitate to say, that those who call themselves Abolitionists should at once effectually withdraw their support, both in person and property, from the government of Massachusetts, and not wait till they constitute a majority of one, before they suffer the right to prevail through them. I think that it is enough if they have God on their side, without waiting for that other one. Moreover, any man more right than his neighbors constitutes a majority of one already.

I meet this American government, or its representative, the State government, directly, and face to face, once a year — no more — in the person of its tax-gatherer; this is the only mode in which a man situated as I am necessarily meets it; and it then says distinctly, Recognize me; and the simplest, the most effectual, and, in the present posture of affairs, the indispensablest mode of treating with it on this head, of expressing your little satisfaction with and love for it, is to deny it them. My civil neighbor, the tax-gatherer, is the very man I have to deal with — for it is, after all, with men and not with parchment that I quarrel — and he has voluntarily chosen to be an agent of the government. How shall he ever know well what he is and does as an officer of the government, or as a man, until he is obliged to consider whether he shall treat me, his neighbor, for whom he has respect, as a neighbor and well-disposed man, or as a maniac and disturber of the peace, and see if he can get over this obstruction to his neighborliness without a ruder and more impetuous thought or speech corresponding with his action. I know this well, that if one thousand, if one hundred, if ten men whom I could name — if ten *honest* men only — ay, if one HONEST man, in this State of Massachusetts, *ceasing to hold slaves,* were actually to withdraw from this copartnership, and be locked up in the country jail therefor, it would be the abolition of slavery in America. . . .

Under a government which imprisons any unjustly, the true place for a just man is in prison

Under a government which imprisons any unjustly, the true place for a just man is also in prison. The proper place to-day, the only place which Massachusetts has provided for her freer and less desponding spirits, is in her prisons, to be put out and locked out of the State by her own act, as they have already put themselves out by their principles. It is there that the fugitive slave, and the Mexican prisoner on parole, and the Indian come to plead the wrongs of his race, should find them; on that separate, but more free and honorable, ground, where the State places those who are not *with* her, but *against* her — the only house in a slave State in which a free man can abide with honor. If any think that their influence would be lost there, and their voices no longer afflict the ear of the State, that they would not be as an enemy within its walls, they do not know by how much truth is stronger than error, nor how much more eloquently and effectively he can combat injustice who has experienced a little in his own person. Cast your whole vote, not a strip

of paper merely, but your whole influence. A
minority is powerless while it conforms to the
majority; it is not even a minority then; but it is
irresistible when it clogs by its whole weight. If
the alternative is to keep all just men in prison, or
give up war and slavery, the State will not hesitate which to choose. If a thousand men were not
to pay their tax-bills this year, that would not be a
violent and bloody measure, as it would be to pay
them, and enable the State to commit violence
and shed innocent blood. This is, in fact, the definition of a peaceable revolution, if any such is possible. If the tax-gatherer, or any other public officer, asks me, as one has done, "But what shall I
do?" my answer is, "If you really wish to do anything, resign your office." When the subject has
refused allegiance, and the officer has resigned
his office, then the revolution is accomplished.
But even suppose blood should flow. Is there not
a sort of blood shed when the conscience is
wounded? Through this wound a man's real
manhood and immortality flow out, and he bleeds
to an everlasting death. I see this blood flowing
now. . . .

I have paid no poll-tax for six years. I was put
into a jail once on this account, for one night; and,
as I stood considering the walls of solid stone, two
or three feet thick, the door of wood and iron, a
foot thick, and the iron grating which strained the
light, I could not help being struck with the fool-
ishness of that institution which treated me as if I
were mere flesh and blood and bones, to be locked

up. I wondered that it should have concluded at length that this was the best use it could put me to, and had never thought to avail itself of my services in some way. I saw that, if there was a wall of stone between me and my townsmen, there was a still more difficult one to climb or break through, before they could get to be as free as I was. I did not for a moment feel confined, and the walls seemed a great waste of stone and mortar. I felt as if I alone of all my townsmen had paid my tax. They plainly did not know how to treat me, but behaved like persons who are underbred. In every threat and in every compliment there was a blunder; for they thought that my chief desire was to stand the other side of that stone wall. I could not but smile to see how industriously they locked the door on my meditations, which followed them out again without let or hindrance, and *they* were really all that was dangerous. As they could not reach me, they had resolved to punish my body; just as boys, if they cannot come at some person against whom they have a spite, will abuse his dog. I saw that the State was half-witted, that it was timid as a lone woman with her silver spoons, and that it did not know its friends from its foes, and I lost all my remaining respect for it, and pitied it. . . .

I do not want to set myself up as better than my neighbors

I do not wish to quarrel with any man or nation. I do not wish to split hairs, to make fine distinctions, or set myself up as better than my neighbors. I seek rather, I may say, even an excuse for conforming to the laws of the land. I am but too ready to conform to them. Indeed, I have reason to suspect myself on this head; and each year, as the tax-gatherer comes round, I find myself disposed to review the acts and position of the general and state governments, and the spirit of the people, to discover a pretext for conformity. ... I believe that the State will soon be able to take all my work of this sort out of my hands, and then I shall be no better a patriot than my fellow-countrymen. Seen from a lower point of view, the Constitution, with all its faults, is very good; the law and the courts are very respectable; even this State and this American government are, in many respects, very admirable, and rare things, to be thankful for, such as a great many have described them; but seen from a point of view a little higher, they are what I have described them; seen from a higher still, and the highest, who shall say what they are, or that they are worth looking at or thinking of at all?

The Constitution, with all its faults, is very good

However, the government does not concern me much, and I shall bestow the fewest possible thoughts on it. It is not many moments that I live under a government, even in this world. If a man is thought-free, fancy-free, imagination-free, that which *is not* never for a long time appearing *to be* to him, unwise rulers or reformers cannot fatally interrupt him. . . .

The authority of government, even such as I am willing to submit to — for I will cheerfully obey those who know and can do better than I, and in many things even those who neither know nor can do so well — is still an impure one: to be strictly just, it must have the sanction and consent of the governed. It can have no pure right over my person and property but what I concede to it. The progress from an absolute to a limited monarchy, from a limited monarchy to a democracy, is a progress toward a true respect for the individual. Even the Chinese philosopher was wise enough to regard the individual as the basis of the empire. Is a democracy, such as we know it, the last improvement possible in government? Is it not possible to take a step further towards recognizing and organizing the rights of man? There will never be a really free and enlightened State, until the State comes to recognize the individual as a higher and independent power, from which all its own power and authority are de-rived, and treats him accordingly. I please myself with imagining a State at last which can afford to be just to all men, and to treat the individual with respect as a neighbor; which even would not think it inconsistent with its own repose if a few were to live aloof from it, not meddling with it, nor embraced by it, who fulfilled all the duties of neighbors and fellowmen. A State which bore this kind of fruit, and suffered it to drop off as fast as it ripened, would prepare the way for a still more perfect and glorious State, which also I have imagined, but not yet anywhere seen.

FREDERICK DOUGLASS

The individual whom African Americans regard as their race's second greatest leader, after Martin Luther King, Jr., is Frederick Douglass (1817? –1895). Before Douglass, no one had ever stated the case for the abolition of slavery so forcefully and convincingly.

No one presented the case for abolition more forcefully

The son of an unknown white man and a slave named Harriet Bailey (Douglass was the name he took when he won his freedom), he was born on a plantation in Talbot County, Maryland. As a young man, he experienced the usual hardships and indignities of a slave, first as a field hand, later as a houseboy in Baltimore, still later as a shipyard worker on the city docks. In 1838, he managed to escape to New Bedford, Massachusetts, where he was soon employed as an agent of the Massachusetts Anti-Slavery Society.

Douglass became a noted reformer and author and one of the truly heroic figures of the abolitionist movement. He bore violence and insult with courage and determination, fighting for more than mere emancipation; social and economic equality were his aims — as they are still the aims of African Americans today. He published an anti-slavery newspaper, the North Star, *as well as several versions of his autobiography, the last being* Life and Times of Frederick Douglass *(1855). During the Civil War, he helped recruit black men for the Union army and on several occasions*

Social and economic equality were his aims

discussed the problem of slavery with Abraham Lincoln. But according to contemporary accounts, it was as a fiery orator against slavery, and for freedom, that Douglass particularly excelled. Here is one of his most famous speeches.

SPEECH AT
ROCHESTER, NEW YORK
JULY 4, 1852

Why am I called upon to speak here today?

Fellow citizens, pardon me, allow me to ask, why am I called upon to speak here today? What have I, or those I represent, to do with your national Independence? Are the great principles of political freedom and of natural justice, embodied in that Declaration of Independence, extended to us? and am 1, therefore, called upon to bring our humble offering to the national altar, and to confess the benefits and express devout gratitude for the blessings resulting from your independence to us?

Would to God, both for your sakes and ours, that an affirmative answer could be truthfully returned to these questions! Then would my task be light, and my burden easy and delightful. For who is there so cold that a nation's sympathy could not warm him? Who so obdurate and dead to the claims of gratitude that would not thankfully acknowledge such priceless benefits? Who so stolid and selfish that would not give his voice to swell the hallelujahs of a nation's jubilee, when the chains of servitude had been torn from his limbs? I am not that man. In a case like that the dumb might eloquently speak and the "lame man leap as an hart."

But such is not the state of the case. I say it with a sad sense of the disparity between us. I am not included within the pale of this glorious anniversary! Your high independence only reveals the immeasurable distance between us. The blessings in which you, this day, rejoice are not enjoyed in common. The rich inheritance of justice, liberty, prosperity, and independence bequeathed by your fathers is shared by you, not by me. The sunlight that brought light and healing to you has brought stripes and death to me. This Fourth of July is yours, not mine. You may rejoice, I must mourn. To drag a man in fetters into the grand illuminated temple of liberty, and call upon him to join you in joyous anthems, were inhuman mockery and sacrilegious irony. Do you mean, citizens, to mock me by asking me to speak today? If so, there is a parallel to your conduct. And let me warn you that it is dangerous to copy the example of a nation whose crimes, towering up to heaven, were thrown down by the breath of the Almighty, burying that nation in irrevocable ruin! I can today take up the plaintive lament of a peeled and woe-smitten people!

The Fourth of July is yours, not mine

"By the rivers of Babylon, there we sat down. Yea! we wept when we remembered Zion. We hanged our harps upon the willows in the midst thereof. For there, they that carried us away captive, required of us a song; and they who wasted us required of us mirth, saying, sing us one of the songs of Zion. How can we sing the Lord's song in a strange land? If I forget thee, O Jerusalem, let my right hand forget her cunning. If I do not remember thee, let my tongue cleave to the roof of my mouth."

How can we sing the Lord's song in a strange land?

Fellow citizens, above your national, tumultuous joy, I hear the mournful wail of millions! whose chains, heavy and grievous yesterday, are, today, rendered more intolerable by the jubilee shouts that reach them. If I do forget, if I do not faithfully remember those bleeding children of sorrow this day, "may my right hand forget her cunning, and may my tongue cleave to the roof of my mouth"! To forget them, to pass lightly over their wrongs, and to chime in with the popular theme would be treason most scandalous and shocking, and would make me a reproach before God and the world. My subject, then, fellow citizens, is *American slavery*. I shall see this day and its popular characteristics from the slave's point of view. Standing there identified with the American bondman, making his wrongs mine. I do not hesitate to declare with all my soul that the character and conduct of this nation never looked blacker to me than on this Fourth of July! Whether we turn to the declarations of the past or to the professions of the present, the conduct of the nation seems equally hideous and revolting. America is false to the past, false to the present, and solemnly binds herself to be false to the future. Standing with God and the crushed and bleeding slave on this occasion, I will, in the name of humanity which is outraged, in the name of liberty which is fettered, in the name of the Constitution and the Bible which are disregarded and trampled upon, dare to call in question and to denounce, with all the emphasis I can command, everything that serves to perpetuate slavery — the great sin and shame of America! "I will not equivocate, I will not excuse"; I will use the severest language I can command; and yet not one word shall escape me that any man, whose judgment is not blinded by prejudice, or who is not at heart a slaveholder, shall not confess to be right and just.

I will denounce everything that serves to perpetuate slavery

But I fancy I hear someone of my audience say, "It is just in this circumstance that you and your brother abolitionists fail to make a favorable impression on the public mind. Would you argue more and denounce less, would you persuade more and rebuke less, your cause would be much more likely to succeed." But, I submit, where all is plain, there is nothing to be argued. What point in the antislavery creed would you have me argue? On what branch of the subject do the people of this country need light? Must I undertake to prove that the slave is a man? That point is conceded already. Nobody doubts it. The slaveholders themselves acknowledge it in the enactment of laws for their government. They acknowledge it when they punish disobedience on the part of the slave. There are seventy-two crimes in the state of Virginia which, if committed by a black man (no matter how ignorant he be), subject him to the punishment of death; while only two of the same crimes will subject a white man to the like punishment. What is this but the acknowledgment that the slave is a moral, intellectual, and responsible being? The manhood of the slave is conceded. It is admitted in the fact that the Southern statute books are covered with enactments forbidding, under severe fines and penalties, the teaching of the slave to read or to write. When you can point to any such laws in reference to the beasts of the field, then I may consent to argue the manhood of the slave. When the dogs in your streets, when the fowls of the air, when the cattle on your hills, when the fish of the sea and the reptiles that crawl shall be unable to distinguish the slave from a brute, then will I argue with you that the slave is a man!

The slave is a moral, intellectual, responsible being

For the present, it is enough to affirm the equal manhood of the Negro race. Is it not astonishing that, while we are plowing, planting, and reaping, using all kinds of mechanical tools, erecting houses, constructing bridges, building ships, working in metals of brass, iron, copper, silver, and gold; that, while we are reading, writing, and ciphering, acting as clerks, merchants, and secretaries, having among us lawyers, doctors, ministers, poets, authors, editors, orators, and teachers; that, while we are engaged in all manner of enterprises common to other men, digging gold in California, capturing the whale in the Pacific, feeding sheep and cattle on the hillside, living, moving, acting, thinking, planning, living in families as husbands, wives, and children, and, above all, confessing and worshiping the Christian's God, and looking hopefully for life and immortality beyond the grave, we are called upon to prove that we are men!

Would you have me argue that man is entitled to liberty? that he is the rightful owner of his own body? You have already declared it. Must I argue the wrongfulness of slavery? Is that a question for republicans? Is it to be settled by the rules of logic and argumentation, as a matter beset with great difficulty, involving a doubtful application of the principle of justice, hard to be understood? How should I look today, in the presence of Americans, dividing and subdividing a discourse, to show that men have a natural right to freedom? speaking of it relatively and positively, negatively and affirmatively? To do so would be to make myself ridiculous and to offer an insult to your understanding. There is not a man beneath the canopy of heaven that does not know that slavery is wrong for him.

What, am I to argue that it is wrong to make men brutes, to rob them of their liberty, to work them without wages, to keep them ignorant of their relations to their fellow men, to beat them

Must I argue the wrongfulness of slavery?

with sticks, to flay their flesh with the lash, to load their limbs with irons, to hunt them with dogs, or sell them at auction, to sunder their families, to knock out their teeth, to burn their flesh, to starve them into obedience and submission to their masters? Must I argue that a system thus marked with blood, and stained with pollution, is wrong? No! I will not. I have better employment for my time and strength than such arguments would imply.

Must I argue that a system marked with blood, stained with pollution, is wrong?

What, then, remains to be argued? Is it that slavery is not divine; that God did not establish it; that our doctors of divinity are mistaken? There is blasphemy in the thought. That which is inhuman cannot be divine! Who can reason on such a proposition? They that can may; I cannot. The time for such argument is past.

At a time like this, scorching iron, not convincing argument, is needed. O! had I the ability, and could I reach the nation's ear, I would today pour out a fiery stream of biting ridicule, blasting reproach, withering sarcasm, and stern rebuke. For it is not light that is needed, but fire; it is not the gentle shower, but thunder. We need the storm, the whirlwind, and the earthquake. The feeling of the nation must be quickened; the conscience of the nation must be roused; the propriety of the nation must be startled; the hypocrisy of the nation must be exposed; and its crimes against God and man must be proclaimed and denounced.

What, to the American slave, is your Fourth of

July? I answer: a day that reveals to him, more than all other days in the year, the gross injustice and cruelty to which he is the constant victim. To him, your celebration is a sham; your boasted liberty, an unholy license; your national greatness, swelling vanity; your sounds of rejoicing are empty and heartless; your denunciation of tyrants, brass-fronted impudence; your shouts of liberty and equality, hollow mockery; your prayers and hymns, your sermons and thanksgivings, with all your religious parade and solemnity, are, to Him, mere bombast, fraud, deception, impiety, and hypocrisy — a thin veil to cover up crimes which would disgrace a nation of savages. There is not a nation of savages. There is not a nation on the earth guilty of practices more shocking and bloody than are the people of the United States at this very hour.

Go where you may, search where you will, roam through all the monarchies and despotisms of the Old World, travel through South America, search out every abuse, and when you have found the last, lay your facts by the side of the everyday practices of this nation, and you will say with me that, for revolting barbarity and shameless hypocrisy, America reigns without a rival.

JOHN STUART MILL

It's a little-known fact, but London, England, and 1849 were a particularly significant place and time. In that city and at that time were published three of the most important writings in the history of western civilization: Karl Marx's A Contribution to the Critique of Political Economy, whose introductory essay contains the clearest statement of the materialist interpretation of history — what we call marxism or communism today; Charles Darwin's monumental announcement of the theory of evolution, On the Origin of Species; and John Stuart Mill's On Liberty. It is doubtful that any other works from the nineteenth or twentieth centuries have excited as much attention, given rise to so much controversy, and had such profound effects — Marx's book on economics and sociology, Darwin's book on science and religion, Mill's book on political theory and the development of democratic thought and institutions.

The finest work ever written on the case for man's right to think and act for himself.

In the opinion of many knowledgeable observers, On Liberty is the finest work ever written on the case for man's right to think and act for himself. Others regard it as one of the world's great pieces of social criticism. Some believe that On Liberty should be included in the exalted company of such classics as Plato's Republic, Aristotle's Politics, Machiavelli's The Prince, Hobbes's Leviathan, and Rousseau's The Social Contract.

So who is this man Mill? And why should a book he wrote more than one hundred and fifty years ago have relevance and meaning for us in twenty-first-century America?

John Stuart Mill (1806–1873) was a leader of

*the utilitarian movement in Britain. The majority
of his life was spent in administrative positions in
the English government; he also served a three-
year term in Parliament. Mill authored many essays
and several substantial treatises. His major writings include his greatest philosophical work,* System of Logic *(1843);* Principles of Political Economy *(1848), which applies economic principles to
social conditions;* On Liberty *(1859);* Utilitarian-
ism *(1863);* The Subjection of Women *(1869);
and* Autobiography *(1873).*

On Liberty *is Mill's most famous political writing. Published in 1859, it has been reprinted dozens of times in a number of languages, and its
fame has continued to grow.*

In his Autobiography, *Mill refers to* On Liberty *as having but one very simple principle. Let
me set forth his exact words for you. Keep in
mind that although Mill may have regarded his
principle as being simple, putting its words into
action in the political arena has over the years
proved to be complex and controversial.*

*That principle is, that the sole end for
which mankind are warranted, individually
or collectively, in interfering with the liberty of action of any of their number, is self-
protection. That the only purpose for which
power can be rightfully exercised over any
member of a civilised community, against
his will, is to prevent harm to others. His*

own good, either physical or moral, is not a sufficient warrant. He cannot rightfully be compelled to do or forbear because it will be better for him to do so, because it will make him happier, because, in the opinions of others, to do so would be wise, or even right. These are good reasons for remonstrating with him, or reasoning with him, or persuading him, or entreating him, but not for compelling him, or visiting with him any evil in case he do otherwise. To justify that, the conduct from which it is desired to deter him must be calculated to produce evil to someone else. The only part of the conduct of anyone, for which he is amenable to society, is that which concerns others. In the part which merely concerns himself, his independence is, of right, absolute. Over himself, over his own body and mind, the individual is sovereign.

The rest of the book is an elaboration of this principle: that the liberty of the individual should be absolute except in the one case where liberty does harm to another.

Liberty should be absolute except where it does harm

"Mill pushed to the forefront," wrote the historian David Spitz, "the question that most concerns those who value liberty and are committed to the principle of democracy: namely, how in democratic states can individuals and minorities be protected against the possible tyranny of

majorities? This is why, for more than a century, every serious debate on these questions has turned on the name and work of John Stuart Mill."[15]

FROM *ON LIBERTY*
1859

The object of this Essay is to assert one very simple principle. . . . That principle is, that the sole end for which mankind are warranted, individually or collectively, in interfering with the liberty of action of any of their number, is self-protection. That the only purpose for which power can be rightfully exercised over any member of a civilized community, against his will, is to prevent harm to others. His own good, either physical or moral, is not a sufficient warrant. He cannot rightfully be compelled to do or forbear because it will be better for him to do so, because it will make him happier, because, in the opinion of others, to do so would be wise, or even right. There are good reasons for remonstrating with him, or reasoning with him, or visiting with him any evil in case he do otherwise. To justify that, the conduct from which it is desired to deter him, must be calculated to produce evil to someone else. The only part of the conduct of anyone, for which he is amenable to society, is that which concerns others. In

The sole end for which mankind are warranted in interfering with liberty is self-protection

15 JOHN STUART MILL, ON LIBERTY, David Spitz, ed., W.W. Norton, New York, 1975, x.

the part which merely concerns himself, his independence is, of right, absolute. Over himself, over his own body and mind, the individual is sovereign. . . .

IV

WRITINGS FROM THE CIVIL WAR AND RECONSTRUCTION PERIODS

ABRAHAM LINCOLN

You may recall that earlier in the book I posed this question: if George Washington had not accepted Congress's request for him to take command of the Continental army, would we have a United States of America today?

Well, here's another: What if Abe Lincoln had not made his appearance in our history at the precise time that he did? Would we be a country? Or two? Or three? Or a dozen or more relatively small, weak states, competing and warring with each other to the detriment of all?

What if Lincoln had not come along when he did?

Instead, what we have is a union, a single country, united in purpose and with freedom of opportunity for all.

Because of that . . . because of this man, when I think about choosing the greatest American hero in all our history (and no, I haven't forgotten the great things Washington and Jefferson and Madison and all the other Founding Fathers did for us; but the reality remains that every single one of them was indelibly tainted by the sin of

The greatest American hero in our history

slavery), my thoughts invariably turn to Abraham Lincoln.

The story of Abe Lincoln's life is too well known to require retelling here. Every schoolboy knows of Lincoln's birth in 1809 in a pioneer's log cabin in Kentucky; of his meager schooling and his arduous efforts to educate himself; of his failure as a storekeeper in New Salem, Illinois; and at least something of his career in politics, which was ended by a bullet fired by John Wilkes Booth six weeks after Lincoln began his second term as president of the United States, in 1865.

Lincoln has become the purest and noblest symbol of American democracy, almost as much because of what he said as because of what he did. For in his later years, Lincoln spoke and wrote magnificently, sometimes in homespun phrases, rich in the humor of the frontier, and sometimes in words profoundly dignified and serious, invested with an emotion that was almost mystical. Several of his speeches must rank with the world's masterpieces of oratory; others, straightforward and simple, express perfectly the ideas for which large numbers of Americans would prove willing to die.

His speeches rank with the world's masterpieces of oratory

From the moment this extraordinary individual made his appearance on the stage of American politics, nothing was ever to be the same. You can see this from his earliest days. Here's his first public writing, the announcement of his candidacy for the Illinois legislature, written about

March 1, 1832, in Lincoln's inimitable style:

> *Fellow-Citizens: I presume you all know*
> *who I am. I am humble Abraham Lincoln.*
> *I have been solicited by many friends to*
> *become a candidate for the Legislature.*
> *My politics are short and sweet, like the old*
> *woman's dance. . . .*

We are fortunate that Lincoln was a man not only of heroic deeds but of incomparable, memorable words, phrases, and verbal images. Of course, we cannot now experience the force of his personal company. But we can experience the beauty and power of his language; the logic, strength, and hard common sense of his reasoning. It is seldom noted by those who focus on Lincoln's political accomplishments, but he may well have been one of the finest prose writers in American history.

One of the finest prose writers in American history

In each of the major periods of his career — as a state legislator and lawyer in Illinois, during his fight against the extension of slavery into the western territories, and finally, during the years he spent preserving the Union as president of the United States — Lincoln left behind words to be remembered by. And what words they were!

> *"A house divided against itself cannot*
> *stand." I believe this government cannot*
> *endure permanently half slave and half*

free. I do not expect the Union to be dissolved — I do not expect the house to fall — but I do expect it will cease to be divided. It will become all one thing, or all the other. (From Springfield Speech, June 16, 1858).

We are not enemies, but friends. We must not be enemies. Though passion may have strained, it must not break our bonds of affection. The mystic chords of memory, stretching from every battlefield and patriot grave to every living heart and hearthstone all over this broad land, will yet swell the chorus of the Union when again touched, as surely they will be, by the better angels of our nature. (From First Inaugural Address, March 4, 1861)

We here highly resolve that these dead shall not have died in vain; that this nation, under God, shall have a new birth of freedom; and that government of the people, by the people, for the people, shall not perish from the earth. (From Gettysburg Address, November 19, 1863)

With malice toward none; with charity for all; with firmness in the right, as God gives us to see the right, let us strive on to finish the work we are in; to bind up the nation's wounds; to care for him who shall have borne the battle, and for his widow, and his orphan — to do all which may achieve and cherish a just and lasting peace among ourselves, and with all nations. (From Second Inaugural Address, March 4, 1865)

Here are the six Lincoln writings that are generally regarded as being his finest:

FROM SPEECH DELIVERED AT SPRINGFIELD, ILLINOIS JUNE 16, 1858

Mr. President and Gentlemen of the Convention: If we could first know where we are, and whither we are tending, we could better judge what to do, and how to do it. We are now far into the fifth year since a policy was initiated with the avowed object and confident promise of putting an end to slavery agitation. Under the operation of that policy, that agitation has not only not ceased, but has constantly augmented. In my opinion, it will not cease until a crisis shall have been reached and passed. "A house divided against itself can not stand." I believe this government cannot endure permanently half slave and half free. I do not expect the Union to be dissolved — I do not expect the house to fall — but I do expect it will cease to be divided. It will become all one thing,

This government cannot endure permanently half slave and half free

or all the other. Either the opponents of slavery will arrest the further spread of it, and place it where the public mind shall rest in the belief that it is in course of ultimate extinction; or its advocates will push it forward till it shall become alike lawful in all the States, old as well as new, North as well as South. Have we no tendency to the latter condition?

Let any one who doubts carefully contemplate that now almost complete legal combination — piece of machinery, so to speak — compounded of the Nebraska doctrine and the Dred Scott decision. Let him consider not only what work the machinery is adapted to do, and how well adapted; but also let him study the history of its construction, and trace, if he can, or rather fail, if he can, to trace the evidences of design and concert of action among its chief architects, from the beginning.

The new year of 1854 found slavery excluded from more than half the States by State constitutions, and from most of the national territory by congressional prohibition. Four days later commenced the struggle which ended in repealing that congressional prohibition. This opened all the national territory to slavery, and was the first point gained.

But, so far, Congress only had acted; and an indorsement by the people, real or apparent, was indispensable to save the point already gained and give chance for more.

This necessity had not been overlooked, but had been provided for, as well as might be, in the notable argument of "squatter sovereignty," otherwise called "sacred right of self-government," which latter phrase, though expressive of the only rightful basis of any government, was so perverted in this attempted use of it as to amount to just this: That if any one man choose to enslave another, no third man shall be allowed to object. That argument was incorporated into the Nebraska Bill itself, in the language which follows: "It being the true intent and meaning of this act not to legislate slavery into any Territory or State, nor to exclude it therefrom; but to leave the people thereof perfectly free to form and regulate their domestic institutions in their own way, subject only to the Constitution of the United States." Then opened the roar of loose declamation in favor of "squatter sovereignty" and "sacred right of self-government." "But," said opposition members, "let us amend the bill so as to expressly declare that the people of the territory may exclude slavery." "Not we," said the friends of the measure; and down they voted the amendment.

While the Nebraska Bill was passing through Congress, a law case involving the question of a negro's freedom, by reason of his owner having voluntarily taken him first into a free State and then a Territory covered by the congressional prohibition, and held him as a slave for a long time in each, was passing through the U.S. Circuit Court for the District of Missouri; and both the Nebraska Bill and law suit were brought to a decision in the same month of May, 1854. The negro's name was "Dred Scott," which name now designates the decision finally made in the case. Before the then next Presidential election, the law case came to and was argued in the Supreme Court of the United States; . . .

The Dred Scott decision

The several points of the Dred Scott decision . . . constitute the piece of machinery in its present state of advancement. The working points of that machinery are:

(1) That no negro slave, imported as such from Africa, and no descendant of such slave, can ever be a citizen of any State, in the sense of that term as used in the Constitution of the United States. This point is made in order to deprive the negro in every possible event of the benefit of this provision of the United States Constitution which declares that, "the citizens of each State shall be entitled to all the privileges and immunities of citizens in the several States."

(2) That, "subject to the Constitution of the United States," neither Congress nor a territorial legislature can exclude slavery from any United States Territory. This point is made in order that individual men may fill up the Territories with slaves, without danger of losing them as property, and thus enhance the chances of permanency to the institution through all the future.

(3) That whether the holding a negro in actual

slavery in a free State makes him free as against the holder, the United States courts will not decide, but will leave it to be decided by the courts of any slave State the Negro may be forced into by the master. This point is made not to be pressed immediately, but, if acquiesced in for a while, and apparently indorsed by the people at an election, then to sustain the logical conclusion that what Dred Scott's master might lawfully do with Dred Scott in the free State of Illinois, every other master may lawfully do with any other one or one thousand slaves in Illinois or in any other free State.

Auxiliary to all this, and working hand in hand with it, the Nebraska doctrine, or what is left of it, is to educate and mould public opinion, at least Northern public opinion, not to care whether slavery is voted down or voted up. This shows exactly where we now are, and partially, also, whither we are tending.

It will throw additional light on the latter, to go back and run the mind over the string of historical facts already stated. Several things will now appear less dark and mysterious than they did when they were transpiring. The people were to be left "perfectly free," "subject only to the Constitution." What the Constitution had to do with it outsiders could not then see. Plainly enough now, it was an exactly fitted niche for the Dred Scott decision to afterward come in, and declare the perfect freedom of the people to be just no freedom at all. Why was the amendment expressly declaring the right of the people to exclude slavery voted down? Plainly enough now, the adoption of it would have spoiled the niche for the Dred Scott decision. . . .

It should not be overlooked that, by the Nebraska bill, the people of a State as well as Territory were to be left "perfectly free," "subject only to the Constitution." Why mention a State? They were legislating for Territories, and not for or about States. Certainly the people of a State are and ought to be subject to the Constitution of the United States; but what is mention of this lugged into this merely territorial law? Why are the people of a Territory and the people of a State therein lumped together; and their relation to the Constitution therein treated as being precisely the same? While the opinion of the court, by Chief Justice Taney, in the Dred Scott case, and the separate opinions of all the concurring judges, expressly declare that the Constitution of the United States neither permits Congress nor a territorial legislature to exclude slavery from any United States Territory, they all omit to declare whether or not the same Constitution permits a State, or the people of a State, to exclude it. . . . Put this and that together, and we have another nice little niche, which we may, ere long, see filled with another Supreme Court decision, declaring that the Constitution of the United States does not permit a State to exclude slavery from its limits. And this may especially be expected if the doctrine of "care not whether slavery be voted down or voted up" shall gain upon the public mind sufficiently to give promise that such a decision can be maintained when made.

Such a decision is all that slavery now lacks of being alike lawful in all the States. Welcome, or unwelcome, such decision is probably coming, and will soon be upon us, unless the power of the present political dynasty shall be met and overthrown. We shall lie down pleasantly dreaming that the people of Missouri are on the verge of making their State free, and we shall awake to the reality instead that the Supreme Court has made Illinois a slave State. To meet and overthrow the power of that dynasty is the work now before all those who would prevent that consummation. That is what we have to do. How can we best do it? . . .

Our cause, then, must be intrusted to, and conducted by, its own undoubted friends — those whose hands are free, whose hearts are in the work, who do care for the result. Two years ago the Republicans of the nation mustered over thirteen hundred thousand strong. We did this under the single impulse of resistance to a common danger, with every external circumstance against us. Of strange, discordant, and even hostile elements, we gathered from the four winds, and formed and fought the battle through, under the constant hot fire of a disciplined, proud, and pampered enemy. Did we brave all then to falter now? — now, when

We shall awake to the reality that the Supreme Court has made Illinois a slave State

that same enemy is wavering, dissevered, and belligerent? The result is not doubtful. We shall not fail — if we stand firm, we shall not fail. Wise counsels may accelerate or mistakes delay it, but, sooner or later, the victory is sure to come.

If we stand firm, we shall not fail

FROM ADDRESS AT COOPER INSTITUTE, NEW YORK, NEW YORK, FEBRUARY 27, 1860

Mr. President and Fellow-citizens of New York: The facts which I shall deal with this evening are mainly old and familiar; nor is there anything new in the general use I shall make of them. If there shall be any novelty, it will be in the mode of presenting the facts, and the inferences and observations following that presentation. In his speech last autumn at Columbus, Ohio, as reported in the "New York Times," Senator Douglas said:

"Our fathers, when they framed the government under which we live, understood this question just as well, and even better, than we do now."

I fully indorse this, and I adopt it as a text for this discourse. I so adopt it because it furnishes a precise and an agreed starting point for the discussion between Republicans and that wing of the Democracy headed by Senator Douglas. It simply leaves the inquiry: What was the understanding those fathers had of the question mentioned?

What is the frame of government under which we live? The answer must be, "The Constitution of the United States." That Constitution consists of the original, framed in 1787, and under which the present government first went into operation, and twelve subsequently framed amendments, the first ten of which were framed in 1789.

Who were our fathers that framed the Constitution? I suppose the "thirty-nine" who signed the original instrument may be fairly called our fathers who framed that part of the present Government. It is almost exactly true to say they framed it, and it is altogether true to say they fairly represented the opinion and the sentiment of the whole nation at that time. Their names, being familiar to nearly all, and accessible to quite all, need not now be repeated.

I take these "thirty-nine," for the present, as being "our fathers who framed the government under which we live." What is the question, which according to the text, those fathers understood "just as well, and even better, than we do now"?

It is this: Does the proper division of local from Federal authority, or anything in the Constitution, forbid our Federal Government to control as to slavery in our Federal Territories?

Upon this, Senator Douglas holds the affirmative, and Republicans the negative. This affirmative and denial form an issue; and this issue — this question — is precisely what the text declares our fathers understood "better than we." Let us now inquire whether the "thirty-nine," or any of them, ever acted upon this question; and if they did, how they acted upon it — how they expressed that better understanding. . . .

Who were the fathers that framed the Constitution?

In 1789, by the first Congress which sat under the Constitution, an act was passed to enforce the Ordinance of '87, including the prohibition of slavery in the Northwestern Territory. . . . [The bill] went through all its stages without a word of opposition, and finally passed both branches without yeas and nays, which is equivalent to a unanimous passage. In this Congress there were sixteen of the thirty-nine fathers who framed the original Constitution. . . .

Nothing forbade Congress to prohibit slavery in the Federal territory

This shows that, in their understanding, no line dividing local from Federal authority, nor anything in the Constitution, properly forbade Congress to prohibit slavery in the Federal territory; else both their fidelity to correct principle, and their oath to support the Constitution, would have constrained them to oppose the prohibition.

Again, George Washington, another of the "thirty-nine," was then President of the United States, and as such approved and signed the bill, thus completing its validity as a law, and thus showing that, in his understanding, no line dividing local from Federal authority, nor anything in the Constitution, forbade the Federal Government to control as to slavery in federal territory. . . .

The sum of the whole [evidence] is that of our thirty-nine fathers who framed the original Constitution . . . a clear majority of the whole . . . certainly understood that no proper division of local from Federal authority, nor any part of the Constitution, forbade the Federal Government to control slavery in the Federal Territories; while all the rest probably had the same understanding. Such, unquestionably, was the understanding of our fathers who framed the original Constitution; and the text affirms that they understood the question "better than we."

But, so far, I have been considering the understanding of the question manifested by the framers of the original Constitution. In and by the original instrument, a mode was provided for amending it; and, as I have already stated, the present frame of "the government under which we live" consists of that original, and twelve amendatory articles framed and adopted since. Those who now insist that Federal control of slavery in Federal Territories violates the Constitution, point us to the provisions which they suppose it thus violates; and, as I understand, they all fix upon provisions in these amendatory articles, and not in the original instrument. The Supreme Court, in the Dred Scott case, plant themselves upon the fifth amendment, which provides that no person shall be deprived of "life, liberty, or property without due process of law;" while Senator Douglas and his peculiar adherents plant themselves upon the tenth amendment, providing that "the powers not delegated to the United States by the Constitution" "are reserved to the States respectively, or to the people."

Now, it so happens that these amendments

were framed by the first Congress which sat
under the Constitution — the identical Congress
which passed the act, already mentioned, enforcing the prohibition of slavery in the Northwestern
Territory. Not only was it the same Congress, but
they were the identical, same individual men
who, at the same session, and at the same time
within the session, had under consideration, and
in progress toward maturity, these constitutional
amendments, and this act prohibiting slavery in
all the territory the nation then owned. The constitutional amendments were introduced before,
and passed after, the act enforcing the ordinance
of '87; so that, during the whole pendency of the
act to enforce the ordinance, the constitutional
amendments were also pending.

The seventy-six members of that Congress,
including sixteen of the framers of the original
Constitution . . . were preeminently our fathers
who framed that part of "the government under
which we live" which is now claimed as forbidding
the Federal Government to control slavery in the
Federal Territories.

Is it not a little presumptuous in any one at
this day to affirm that the two things which that
Congress deliberately framed, and carried to maturity at the same time, are absolutely inconsistent with each other? And does not such affirmation become impudently absurd when coupled
with the other affirmation, from the same mouth,
that those who did the two things alleged to be

inconsistent, understood whether they really were inconsistent better than we — better than he who affirms that they are inconsistent?

It is surely safe to assume that the thirty-nine framers of the original Constitution, and the seventy-six members of the Congress which framed the amendments thereto, taken together, do certainly include those who may be fairly called "our fathers who framed the Government under which we live." And so assuming, I defy any man to show that any one of them ever, in his whole life, declared that, in his understanding, any proper division of local from Federal authority, or any part of the Constitution, forbade the Federal Government control as to slavery in the Federal Territories. I go a step further. I defy any one to show that any living man in the whole world ever did, prior to the beginning of the present century (and I might almost say prior to the beginning of the last half of the present century), declare that, in his understanding, any proper division of local from Federal authority, or any part of the Constitution, forbade the Federal Government to control as to slavery in the Federal Territories. To those who now so declare I give not only "our fathers who framed the Government under which we live," but with them all other living men within the century in which it was framed, among whom to search, and they shall not be able to find the evidence of a single man agreeing with them. . . .

And now, if they would listen, — as I suppose they will not — I would address a few words to the Southern people.

I would address a few words to the Southern people

I would say to them: You consider yourselves a reasonable and a just people; and I consider that in the general qualities of reason and justice you are not inferior to any other people. Still, when you speak of us Republicans, you do so only to denounce us as reptiles, or, at the best, as no better than outlaws. You will grant a hearing to pirates or murderers, but nothing like it to "Black Republicans." In all your contentions with one another, each of you deems an unconditional condemnation of "Black Republicanism" as the first thing to be attended to. Indeed, such condemnation of us seems to be an indispensable prerequisite — license, so to speak — among you to be admitted or permitted to speak at all. Now can you or not be prevailed upon to pause and to consider whether this is quite just to us, or even to yourselves? Bring forward your charges and specifications, and then be patient long enough to hear us deny or justify.

You say we are sectional. We deny it. That makes an issue; and the burden of proof is upon you. You produce your proof; and what is it? Why, that our party has no existence in your section — gets no votes in your section. . . . The fact that we get no votes in your section is a fact of your making, and not of ours. . . .

Some of you delight to flaunt in our faces the

warning against sectional parties given by Washington in his Farewell Address. Less than eight years before Washington gave that warning, he had, as President of the United States, approved and signed an act of Congress enforcing the prohibition of slavery in the Northwestern Territory, which act embodied the policy of the government upon that subject up to and at the very moment he penned that warning; and about one year after he penned it he wrote Lafayette that he considered that prohibition a wise measure, expressing in the same connection his hope that we should some time have a confederacy of free States.

Bearing this in mind, and seeing that sectionalism has since arisen upon this same subject, is that warning a weapon in your hands against us, or in our hands against you? Could Washington himself speak, would he cast the blame of that sectionalism upon us, who sustain his policy, or upon you, who repudiate it? We respect that warning of Washington, and we commend it to you, together with his example pointing to the right application of it.

We respect that warning of Washington, and we commend it to you

But you say you are conservative — eminently conservative — while we are revolutionary, destructive, or something of the sort. What is conservatism? Is it not adherence to the old and tried, against the new and untried? We stick to, contend for, the identical old policy on the point in controversy which was adopted by "our fathers who framed the government under which we live;"

while you with one accord reject, and scout, and spit upon that old policy, and insist upon substituting something new. . . .

Again, you say we have made the slavery question more prominent than it formerly was. We deny it. We admit that it is more prominent, but we deny that we made it so. It was not we, but you, who discarded the old policy of the fathers. We resisted, and still resist, your innovation; and thence comes the greater prominence of the question. . . .

You charge that we stir up insurrections among your slaves. We deny it

You charge that we stir up insurrections among your slaves. We deny it; and what is your proof? Harper's Ferry! John Brown!! John Brown was no Republican; and you have failed to implicate a single Republican in his Harper's Ferry enterprise. If any member of our party is guilty in that matter, you know it, or you do not know it. If you do know it, you are inexcusable for not designating the man and proving the fact. If you do not know it, you are inexcusable for asserting it, and especially for persisting in the assertion after you have tried and failed to make the proof. You need not be told that persisting in a charge which one does not know to be true, is simply malicious slander.

No Republican aided or encouraged the Harper's Ferry affair

Some of you admit that no Republican designedly aided or encouraged the Harper's Ferry affair, but still insist that our doctrines and declarations necessarily lead to such results. We do not believe it. We know we hold no doctrine, and make no declaration, which were not held to and made by "our fathers who framed the government under which we live.". . . . Republican doctrines and declarations are accompanied with a continual protest against any interference whatever with your slaves, or with you about your slaves. Surely, this does not encourage them to revolt. True, we do, in common with "our fathers who framed the government under which we live," declare our belief that slavery is wrong; but the slaves do not hear us declare even this. For anything we say or do, the slaves would scarcely know there is a Republican party. . . .

Slave insurrections are no more common now than they were before the Republican party was organized. . . . In the present state of things in the United States, I do not think a general, or even a very extensive, slave insurrection is possible. The indispensable concert of action cannot be attained. The slaves have no means of rapid communication; nor can incendiary freemen, black or white, supply it. The explosive materials are everywhere in parcels; but there neither are, nor can be supplied, the indispensable connecting trains.

Much is said by Southern people about the affection of slaves for their masters and mistresses; and a part of it, at least, is true. A plot for an uprising could scarcely be devised and communicated to twenty individuals before some one of them, to save the life of a favorite master or mistress, would divulge it. . . . Occasional poisonings

I do not think a slave insurrection is possible

from the kitchen, and open or stealthy assassinations in the field, and local revolts extending to a score or so, will continue to occur as the natural results of slavery; but no general insurrection of slaves, as I think, can happen in this country for a long time. Whoever much fears, or much hopes, for such an event, will be alike disappointed.

In the language of Mr. Jefferson, uttered many years ago, "It is still in our power to direct the process of emancipation and deportation peaceably, and in such slow degrees, as that the evil will wear off insensibly; and their places be . . . filled up by free white laborers. If, on the contrary, it is left to force itself on, human nature must shudder at the prospect held up."

Mr. Jefferson did not mean to say, nor do I, that the power of emancipation is in the Federal Government. He spoke of Virginia; and, as to the power of emancipation, I speak of the slaveholding States only. The Federal Government, however, as we insist, has the power of restraining the extension of the institution — the power to insure that a slave insurrection shall never occur on any American soil which is now tree from slavery.

The Federal Government has the power of restraining the extension of slavery

John Brown's effort was peculiar. It was not a slave insurrection. It was an attempt by white men to get up a revolt among slaves, in which the slaves refused to participate. In fact, it was so absurd that the slaves, with all their ignorance, saw plainly enough it could not succeed. That affair, in its philosophy, corresponds with the many attempts, related in history, at the assassination of kings and emperors. An enthusiast broods over the oppression of a people till he fancies himself commissioned by Heaven to liberate them. He ventures the attempt, which ends in little else than his own execution. Orsini's attempt on Louis Napoleon, and John Brown's attempt at Harper's Ferry, were, in their philosophy, precisely the same. The eagerness to cast blame on old England in the one case, and on New England in the other, does not disprove the sameness of the two things.

And how much would it avail you, if you could . . . break up the Republican organization? Human action can be modified to some extent, but human nature cannot be changed. There is a judgment and a feeling against slavery in this nation, which cast at least a million and a half of votes. You cannot destroy that judgment and feeling — that sentiment — by breaking up the political organization which rallies around it. . . . Would the number of John Browns be lessened or enlarged by the operation?

But you will break up the Union rather than submit to a denial of your Constitutional rights. . . .

Your purpose, then, plainly stated, is that you will destroy the government, unless you be allowed to construe and enforce the Constitution as you please, on all points in dispute between you and us. You will rule or ruin in all events. . . .

[Do] you really feel yourselves justified to

break up this Government unless such a court decision as yours is shall be at once submitted to as a conclusive and final rule of political action? But you will not abide the election of a Republican President! In that supposed event, you say, you will destroy the Union; and then, you say, the great crime of having destroyed it will be upon us! That is cool. A highwayman holds a pistol to my ear, and mutters through his teeth, "Stand and deliver, or I shall kill you, and then you will be a murderer!"

To be sure, what the robber demanded of me — my money — was my own; and I had a clear right to keep it; but it was no more my own than my vote is my own; and the threat of death to me, to extort my money, and the threat of destruction to the Union, to extort my vote, can scarcely be distinguished in principle.

A few words now to Republicans. It is exceedingly desirable that all parts of this great Confederacy shall be at peace, and in harmony one with another. Let us Republicans do our part to have it so. Even though much provoked, let us do nothing through passion and ill-temper. Even though the Southern people will not so much as listen to us, let us calmly consider their demands, and yield to them if in our deliberate view of our duty, we possibly can. Judging by all they say and do, and by the subject and nature of their controversy with us, let us determine, if we can, what will satisfy them.

[Do] you really feel yourself justified to break up this Government?

Will they be satisfied if the Territories be unconditionally surrendered to them? We know they will not. In all their present complaints against us, the Territories are scarcely mentioned. Invasions and insurrections are the rage now. Will it satisfy them if, in the future, we have nothing to do with invasions and insurrections? We know it will not. We so know, because we know we never had anything to do with invasions and insurrections; and yet this total abstaining does not exempt us from the charge and the denunciation.

The question recurs, What will satisfy them? Simply this: we must not only let them alone, but we must somehow convince them that we do let them alone. This, we know by experience, is no easy task. We have been so trying to convince them from the very beginning of our organization, but with no success. In all our platforms and speeches we have constantly protested our purpose to let them alone; but this has had no tendency to convince them. . . .

These natural and apparently adequate means all failing, what will convince them? This, and this only: cease to call slavery wrong, and join them in calling it right. And this must be done thoroughly — done in acts as well as in words. Silence will not be tolerated — we must place ourselves avowedly with them. Senator Douglas's new sedition law must be enacted and enforced, suppressing all declarations that slavery is wrong, whether made in politics, in presses, in pulpits, or in private. We

We have constantly protested our purpose to let them alone

must arrest and return their fugitive slaves with greedy pleasure. . . . The whole atmosphere must be disinfected from all taint of opposition to slavery, before they will cease to believe that all their troubles proceed from us. . . .

Holding, as they do, that slavery is morally right and socially elevating, they cannot cease to demand a full national recognition of it as a legal right and a social blessing.

Nor can we justifiably withhold this on any ground save our conviction that slavery is wrong. If slavery is right, all words, acts, laws, and constitutions against it are themselves wrong, and should be silenced and swept away. If it is right, we cannot justly object to its nationality — its universality; if it is wrong, they cannot justly insist upon its extension — its enlargement. All they ask we could readily grant, if we thought slavery right; all we ask they could as readily grant if they thought it wrong. Their thinking it right and our thinking it wrong is the precise fact upon which depends the whole controversy. Thinking it right, as they do, they are not to blame for desiring its **Thinking** full recognition as being right; but thinking it **that slavery** wrong, as we do, can we yield to them? Can we **is wrong, can** cast our votes with their view, and against our **we yield to** own? In view of our moral, social, and political **them?** responsibilities, can we do this?

Wrong as we think slavery is, we can yet afford to let it alone where it is, because that much is due to the necessity arising from its actual presence in the nation; but can we, while our votes will prevent it, allow it to spread into the national Territories, and to overrun us here in these free States? If our sense of duty forbids this, then let us stand by our duty fearlessly and effectively. Let us be diverted by none of those sophistical contrivances wherewith we are so industriously plied and belabored — contrivances such as groping for some middle ground between the right and the wrong; vain as the search for a man who should be neither a living man nor a dead man; such as a policy of "don't care" on a question about which all true men do care; such as Union appeals beseeching true Union men to yield to Disunionists, reversing the divine rule, and calling, not the sinners, but the righteous to repentance; such as invocations to Washington, imploring men to unsay what Washington said and undo what Washington did.

Neither let us be slandered from our duty by false accusations against us, nor frightened from it by menaces of destruction to the government, nor of dungeons to ourselves. Let us have faith that right makes might, and in that faith let us to the end dare to do our duty as we understand it.

Let us have faith that right makes might

FROM FIRST
INAUGURAL ADDRESS
MARCH 4, 1861

Fellow-citizens of the United States: In compliance with a custom as old as the government itself, I appear before you to address you briefly, and to take in your presence the oath prescribed by the Constitution of the United States to be taken by the President "before he enters on the execution of his office.". . .

Apprehension seems to exist among the people of the Southern States that by the accession of a Republican administration their property and their peace and personal security are to be endangered. There has never been any reasonable cause for such apprehension. Indeed, the most ample evidence to the contrary has all the while existed and been open to their inspection. It is found in nearly all the published speeches of him who now addresses you. I do but quote from one of those speeches when I declare that "I have no purpose, directly or indirectly, to interfere with the institution of slavery in the States where it exists. I believe I have no lawful right to do so, and I have no inclination to do so." Those who nominated and elected me did so with full knowledge that I had made this and many similar declarations, and had never recanted them. And, more than this, they placed in the platform for my acceptance, and as a law to themselves and to me, the clear and emphatic resolution which I now read:

> "Resolved, That the maintenance inviolate of the rights of the States, and especially the right of each State to order and control its own domestic institutions according to its own judgment exclusively, is essential to that balance of power on which the perfec-

The people of the Southern states think they will be endangered by a Republican government

tion and endurance of our political fabric
depend, and we denounce the lawless invasion by armed force of the soil of any State
or Territory, no matter under what pretext,
as among the gravest of crimes."

I now reiterate these sentiments; and, in doing
so, I only press upon the public attention the most
conclusive evidence of which the ease is suscepti-
ble, that the property, peace, and security of no
section are to be in any wise endangered by the
now incoming administration. I add, too, that all
the protection which, consistently with the Constitution and the laws, can be given, will be cheerfully given to all the States when lawfully
demanded, for whatever cause — as cheerfully to
one section as to another.

There is much controversy about the deliver-
ing up of fugitives from service or labor. The
clause I now read is as plainly written in the Constitution as any other of its provisions:

"No person held to service or labor in one
State, under the laws thereof, escaping into
another, shall in consequence of any law or
regulation therein be discharged from such
service or labor, but shall be delivered up on
claim of the party to whom such service or
labor may be due".

It is scarcely questioned that this provision was
intended by those who made it for the re-claim-
ing of what we call fugitive slaves; and the intention of the lawgiver is the law. All members of

Congress swear their support to the whole Constitution — to this provision as much as to any other. . . .

There is some difference of opinion whether this clause should be enforced by national or by State authority; but surely that difference is not a very material one. If the slave is to be surrendered, it can be of but little consequence to him or to others by which authority it is done. . . .

I take this oath today with no mental reservations

I take the official oath to-day with no mental reservations, and with no purpose to construe the Constitution or laws by any hypercritical rules. And while I do not choose now to specify particular acts of Congress as proper to be enforced, I do suggest that it will be much safer for all, both in official and private stations, to conform to and abide by all those acts which stand unrepealed, than to violate any of them, trusting to find impunity in having them held to be unconstitutional.

It is seventy-two years since the first inauguration of a President under our National Constitution. During that period fifteen different and greatly distinguished citizens have, in succession, administered the executive branch of the government. They have conducted it through many perils, and generally with great success. Yet, with all this scope of precedent, I now enter upon the same task for the brief constitutional term of four years under great and peculiar difficulty. A disruption of the Federal Union, heretofore only menaced, is now formidably attempted.

I hold that, in contemplation of universal law and of the Constitution, the Union of these States is perpetual. Perpetuity is implied, if not expressed, in the fundamental law of all national governments. It is safe to assert that no government proper ever had a provision in its organic law for its own termination. Continue to execute all the express provisions of our National Constitution, and the Union will endure forever — it being impossible to destroy it except by some action not provided for in the instrument itself.

In legal contemplation the Union is perpetual

Again, if the United States be not a government proper, but an association of States in the nature of contract merely, can it, as a contract, be peaceably unmade by less than all the parties who made it? One party to a contract may violate it — break it, so to speak; but does it not require all to lawfully rescind it?

Descending from these general principles, we find the proposition that, in legal contemplation the Union is perpetual confirmed by the history of the Union itself. The Union is much older than the Constitution. It was formed, in fact, by the Articles of Association in 1774. It was matured and continued by the Declaration of Independence in 1776. It was further matured, and the faith of all the then thirteen States expressly plighted and engaged that it should be perpetual, by the Articles of Confederation in 1778. And, finally, in 1787 one of the declared objects for ordaining and establishing the Constitution was "to form a more perfect Union."

But if the destruction of the Union by one or by a part only of the States be lawfully possible, the Union is less perfect than before the Constitution, having lost the vital element of perpetuity.

No State upon its own mere motion can lawfully get out of the Union

It follows from these views that no State upon its own mere motion can lawfully get out of the Union; that resolves and ordinances to that effect are legally void; and that acts of violence, within any State or States, against the authority of the United States, are insurrectionary or revolutionary, according to circumstances.

I therefore consider that, in view of the Constitution and the laws, the Union is unbroken; and to the extent of my ability I shall take care, as the Constitution itself expressly enjoins upon me, that the laws of the Union be faithfully executed in all the States. Doing this I deem to be only a simple duty on my part; and I shall perform it so far as practicable, unless my rightful masters, the American people, shall withhold the requisite means, or in some authoritative manner direct the contrary. I trust this will not be regarded as a menace, but only as the declared purpose of the Union that it will constitutionally defend and maintain itself.

In doing this there needs to be no bloodshed or violence; and there shall be none, unless it be forced upon the national authority. The power confided to me will be used to hold, occupy, and possess the property and places belonging to the government, and to collect the duties and imposts; but beyond what may be necessary for these objects, there will be no invasion, no using of force against or among the people anywhere. Where hostility to the United States, in any interior locality, shall be so great and universal as to prevent competent resident citizens from holding the Federal offices, there will be no attempt to force obnoxious strangers among the people for that object. While the strict legal right may exist in the government to enforce the exercise of these offices, the attempt to do so would be so irritating, and so nearly impracticable withal, that I deem it better to forego for the time the uses of such offices.

The mails, unless repelled, will continue to be furnished in all parts of the Union. So far as possible, the people everywhere shall have that sense of perfect security which is most favorable to calm thought and reflection. The course here indicated will be followed unless current events and experience shall show a modification or change to be proper, and in every case and exigency my best discretion will be exercised according to circumstances actually existing, and with a view and a hope of a peaceful solution of the national troubles and the restoration of fraternal sympathies and affections.

That there are persons in one section or anoth-

er who seek to destroy the Union at all events,
and are glad of any pretext to do it, I will neither
affirm nor deny; but if there be such, I need
address no word to them. To those, however, who
really love the Union may I not speak?

To those
who love the
Union may I
not speak?

Before entering upon so grave a matter as the
destruction of our national fabric, with all its benefits, its memories, and its hopes, would it not be
wise to ascertain precisely why we do it? Will you
hazard so desperate a step while there is any possibility that any portion of the ills you fly from
have no real existence? Will you, while the certain ills you fly to are greater than all the real
ones you fly from — will you risk the commission
of so fearful a mistake?

All profess to be content in the Union if all
constitutional rights can be maintained. Is it true,
then, that any right, plainly written in the Constitution, has been denied? I think not. Happily the
human mind is so constituted that no party can
reach to the audacity of doing this. Think, if you
can, of a single instance in which a plainly written
provision of the Constitution has ever been
denied. If by the mere force of numbers a majority should deprive a minority of any clearly written constitutional right, it might, in a moral point
of view, justify revolution — certainly would if
such a right were a vital one. But such is not our
case. All the vital rights of minorities and of individuals are so plainly assured to them by affirma-
tions and negations, guarantees and prohibitions,

in the Constitution, that controversies never arise concerning them. But no organic law can ever be framed with a provision specifically applicable to every question which may occur in practical administration. No foresight can anticipate, nor any document of reasonable length contain, express provisions for all possible questions. Shall fugitives from labor be surrendered by national or by State authority? The Constitution does not expressly say. *May* Congress prohibit slavery in the Territories? The Constitution does not expressly say. *Must* Congress protect slavery in the Territories? The Constitution does not expressly say. From questions of this class spring all our constitutional controversies, and we divide upon them into majorities and minorities. If the minority will not acquiesce, the majority must, or the government must cease. There is no other alternative; for continuing the government is acquiescence on one side or the other.

If a minority in such case will secede rather than acquiesce, they make a precedent which in turn will divide and ruin them; for a minority of their own will secede from them whenever a majority refuses to be controlled by such minority. For instance, why may not any portion of a new confederacy a year or two hence arbitrarily secede again, precisely as portions of the present Union now claim to secede from it? All who cherish disunion sentiments are now being educated to the exact temper of doing this.

Is there such perfect identity of interests among the States to compose a new Union, as to produce harmony only, and prevent renewed secession?

The central idea of secession is anarchy

Plainly, the central idea of secession is the essence of anarchy. A majority held in restraint by constitutional checks and limitations, and always changing easily with deliberate changes of popular opinions and sentiments, is the only true sovereign of a free people. Whoever rejects it does, of necessity, fly to anarchy or to despotism. Unanimity is impossible; the rule of a minority, as a permanent arrangement, is wholly inadmissible; so that, rejecting the majority principle, anarchy or despotism in some form is all that is left.

I do not forget the position, assumed by some, that constitutional questions are to be decided by the Supreme Court; nor do I deny that such decisions must be binding, in any case, upon the parties to a suit, as to the object of that suit, while they are also entitled to very high respect and consideration in all parallel cases by all other departments of the government. And while it is obviously possible that such decision may be erroneous in any given case, still the evil effect following it, being limited to that particular case, with the chance that it may be overruled and never become a precedent for other cases, can better be borne than could the evils of a different practice. At the same time, the candid citizen must confess that if the policy of the government, upon vital questions affecting the whole people, is to be irrevocably fixed by decisions of the Supreme Court, the instant they are made, in ordinary litigation between parties in personal actions, the people will have ceased to be their own rulers, having to that extent practically resigned their government into the hands of that eminent tribunal. Nor is there in this view any assault upon the court or the judges. It is a duty from which they may not shrink to decide cases properly brought before them, and it is no fault of theirs if others seek to turn their decisions to political purposes.

There is in this view no assault upon the court or the judges

One section of our country believes slavery is right, and ought to be extended, while the other believes it is wrong, and ought not to be extended. This is the only substantial dispute. The fugitive-slave clause of the Constitution, and the law for the suppression of the foreign slave-trade, are each as well enforced, perhaps, as any law can ever be in a community where the moral sense of the people imperfectly supports the law itself. The great body of the people abide by the dry legal obligation in both cases, and a few break over in each. This, I think, cannot be perfectly cured; and it would be worse in both cases after the separation of the sections than before. The foreign slave-trade, now imperfectly suppressed, would be ultimately revived, without restriction, in one section, while fugitive slaves, now only partially surrendered, would not be surrendered at all by the other.

Physically speaking, we cannot separate

Physically speaking, we cannot separate. We cannot remove our respective sections from each other, nor build an impassable wall between them. A husband and wife may be divorced, and go out of the presence and beyond the reach of each other; but the different parts of our country cannot do this. They cannot but remain face to face, and intercourse, either amicable or hostile, must continue between them. Is it possible, then, to make that intercourse more advantageous or more satisfactory after separation than before? Can aliens make treaties easier than friends can make laws? Can treaties be more faithfully enforced between aliens than laws can among friends? Suppose you go to war, you cannot fight always; and when after much loss on both sides, and no gain on either, you cease fighting, the identical old questions as to terms of intercourse are again upon you.

Whenever the people shall grow weary of the existing government, they can exercise their constitutional right of amending it

This country, with its institutions, belongs to the people who inhabit it. Whenever they shall grow weary of the existing government, they can exercise their constitutional right of amending it, or their revolutionary right to dismember or overthrow it. I cannot be ignorant of the fact that many worthy and patriotic citizens are desirous of having the National Constitution amended. While I make no recommendation of amendments, I fully recognize the rightful authority of the people over the whole subject, to be exercised in either of the modes prescribed in the instrument itself; . . . I understand a proposed amendment to the

Constitution — which amendment, however, I
have not seen — has passed Congress, to the
effect that the Federal Government shall never
interfere with the domestic institutions of the
States, including that of persons held to service.
To avoid misconstruction of what I have said, I
depart from my purpose not to speak of particular
amendments so far as to say that, holding such a
provision to now be implied constitutional law, I
have no objection to its being made express and
irrevocable.

The chief magistrate derives all his authority
from the people, and they have conferred none
upon him to fix terms for the separation of the
States. The people themselves can do this also if
they choose; but the executive, as such, has nothing to do with it. His duty is to administer the present government, as it came to his hands, and to
transmit it, unimpaired by him, to his successor.

Why should there not be a patient confidence
in the ultimate justice of the people? Is there any
better or equal hope in the world? In our present
differences is either party without faith of being
in the right? If the Almighty Ruler of Nations,
with his eternal truth and justice, be on your side
of the North, or on yours of the South, that
truth and that justice will surely prevail by the
judgment of this great tribunal of the American
people.

By the frame of the government under which
we live, this same people have wisely given their
public servants but little power for mischief, and

have, with equal wisdom, provided for the return of that little to their own hands at very short intervals. While the people retain their virtue and vigilance, no administration, by any extreme of wickedness or folly, can very seriously injure the government in the short space of four years.

My country-men, one and all, think calmly and well upon this whole subject

My countrymen, one and all, think calmly and well upon this whole subject. Nothing valuable can be lost by taking time. If there be an object to hurry any of you in hot haste to a step which you would never take deliberately, that object will be frustrated by taking time; but no good object can be frustrated by it. Such of you as are now dissatisfied, still have the old Constitution unimpaired, and, on the sensitive point, the laws of your own framing under it; while the new administration will have no immediate power, if it would, to change either. If it were admitted that you who are dissatisfied hold the right side in the dispute, there still is no single good reason for precipitate action. Intelligence, patriotism, Christianity, and a firm reliance on Him who has never yet forsaken this favored land, are still competent to adjust in the best way all our present difficulty.

In your hands is the momentous issue of civil war

In your hands, my dissatisfied fellow-countrymen, and not in mine, is the momentous issue of civil war. The government will not assail you. You can have no conflict without being yourselves the aggressors. You have no oath registered in heaven to destroy the government, while I shall have the most solemn one to "preserve, protect, and defend it."

I am loath to close. We are not enemies, but friends. We must not be enemies. Though passion may have strained, it must not break our bonds of affection. The mystic chords of memory, stretching from every battle-field and patriot grave to every living heart and hearthstone all over this broad land, will yet swell the chorus of the Union when again touched, as surely they will be, by the better angels of our nature.

The mystic chords of memory will be touched by the better angels of our nature

THE EMANCIPATION
PROCLAMATION
JANUARY 1, 1863

Whereas, on the twenty-second day of September, in the year of our Lord one thousand eight hundred and sixty-two, a proclamation was issued by the President of the United States, containing, among other things, the following, to wit:

"That on the first day of January, in the year of our Lord one thousand eight hundred and sixty-three, all persons held as slaves within any State, or designated part of a State, the people whereof shall then be in rebellion against the United States, shall be then, thenceforward and forever free; and the Executive Government of the United States, including the military and naval authority thereof, will recognize and maintain the freedom of such persons, and will do no act or acts to repress such persons, or any of them, in any efforts they may make for their actual freedom.

"That the Executive will, on the first day of

January aforesaid, by proclamation, designate the States and parts of States, if any, in which the people thereof respectively shall then be in rebellion against the United States, and the fact that any State, or the people thereof, shall on that day be in good faith represented in the Congress of the United States by members chosen thereto at elections wherein a majority of the qualified voters of such State shall have participated, shall, in the absence of strong countervailing testimony be deemed conclusive evidence that such State and the people thereof are not then in rebellion against the United States."

Now, therefore I, Abraham Lincoln, President of the United States, by virtue of the power in me vested as commander-in-chief of the army and navy of the United States in time of actual armed rebellion against authority and government of the United States, and as a fit and necessary war measure for suppressing said rebellion, do on this first day of January, in the year of our Lord one thousand eight hundred and sixty-three, and in accordance with my purpose so to do publicly proclaimed for the full period of 100 days, from the day first above mentioned, order and designate as the States and parts of States wherein the people thereof, respectively, are this day in rebellion against the United States, the following, to wit:

Arkansas, Texas, Louisiana (except the Parishes of St. Bernard, Plaquemine, Jefferson, St. Johns, St. Charles, St. James, Ascension, Assumption,

Terrebonne, Lafourche, St. Mary, St. Martin, and Orleans, including the City of New Orleans), Mississippi, Alabama, Florida, Georgia, South Carolina, North Carolina, and Virginia, (except the forty-eight counties designated as West Virginia and also the counties of Berkeley, Accomac, Northampton, Elizabeth City, York, Princess Ann, and Norfolk, including the cities of Norfolk and Portsmouth) and which excepted parts are for the present left precisely as if this proclamation were not issued.

And by virtue of the power and for the purpose aforesaid, I do order and declare that all persons held as slaves within said designated States, and parts of States are, and henceforward shall be, free; and that the Executive Government of the United States, including the military and naval authorities thereof, will recognize and maintain the freedom of said persons.

All persons within said designated States shall be free

And I hereby enjoin upon the people so declared to be free to abstain from all violence, unless in necessary self-defense; and I recommend to them that in all cases when allowed, they labor faithfully for reasonable wages.

And I further declare and make known, that such persons of suitable condition, will be received into the armed service of the United States to garrison forts, positions, stations and other places, and to man vessels of all sorts in said service.

And upon this act, sincerely believed to be an act of justice, warranted by the Constitution upon military necessity, I invoke the considerate judgment of mankind and the gracious favor of Almighty God.

In witness whereof, I have hereunto set my hand, and caused the seal of the United States to be affixed.

(L.S) Done at the city of Washington, this first day of January, in the year of our Lord one thousand eight hundred and sixty-three, and of the independence of the United States of America the eighty-seventh.

THE GETTYSBURG ADDRESS
NOVEMBER 19, 1863

Four score and seven years ago our fathers brought forth on this continent a new nation, conceived in liberty, and dedicated to the proposition that all men are created equal.

Now we are engaged in a great civil war, testing whether that nation or any nation so conceived and so dedicated, can long endure. We are met on a great battlefield of that war. We have come to dedicate a portion of that field, as a final resting-place for those who here gave their lives that that nation might live. It is altogether fitting and proper that we should do this.

We cannot dedicate — we cannot consecrate — we cannot hallow — this ground

But, in a larger sense, we cannot dedicate — we cannot consecrate — we cannot hallow — this ground. The brave men, living and dead, who struggled here have consecrated it far above our poor power to add or detract. The world will little note nor long remember what we say here, but it can never forget what they did here. It is for us, the living, rather, to be dedicated here to the unfinished work which they who fought here have thus far so nobly advanced. It is rather for us to be here dedicated to the great task remaining before us — that from these honored dead we take increased devotion to that cause for which they gave the last full measure of devotion; that we here highly resolve that these dead shall not have died in vain; that this nation, under God, shall have a new birth of freedom; and that government of the people, by the people, for the people, shall not perish from the earth.

SECOND INAUGURAL ADDRESS
MARCH 4, 1865

Fellow-Countrymen: At this second appearing to take the oath of the presidential office, there is less occasion for an extended address than there was at the first. Then a statement, somewhat in detail, of a course to be pursued, seemed fitting and proper. Now, at the expiration of four years, during which public declarations have been constantly called forth on every point and phase of the great contest which still absorbs the attention and engrosses the energies of the nation, little that is new could be presented. The progress of our arms, upon which all else chiefly depends, is as well known to the public as to myself, and it is, I trust, reasonably satisfactory and encouraging to all. With high hope for the future, no prediction in regard to it is ventured.

On the occasion corresponding to this four years ago all thoughts were anxiously directed to an impending civil war. All dreaded it — all sought to avert it. While the inaugural address was being delivered from this place, devoted altogether to saving the Union without war, insurgent agents were in the city seeking to destroy it without war — seeking to dissolve the Union, and divide effects, by negotiation. Both parties deprecated war; but one of them would make war rather than let the nation survive, and the other would accept war rather than let it perish. And the war came.

One-eighth of the whole population were colored slaves, not distributed generally over the Union, but localized in the southern part of it. These slaves constituted a peculiar and powerful interest. All knew that this interest was, somehow, the cause of war. To strengthen, perpetuate, and extend this interest was the object for which the insurgents would rend the Union even by war; while the Government claimed no right to do more than to restrict the territorial enlargement of it.

Neither party expected for the war the magnitude or the duration which it has already attained. Neither anticipated that the cause of the conflict might cease with, or even before, the conflict itself should cease. Each looked for an easier triumph, and a result less fundamental and astounding. Both read the same Bible, and pray to the same

One party would make war rather than let the nation survive; and the other would accept war rather than let it perish

God; and each invokes his aid against the other.

It may seem strange that any men should dare to ask a just God's assistance in wringing their bread from the sweat of other men's faces, but let us judge not, that we be not judged. The prayers of both could not be answered — that of neither has been answered fully.

The Almighty has His own purposes. "Woe unto the world because of offenses; for it must needs be that offenses come, but woe to that man by whom the offenses cometh." If we shall suppose that American slavery is one of those offenses which, in the providence of God, must needs come, but which, having continued through his appointed time, he now wills to remove, and that he gives to both North and South this terrible war, as the woe due to those by whom the offense came, shall we discern therein any departure from those divine attributes which the believers in a living God always ascribe to him? Fondly do we hope — fervently do we pray — that this mighty scourge of war may speedily pass away. Yet, if God wills that it continue until all the wealth piled by the bondsman's two hundred and fifty years of unrequited toil shall be sunk, and until every drop of blood drawn with the lash shall be paid by another drawn with the sword, as was said three thousand years ago, so still it must be said "the judgments of the Lord are true and righteous altogether."

With malice toward none, with charity for all; with firmness in the right as God gives us to see

Fondly do we hope that this scourge of war may speedily pass away

Let us strive on to finish the work we are in

the right, let us strive on to finish the work we are in; to bind up the nation's wounds, to care for him who shall have borne the battle, and for his widow, and his orphan — to do all which may achieve and cherish a just and lasting peace among ourselves and with all nations

FROM DEBATE OF THE FOURTEENTH AMENDMENT IN CONGRESS

The Bill of Rights should be viewed today not as ten amendments but as eleven — the original ten ratified in 1791, plus the Fourteenth, ratified in 1868 during the Reconstruction era following the Civil War. This is because in the process of debating and enacting the amendment, the Thirty-ninth Congress also redefined (or, as you might say, in reference to the political climate of 1866, reconstructed) most of the rights in the Founding Fathers' original Bill of Rights, including the First Amendment's rights to freedom of expression, assembly, and religion; the Second Amendment's right to keep and bear arms; and the Fifth, Sixth, and Seventh Amendments' rights to grand, petit, and civil juries. Today in the legal discourse of our legislators, judges, and lawyers there exist a number of significant legal terms — due process, equal protection, privileges and immunities, to name a few — that are derived directly from the Fourteenth Amendment. And Supreme Court cases of the last sev-

The amendment made most provisions of the Bill of Rights applicable to the states

enty-five years or so include an impressive array
of landmark decisions in which the Court incorporated the words of the Fourteenth Amendment
into the original Bill of Rights to make its guarantees and prohibitions applicable to the states
as well as to the federal government.

The Fourteenth Amendment consists of five
sections. The section that is critically important
to an understanding of our freedoms is section 1.
(The four remaining sections, which were particularly applicable during the Civil War era, are
largely ignored today.) Section 1 reads as follows:

> All persons born or naturalized in the Unit-
> ed States, and subject to the jurisdiction
> thereof, are citizens of the United States
> and of the State wherein they reside. No
> State shall make or enforce any law which
> shall abridge the privileges and immunities
> of citizens of the United States; nor shall
> any State deprive any person of life, liber-
> ty, or property, without due process of law;
> nor deny to any person within its jurisdic-
> tion the equal protection of the laws.

A draft of The Fourteenth Amendment was
placed before the house of representatives on
December 6, 1865, by Representative John Bingham (1815–1900) of Ohio, perhaps the best constitutional lawyer in the House. In a speech he
gave several years later, Bingham reflected on
the meaning of his draft of the amendment, link-

ing "the privileges and immunities of citizens of the United States" with the Bill of Rights

FROM SPEECH OF JOHN BINGHAM
42ND CONGRESS, 1ST SESSION 1871

[T]he privileges and immunities of citizens of the United States, as contradistinguished from citizens of a State, are chiefly defined in the first eight amendments to the Constitution of the United States. Those eight amendments are as follows. [Bingham then proceeded to read the first eight amendments word for word.] These eight articles I have shown never were limitations upon the power of the States, until made so by the fourteenth amendment. . . .

Bingham's imagery in the Fourteenth Amendment debate also bears notice. For him, the Bill of Rights was not simply "immortal," as he preached in his maiden sermon in support of the amendment, but "sacred," a word that punctuates his most extended meditation on the Bill of Rights:

For Bingham, the Bill of Rights was "immortal" and "sacred"

FROM SPEECH OF JOHN BINGHAM
39TH CONGRESS, 1ST SESSION 1866

As a further security for the enforcement of the Constitution, and especially of this sacred bill of rights, to all the citizens and all the people of the United States, it is further provided that the

members of the several State Legislatures and all
executive and judicial officers, both of the United
States and of the several States, shall be bound by
oath or affirmation to support this Constitution.
The oath, the most solemn compact which man
can make with his Maker, was to bind the State
Legislatures, executive officers, and judges to
sacredly respect the Constitution and all the rights
secured by it. . . .

[The Bill of Rights encompasses] all the sacred
rights of person — those rights dear to freemen
and formidable only to tyrants — and of which the
fathers of the Republic spoke, after God had given
them the victory. . . .

The Bill of
Rights
encompasses
all the
sacred rights
of person

*Two years before Bingham introduced his
amendment, Representative James Wilson (1835–
1920) of Iowa made clear that he too understood
the "privileges and immunities of citizens of the
United States" to include the guarantees of the
first eight amendments of the Bill of Rights. His
words also show that he deemed all rights and
freedoms in the Bill of Rights to be binding on
state governments:*

FROM SPEECH OF JAMES WILSON
38TH CONGRESS, 1ST SESSION
1864

Freedom of religious opinion, freedom of speech and
press, and the right of assemblage for the purpose
of petition belong to every American citizen. . . .

With these rights no State may interfere. . . .

Sir, I might enumerate many other constitutional rights of the citizen which slavery has disregarded and practically destroyed, but I have [said] enough to illustrate my proposition: that slavery . . . denies to the citizens of each State the privileges and immunities of citizens. . . .

The people of the free States should insist on ample protection to their rights, privileges and immunities, which are none other than those which the Constitution was designed to secure to all citizens alike . . . .

After vigorous debate, the house passed the amendment on May 10, 1866. Concurrently, under the leadership of Senator Jacob Howard (1805–1871) of Michigan, the amendment was debated in the Senate. Howard provided a comprehensive analysis of section 1.

FROM SPEECH OF JACOB HOWARD
39TH CONGRESS, 1ST SESSION
1866

[The privileges and immunities of citizens include] the personal rights guarantied and secured by the first eight amendments of the Constitution; such as the freedom of speech and of the press; the right of the people peaceably to assemble and petition the Government for a redress of grievances, a right appertaining to each and all of the people; the right to keep and bear arms; the right to be exempted from the quartering of soldiers in a house without the consent of the owner; the right to be exempt from unreasonable searches and seizures, and from any search or seizure except by virtue of a warrant issued upon a formal oath or affidavit; the right of an accused person to be informed of the nature of the accusation against him, and his right to be tried by an impartial jury of the vicinage [neighborhood]; and also the right to be secure against excessive bail and against cruel and unusual punishments. . . .

[T]he course of decision of our courts and the present settled doctrine is, that all these immunities, privileges, rights, thus guarantied by the Constitution or recognized by it . . . do not operate in the slightest degree as a restraint or prohibition upon State legislation. . . .

[T]hese guarantees . . . stand simply as a bill of rights in the Constitution . . . [and] States are not restrained from violating the principles embraced in them. . . . The great object of the first section of this amendment is, therefore, to restrain the power of the States and compel them at all times to respect these great fundamental guarantees.

The great object of the amendment is to restrain the power of the states

The amendment was passed by the Senate on June 13, 1866. It was then submitted to the states for ratification and was ratified on July 9, 1868, by the required three-fourths of the states — that is, 28 of the 37 states belonging to the Union at the time.

The influence of the Fourteenth Amendment upon our constitutional freedoms is of immense consequence. It is worthy of joining the august company of the Declaration of Independence, the U.S. Constitution, and the Bill of Rights as one of the most important documents in our constitutional history.

V

WRITINGS FROM THE LATE NINETEENTH CENTURY

FREDERICK JACKSON TURNER

Frederick Jackson Turner (1861–1932), a University of Wisconsin historian, delivered his celebrated paper, "The Significance of the Frontier in American History," at a Chicago meeting of the American Historical Association in July 1893. Turner's "frontier thesis," as it came to be known, is today recognized as the seminal work concerning the American frontier and how it has influenced American culture. Turner summed up the thesis in one of his later writings, "Contributions of the West to American Democracy":

The seminal work concerning the American frontier

> *The paths of the pioneers have widened into broad highways. The forest clearing has expanded into affluent commonwealths. Let us see to it that the ideals of the pioneer in his log cabin shall enlarge into the spiritual life of a democracy where civic power shall dominate and utilize individual achievement for the common good.*

Turner was thus arguing that the development of the American frontier served to help shape the

*character of the American people and the nature
of America's public and private institutions. He
believed that the conventional, class-conscious and
property-oriented attitudes of our eastern sea-
board, formed under old European influences,
underwent a dramatic change as the country
expanded from east to west, and this change
molded us into a people who instead honor individualism, nationalism, mobility, and equality in
political, economic, and legal rights.*

FROM "THE SIGNIFICANCE OF THE FRONTIER IN AMERICAN HISTORY" JULY 11, 1893

In a recent bulletin of the Superintendent of the
Census for 1890 appear these significant words:
"Up to and including 1880 the country had a
frontier of settlement, but at present the unset-
tled area has been so broken into by isolated bodies of settlement that there can hardly be said to
be a frontier line. In the discussion of its extent,
its westward movement, etc., it can not, therefore, any longer have a place in the census
reports." This brief official statement marks the
closing of a great historic movement. Up to our
own day American history has been in a large
degree the history of the colonization of the Great
West. The existence of an area of free land, its
continuous recession, and the advance of American settlement westward, explain American
development.

Behind institutions, behind constitutional forms and modifications, lie the vital forces that call these organs into life and shape them to meet changing conditions. The peculiarity of American institutions is the fact that they have been compelled to adapt themselves to the changes of an expanding people — to the changes involved in crossing a continent, in winning a wilderness, and in developing at each area of this progress, out of the primitive economic and political conditions of the frontier, the complexity of city life. Said Calhoun in 1817, "We are great, and rapidly — I was about to say fearfully — growing!" So saying, he touched on the distinguishing feature of American life. All peoples show development: the germ theory of politics has been sufficiently emphasized. In the case of most nations, however, the development has occurred in a limited area; and if the nation has expanded, it has met other growing peoples whom it has conquered. But in the case of the United States we have a different phenomenon. Limiting our attention to the Atlantic coast, we have the familiar phenomenon of the evolution of institutions in a limited area, such as the rise of representative government; the differentiation of simple colonial governments into complex organs; the progress from primitive industrial society, without division of labor, up to manufacturing civilization. But we have in addition to this a recurrence of the process of evolution in each Western area reached in the process of expansion. Thus

American institutions have been compelled to adapt themselves to the changes of an expanding people

American development has exhibited not merely advance along a single line, but a return to primitive conditions on a continually advancing frontier line, and a new development for that area.

American social development has been continually beginning over again on the frontier

American social development has been continually beginning over again on the frontier. This perennial rebirth, this fluidity of American life, this expansion westward with its new opportunities, its continuous touch with the simplicity of primitive society, furnish the forces dominating American character. The true point of view in the history of this nation is not the Atlantic coast, it is the Great West. Even the slavery struggle . . . occupies its important place in American history because of its relation to westward expansion.

In this advance the frontier is the outer edge of the wave — the meeting point between savagery and civilization. Much has been written about the frontier from the point of view of border warfare and the chase, but as a field for the serious study of the economist and the historian it has been neglected.

The American frontier is sharply distinguished from the European frontier, a fortified boundary line running through dense populations. The most significant thing about the American frontier is that it lies at the hither edge of free land. In the census reports it is treated as the margin of that settlement which has a density of two or more people to the square mile. The term is an elastic one, and for our purpose does not need sharp definition. We shall consider the whole frontier belt, including the Indian country and the outer margin of the "settled area" of the census reports. This paper will make no attempt to treat the subject exhaustively; its aim is simply to call attention to the frontier as a fertile field for investigation, and to suggest some of the problems which arise in connection with it.

In the settlement of America we have to observe how European life entered the continent, and how America modified and developed that life and reacted on Europe. Our early history is the study of European germs developing in an American environment. Too exclusive attention has been paid by institutional students to the Germanic origins, too little to the American factors. The frontier is the line of most rapid and effective Americanization. The wilderness masters the colonist. It finds him a European in dress, industries, tools, modes of travel, and thought. It takes him from the railroad car and puts him in the birch canoe. It strips off the garments of civilization, and arrays him in the hunting shirt and the moccasin. It puts him in the log cabin of the Cherokee and the Iroquois, and runs an Indian palisade around him. Before long he has gone to planting Indian corn and plowing with a sharp stick; he shouts the war cry and takes the scalp in orthodox Indian fashion. In short, at the frontier the environment is at first too strong for the man. He must accept the conditions which it furnishes,

The frontier is the line of the most rapid and effective Americanization

or perish, and so he fits himself into the Indian clearings and follows the Indian trails. Little by little he transforms the wilderness, but the outcome is not the old Europe, not simply the development of Germanic germs. . . . The fact is, that here is a new product that is American. At first the frontier was the Atlantic coast. It was the frontier of Europe in a very real sense. Moving westward, the frontier became more and more American. . . . [T]he advance of the frontier has meant a steady movement away from the influence of Europe, a steady growth of independence on American lines. And to study this advance, the men who grew up under these conditions, and the political, economic, and social results of it, is to study the really American part of our history. . . .

Growth of Democracy

The most important effect of the frontier has been in the promotion of democracy

[T]he most important effect of the frontier has been in the promotion of democracy here and in Europe. As has been pointed out, the frontier is productive of individualism. Complex society is precipitated by the wilderness into a kind of primitive organization based on the family. The tendency is anti-social. It produces antipathy to control, and particularly to any direct control. The tax-gatherer is viewed as a representative of oppression. . . . [F]rontier conditions prevalent in the colonies are important factors in the explanation of the American Revolution, where individual liberty was sometimes confused with absence of all effective government. The same conditions aid in explaining the difficulty of instituting a strong government in the period of the confederacy. The frontier individualism has from the beginning promoted democracy.

The frontier States that came into the Union in the first quarter of a century of its existence came in with democratic suffrage [voting] provisions, and had reactive effects of the highest importance upon the older States whose peoples were being attracted there. . . . The rise of democracy as an effective force in the nation came in with Western preponderance under Jackson and William Henry Harrison, and it meant the triumph of the frontier — with all of its good and with all of its evil elements. . . .

The frontier States came into existence with suffrage [voting]

So long as free land exists, the opportunity for a competency exists, and economic power secures political power. But democracy born of free land, strong in selfishness and individualism, intolerant of administrative experience and education, and pressing individual liberty beyond its proper bounds, has its dangers as well as its benefits. Individualism in America has allowed a laxity in regard to governmental affairs which has rendered possible the spoils system and all the manifest evils that follow from the lack of a highly developed civic spirit. In this connection may be noted also the influence of frontier conditions in permitting lax business honor, inflated paper currency and wild-cat banking. . . . A primitive society can hardly be expected to show the intelligent appreciation of the complexity of business interests in a developed society. . . .

Intellectual Traits

From the conditions of frontier life came intellectual traits of profound importance. The works of travelers along each frontier from colonial days onward describe for each certain traits, and these traits have, while softening down, still persisted as survivals in the place of their origin, even when a higher social organization succeeded. The result is that to the frontier the American intellect owes its striking characteristics. That coarseness and strength combined with acuteness and inquisitiveness; that practical, inventive turn of mind, quick to find expedients; that masterful grasp of material things, lacking in the artistic but powerful to effect great ends; that restless, nervous energy; that dominant individualism, working for good and for evil, and withal that buoyancy and exuberance which comes with freedom — these are traits of the frontier, or traits called out elsewhere because of the existence of the frontier. Since the days when the fleet of Columbus sailed into the waters of the New World, America has been another name for opportunity, and the people of the United States have taken their tone from the incessant expansion which has not only been open but has even been forced upon them. He would be a rash prophet who should assert that the expansive character of American life has

To the frontier the American intellect owes it striking characteristics.

now entirely ceased. Movement has been its dominant fact, and, unless this training has no effect upon a people, the American intellect will continually demand a wider field for its exercise. But never again will such gifts of free land offer themselves. For a moment, at the frontier, the bonds of custom are broken, and unrestraint is triumphant. . . . The stubborn American environment is there with its imperious summons to accept its conditions; the inherited ways of doing things are also there; and yet, in spite of environment, and in spite of custom, each frontier did indeed furnish a new field of opportunity, a gate of escape from the bondage of the past; and freshness, and confidence, and scorn of older society, impatience of its restraints and its ideas, and indifference to its lessons, have accompanied the frontier. What the Mediterranean Sea was to the Greeks, breaking the bond of custom, offering new experiences, calling out new institutions and activities, that, and more, the ever retreating frontier has been to the United States directly, and to the nations of Europe more remotely. And now, four centuries from the discovery of America, at the end of a hundred years of life under the Constitution, the frontier has gone, and with its going has closed the first period of American history.

JOHN MARSHALL HARLAN

John Marshall Harlan (1833–1911) served as a colonel in the Union army, as attorney general of

Kentucky, and, for 34 years, as an associate justice of the U.S. Supreme Court. He was a man of strong and independent convictions and a firm defender of civil liberties and civil rights. This is

Perhaps the most famous Supreme Court dissent of all time

most evident in his brilliant dissent from the majority opinion of the Court in the landmark Supreme Court decision Plessy v. Ferguson. *The case arose when a black man, Homer Plessy, was jailed for sitting in the "whites only" car of the East Louisiana Railroad in violation of Louisiana's Separate Car Act that required that he sit in the "colored" car. At his trial, Plessy argued before Judge John Howard Ferguson that the Louisiana law violated his rights under the Thirteenth and Fourteenth Amendments to the Constitution.*

By a vote of 8 to 1, Justice Harlan being the sole dissenter, the Court ruled that the doctrine of "separate but equal" was constitutional under the Fourteenth Amendment, thus giving constitutional sanction to a large number of segregation laws relating to many public areas, including restaurants, bars, theaters, restrooms, and public schools.

Harlan's wisdom would later be confirmed

It was not until 1954, in the equally celebrated case, Brown v. Board of Education,[16] *that Justice Harlan's wisdom was confirmed and the doctrine of "separate but equal" was struck down.*

[16] See page 334.

FROM DISSENT IN
PLESSY V. FERGUSON
1896

By the Louisiana statute, the validity of which is here involved, all railway companies (other than street railway companies) carrying passengers in that state are required to have separate but equal accommodations for white and colored persons, "by providing two or more passenger coaches for each passenger train, *or* by dividing the passenger coaches by *partition* so as to secure separate accommodations." Under this statute, no colored person is permitted to occupy a seat in a coach assigned to white persons; nor any white person to occupy a seat in the coach assigned to colored persons. The managers of the railroad are not allowed to exercise any discretion in the premises, but are required to assign each passenger to some coach or compartment set apart for the exclusive use of his race. If a passenger insists upon going into a coach or compartment not set apart for persons of his race, he is subject to be fined, or to be imprisoned in the parish jail. Penalties are prescribed for the refusal or neglect of the officers, directors, conductors, and employees of railroad companies to comply with the provisions of the act. . . .

[W]e have before us a state enactment that compels, under penalties, the separation of the two races in railroad passenger coaches, and makes it a crime for a citizen of either race to enter a coach that has been assigned to citizens of the other race.

Thus the state regulates the use of a public highway by citizens of the United States solely upon the basis of race.

However apparent the injustice of such legislation may be, we have only to consider whether it is consistent with the Constitution of the United States. . . .

In respect of civil rights, common to all citizens, the Constitution of the United States does not, I think, permit any public authority to know the race of those entitled to be protected in the enjoyment of such rights. Every true man has pride of race, and under appropriate circumstances, when the rights of others, his equals before the law, are not to be affected, it is his privilege to express such pride and to take such action based upon it as to him seems proper. But I deny that any legislative body or judicial tribunal may have regard to the race of citizens when the civil rights of those citizens are involved. Indeed such legislation as that here in question is inconsistent, not only with that equality of rights which pertains to citizenship, national and state, but with the personal liberty enjoyed by every one within the United States. . . .

The 13th Amendment does not permit the withholding or the deprivation of any right necessarily inhering in freedom. It not only struck down the institution of slavery as previously exist-

Every true man has pride of race

The 13th Amendment does not permit the withholding of any right inhering in freedom

ing in the United States, but it prevents the imposition of any burdens or disabilities that constitute badges of slavery or servitude. It decreed universal civil freedom in this country. This court has so adjudged. But that amendment having been found inadequate to the protection of the rights of those who had been in slavery, it was followed by the 14th Amendment, which added greatly to the dignity and glory of American citizenship, and to the security of personal liberty, by declaring that "all persons born or naturalized in the United States, and subject to the jurisdiction thereof, are citizens of the United States and of the state wherein they reside," and that "no state shall make or enforce any law which shall abridge the privileges or immunities of citizens of the United States; nor shall any state deprive any person of life, liberty, or property without due process of law, nor deny to any person within its jurisdiction the equal protection of the laws." These two amendments, if enforced according to their true intent and meaning, will protect all the civil rights that pertain to freedom and citizenship. Finally, and to the end that no citizen should be denied, on account of his race, the privilege of participating in the political control of his country, it was declared by the 15th Amendment that "the right of citizens of the United States to vote shall not be denied or abridged by the United States or by any state on account of race, color, or previous condition of servitude."

These notable additions to the fundamental

These two amendments will protect all the civil rights that pertain to freedom and citizenship

law were welcomed by the friends of liberty throughout the world. They removed the race line from our governmental systems. They had, as this court has said, a common purpose, namely, to secure "to a race recently emancipated, a race that through many generations have been held in slavery, all the civil rights that the superior race enjoy." They declared, in legal effect, this court has further said, "that the law in the states shall be the same for the black as for the white; that all persons, whether colored or white, shall stand equal before the laws of the states, and, in regard to the colored race, for whose protection the amendment was primarily designed, that no discrimination shall be made against them by law because of their color." We also said: "The words of the amendment, it is true, are prohibitory, but they contain a necessary implication of a positive immunity, or right, most valuable to the colored race — the right to exemption from unfriendly legislation against them distinctively as colored — exemption from legal discriminations, implying inferiority in civil society, lessening the security of their enjoyment of the rights which others enjoy, and discriminations which are steps towards reducing them to the condition of a subject race.". . .

The law in the states shall be the same for the black as for the white

The white race deems itself to be the dominant race in this country. And so it is, in prestige, in achievements, in education, in wealth, and in power. So, I doubt not that it will continue to be

for all time, if it remains true to its great heritage
and holds fast to the principles of constitutional
liberty. But in view of the Constitution, in the eye
of the law, there is in this country no superior,
dominant, ruling class of citizens. There is no
caste here. Our Constitution is color-blind, and
neither knows nor tolerates classes among citizens. In respect of civil rights, all citizens are
equal before the law. The humblest is the peer of
the most powerful. The law regards man as man,
and takes no account of his surroundings or of his
color when his civil rights as guaranteed by the
supreme law of the land are involved. It is therefore to be regretted that this high tribunal, the
final expositor of the fundamental law of the land,
has reached the conclusion that it is competent for
a state to regulate the enjoyment by citizens of
their civil rights solely upon the basis of race. . . .

In my opinion, the judgment this day rendered
will, in time, prove to be quite as pernicious as the
decision made by this tribunal in the *Dred Scott
Case*. It was adjudged in that case that the descendants of Africans who were imported into this
country and sold as slaves were not included nor
intended to be included under the word "citizens"
in the Constitution, and could not claim any of the
rights and privileges which that instrument provided for and secured to citizens of the United
States; that at the time of the adoption of the
Constitution they were "considered as a subordinate and inferior class of beings, who had been

*Our Consti-
tution is
color-blind*

subjugated by the dominant race, and, whether emancipated or not, yet remained subject to their authority, and had no rights or privileges but such as those who held the power and the government might choose to grant them.". . . The recent amendments of the Constitution, it was supposed, had eradicated these principles from our institutions. But it seems that we have yet, in some of the states, a dominant race, a superior class of citizens, which assumes to regulate the enjoyment of civil rights, common to all citizens, upon the basis of race. The present decision, it may well be apprehended, will not stimulate aggressions, more or less brutal and irritating, upon the admitted rights of colored citizens, but will encourage the belief that it is possible, by means of state enactments, to defeat the beneficent purposes which the people of the United States had in view when they adopted the recent amendments of the Constitution, by one of which the blacks of this country were made citizens of the United States and of the states in which they respectively reside and whose privileges and immunities, as citizens, the states are forbidden to abridge. Sixty millions of whites are in no danger from the presence here of eight millions of blacks.

The destinies of the two races in this country are indissolubly linked together

The destinies of the two races in this country are indissolubly linked together, and the interests of both require that the common government of all shall not permit the seeds of race hate to be planted under the sanction of law. What can more certainly arouse race hate, what more certainly create and perpetuate a feeling of distrust between these races, than state enactments which in fact proceed on the ground that colored citizens are so inferior and degraded that they cannot be allowed to sit in public coaches occupied by white citizens? That, as all will admit, is the real meaning of such legislation as was enacted in Louisiana.

The sure guaranty of the peace and security of each race is the clear, distinct, unconditional recognition by our governments, national and state, of every right that inheres in civil freedom, and of the equality before the law of all citizens of the United States without regard to race. State enactments, regulating the enjoyment of civil rights, upon the basis of race, and cunningly devised to defeat legitimate result of the war, under the pretense of recognizing equality of rights, can have no other result than to render permanent peace impossible and to keep alive a conflict of races, the continuance of which must do harm to all concerned. This question is not met by the suggestion that social equality cannot exist between the white and black races in this country. That argument, if it can be properly regarded as one, is scarcely worthy of consideration, for social equality no more exists between two races when traveling in a passenger coach or a public highway than when members of the same races sit by each other in a street car or in the jury box, or stand or sit with each other in a political assembly, or when

State enactments keep alive a conflict of races

they use in common the streets of a city or town, or when they are in the same room for the purpose of having their names placed on the registry of voters, or when they approach the ballot-box in order to exercise the high privilege of voting. . . .

The arbitrary separation of citizens, on the basis of race, while they are on a public highway, is a badge of servitude wholly inconsistent with the civil freedom and the equality before the law established by the Constitution. It cannot be justified upon any legal grounds.

If evils will result from the commingling of the two races upon public highways established for the benefit of all, they will be infinitely less than those that will surely come from state legislation regulating the enjoyment of civil rights upon the basis of race. We boast of the freedom enjoyed by our people above all other peoples. But it is difficult to reconcile that boast with a state of the law which, practically, puts the brand of servitude and degradation upon a large class of our fellow citizens, our equals before the law. The thin disguise of "equal" accommodations for passengers in railroad coaches will not mislead anyone, or atone for the wrong this day done.

The result of the whole matter is that while this court has frequently adjudged, and at the present term has recognized the doctrine, that a state cannot, consistently with the Constitution of the United States, prevent white and black citizens, having the required qualifications for jury

The thin disguise of "equal" accommodations will not mislead anyone

service, from sitting in the same jury box, it is now solemnly held that a state may prohibit white and black citizens from sitting in the same passenger coach on a public highway, or may require that they be separated by a "partition" when in the same passenger coach. May it not now be reasonably expected that astute men of the dominant race, who affect to be disturbed at the possibility that the integrity of the white race may be corrupted, or that its supremacy will be imperiled, by contact on public highways with black people, will endeavor to procure statutes requiring white and black jurors to be separated in the jury box by a "partition," and that, upon retiring from the court room to consult as to their verdict, such partition, if it be a movable one, shall be taken to their consultation room, and set up in such way as to prevent black jurors from coming too close to their brother jurors of the white race. If the "partition" used in the court room happens to be stationary, provision could be made for screens with openings through which jurors of the two races could confer as to their verdict without coming into personal contact with each other. I cannot see but that, according to the principles this day announced, such state legislation, although conceived in hostility to, and enacted for the purpose of humiliating, citizens of the United States of a particular race, would be held to be consistent with the Constitution.

I do not deem it necessary to review the decisions of state courts to which reference was made in argument. Some, and the most important, of them are wholly inapplicable, because rendered prior to the adoption of the last amendments of the Constitution, when colored people had very few rights which the dominant race felt obliged to respect. Others were made at a time when public opinion, in many localities, was dominated by the institution of slavery; when it would not have been safe to do justice to the black man: and when, so far as the rights of blacks were concerned, race prejudice was, practically, the supreme law of the land. Those decisions cannot be guides in the era introduced by the recent amendments of the supreme law, which established universal civil freedom, gave citizenship to all born or naturalized in the United States and residing here, obliterated the race line from our systems of governments, national and state, and placed our free institutions upon the broad and sure foundation of the equality of all men before the law.

The statute of Louisiana is inconsistent with the personal liberty of citizens, black and white

I am of opinion that the statute of Louisiana is inconsistent with the personal liberty of citizens, white and black, in that state, and hostile to both the spirit and letter of the Constitution of the United States. If laws of like character should be enacted in the several states of the Union, the effect would be in the highest degree mischievous. Slavery, as an institution tolerated by law would, it is true, have disappeared from our country, but there would remain a power in the states, by sinister legislation, to interfere with the full enjoyment of the blessings of freedom; to regulate civil rights, common to all citizens, upon the basis of race; and to place in a condition of legal inferiority a large body of American citizens, now constituting a part of the political community called the people of the United States, for whom and by whom, through representatives, our government is administered. Such a system is inconsistent with the guarantee given by the Constitution to each state of a republican form of government, and may be stricken down by congressional action, or by the courts in the discharge of their solemn duty to maintain the supreme law of the land, anything in the Constitution or laws of any state to the contrary notwithstanding.

For the reasons stated, I am constrained to withhold my assent from the opinion and judgment of the majority.

THEODORE ROOSEVELT

Our colorful twenty-sixth president, Theodore Roosevelt (1858–1919), was a strong, vigorous, multifaceted man. He held the elective offices of New York State assemblyman, governor of New York, and vice president and president of the United States. He was also police commissioner

A multi-faceted man

of New York City, a member of the U.S. Civil Service Commission, assistant secretary of the Navy, a colonel in the Rough Riders, president of the American Historical Association, and founder of the Boone and Crockett Club and the National Collegiate Athletic Association.

An extraordinarily literate man

While Roosevelt was an exceptional man of action, he was also an extraordinarily literate man. He is said to have read a book a day. He wrote thirty-five books of his own and is reputed to have written one hundred fifty thousand letters during his lifetime, an output exceeding even that of Thomas Jefferson.

Many Roosevelt quotations have become part of our heritage. Here are three of those most often cited.

> It is not the critic who counts: not the man who points out how the strong man stumbles or where the doer of deeds could have done better. The credit belongs to the man who is actually in the arena, whose face is marred by dust and sweat and blood, who strives valiantly, who errs and comes up short again and again, because there is no effort without error or shortcoming, but who knows the great enthusiasms, the great devotions, who spends himself for a worthy cause; who, at the best, knows, in the end, the triumph of high achievement, and who, at the worst, if he fails, at least he fails

while daring greatly, so that his place shall never be with those cold and timid souls who knew neither victory or defeat. (From "The Man in the Arena," April 23, 1910).

Is America a weakling, to shrink from the work of the great world powers? No! The young giant of the West stands on a continent and clasps the crest of an ocean in either hand. Our nation, glorious in youth and strength, looks into the future with eager eyes and rejoices as a strong man to run a race. (From "The Young Giant of the West," June 7, 1897).

I have always been fond of the West African proverb, "Speak softly and carry a big stick; you will go far." (From "The Big Stick," January 26, 1900).

Here is one of Theodore Roosevelt's most powerful writings. It concerns American freedoms and the responsibilities we have to protect and preserve those freedoms, both as individuals and as a nation. Every word of this marvelous piece should forcibly resound in the consciousness of every American, particularly after the tragedy of September 11, 2001, and the hard task that now confronts us of eliminating terrorism from the world.

Roosevelt's words should resound in our consciousness today

FROM THE CHICAGO SPEECH
APRIL 10, 1899

In speaking to you, men of the greatest city of the West, men of the state which gave to the country Lincoln and Grant, men who preeminently and distinctly embody all that is most American in the American character, I wish to preach not the doctrine of ignoble ease but the doctrine of the strenuous life; the life of toil and effort; of labor and strife; to preach that highest form of success which comes not to the man who desires mere easy peace but to the man who does not shrink from danger, from hardship, or from bitter toil, and who out of these wins the splendid ultimate triumph.

I wish to preach the doctrine of the strenuous life

A life of slothful ease, a life of that peace which springs merely from lack either of desire or of power to strive after great things, is as little worthy of a nation as of an individual. I ask only that what every self-respecting American demands from himself and from his sons shall be demanded of the American nation as a whole. Who among you would teach your boys that ease, that peace, is to be the first consideration in their eyes — to be the ultimate goal after which they strive? You men of Chicago have made this city great, you men of Illinois have done your share, and more than your share, in making America great, because you neither preach nor practice such a doctrine. You work yourselves, and you bring up your sons to work. If you are rich and are worth your salt, you will teach your sons that though they may have leisure, it is not to be spent in idleness; for wisely used leisure merely means that those who possess it, being free from the necessity of working for their livelihood, are all the more bound to carry on some kind of non-remunerative work in science, in letters, in art, in exploration, in historical research — work of the type we most need in this country, the successful carrying out of which reflects most honor upon the nation. We do not admire the man of timid peace. We admire the man who embodies victorious effort; the man who never wrongs his neighbor, who is prompt to help a friend, but who has those virile qualities necessary to win in the stern strife of actual life. It is hard to fail, but it is worse never to have tried to succeed. . . .

We do not admire the man of timid peace

As it is with the individual so it is with the nation. It is a base untruth to say that happy is the nation that has no history. Thrice happy is the nation that has a glorious history. Far better it is to dare mighty things, to win glorious triumphs, even though checkered by failure, than to take rank with those poor spirits who neither enjoy much nor suffer much because they live in the gray twilight that knows neither victory nor defeat. If in 1861 the men who loved the Union had believed that peace was the end of all things, and war and strife the worst of all things, and had acted up to their belief, we would have saved hundreds of thousands of lives, we would have saved hundreds of millions of dollars. Moreover, besides saving all the blood and treasure we then lavished, we would have prevented the heartbreak of many women, the dissolution of many homes, and we would have spared the country those months of gloom and shame when it seemed as if our armies marched only to defeat. We would have avoided all this suffering simply by shrinking from strife. And if we had thus avoided it, we would have shown that we were weaklings, and that we were unfit to stand among the great nations of the earth. Thank God for the iron in the blood of our fathers, the men who upheld the wisdom of Lincoln and bore sword or rifle in the armies of Grant! Let us, the children of the men who proved themselves equal to the mighty days, let us, the children of the men who carried the great Civil War to a triumphant conclusion, praise the God of our fathers that the ignoble counsels of peace were rejected; that the suffering and loss, the blackness of sorrow and despair, were unflinchingly faced, and the years of strife endured; for in the end the slave was freed, the Union restored, and the mighty American republic placed once more as a helmeted queen among nations.

Thank God for the iron in the blood of our fathers

We of this generation do not have to face a task such as that our fathers faced, but we have our tasks, and woe to us if we fail to perform them! . . . If we are to be a really great people, we must strive in good faith to play a great part in the world. We cannot avoid meeting great issues. All that we can determine for ourselves is whether we shall meet them well or ill. Last year we could not help being brought face to face with the problem of war with Spain. All we could decide was whether we should shrink like cowards from the contest or enter into it as beseemed a brave and high-spirited people; and, once in, whether failure or success should crown our banners. So it is now. We cannot avoid the responsibilities that confront us in Hawaii, Cuba, Puerto Rico, and the Philippines. All we can decide is whether we shall meet them in a way that will redound to the national credit, or whether we shall make of our dealings with these new problems a dark and shameful page in our history. To refuse to deal with them at all merely amounts to dealing with them badly. We have a given problem to solve. If we undertake the solution there is, of course, always danger that we may not solve it aright; but to refuse to undertake the solution simply renders it certain that we cannot possibly solve it aright.

> **If we are to be a great people, we must strive to play a great part in the world**

The timid man, the lazy man, the man who distrusts his country, the over-civilized man, who has lost the great fighting, masterful virtues, and the ignorant man and the man of dull mind, whose soul is incapable of feeling the mighty lift that thrills "stern men with empires in their brains" — all these, of course, shrink from seeing the nation undertake its new duties; shrink from seeing us build a navy and army adequate to our needs; shrink from seeing us do our share of the world's work. . . . These are the men who fear the strenuous life, who fear the only national life which is really worth leading. . . .

I preach to you, then, my countrymen, that our country calls not for the life of ease, but for the life of strenuous endeavor. The twentieth century looms before us big with the fate of many nations. If we stand idly by, if we seek merely swollen, slothful ease and ignoble peace, if we shrink from the hard contests where men must win at hazard of their lives and at the risk of all they hold dear, then the bolder and stronger peoples will pass us by and will win for themselves the domination of the world. Let us therefore boldly face the life of strife, resolute to do our duty well and manfully; resolute to uphold righteousness by deed and by word; resolute to be both honest and brave, to serve high ideals, yet to use practical methods. Above all, let us shrink from no strife, moral or physical, within or without the nation, provided we are certain that the strife is justified, for it is only through strife, through hard and dangerous endeavor, that we shall ultimately win the goal of true national greatness.

Let us face the life of strife

VI
WRITINGS FROM
THE TWENTIETH
CENTURY

WOODROW WILSON

Woodrow Wilson (1856–1924) — lawyer, college professor, university president, and state governor — was elected as the twenty-eighth president of the United States in 1912. His campaign was based upon an appeal to liberal and reform groups, and his election was a triumph of the little man against the big industrialist. Wilson's first administration witnessed many needed reforms in the tariff structures, banking systems, and industrial policies of the nation. He was reelected to the presidency in 1916, chiefly because of his advocacy of keeping America out of World War I. However, in 1917, in response to the sinking of American ships by German submarines, Wilson asked Congress to declare war against Germany, stating that "the world must be made safe for democracy." After the war, Wilson proposed a comprehensive peace treaty and the concept of a League of Nations, both of which were rejected by Congress. Defeat of these proposals left Wilson an embittered and broken man upon his retirement in 1921.

His most significant writings were a series of speeches from his first presidential campaign, published under the title The New Freedom, *which became a bible of prewar liberal thought.*

FROM *THE NEW FREEDOM*
"LIFE COMES FROM THE SOIL"
1913

Nations are renewed from the bottom, not the top

When I look back on the processes of history, when I survey the genesis of America, I see this written over every page: that the nations are renewed from the bottom, not from the top; that the genius which springs up from the ranks of unknown men is the genius which renews the youth and energy of the people. Everything I know about history, every bit of experience and observation that has contributed to my thought, has confirmed me in the conviction that the real wisdom of human life is compounded out of the experiences of ordinary men. The utility, the vitality, the fruitage of life does not come from the top to the bottom; it comes, like the natural growth of a great tree, from the soil, up through the trunk into the branches to the foliage and the fruit. The great struggling unknown masses of the men who are at the base of everything are the dynamic force that is lifting the levels of society. A nation is as great, and only as great, as her rank and file.

So the first and chief need of this nation of ours to-day is to include in the partnership of government all those great bodies of unnamed men who are going to produce our future leaders and renew the future energies of America. And as I confess that, as I confess my belief in the common man, I know what I am saying. The man who is swimming against the stream knows the strength of it. The man who is in the melee knows what blows are being struck and what blood is being drawn. The man who is on the make is the judge of what is happening in America, not the man who has made good; not the man who has emerged from the flood; not the man who is standing on the bank looking on, but the man who is struggling for his life and for the lives of those who are dearer to him than himself. That is the man whose judgment will tell you what is going on in America; that is the man by whose judgment I, for one, wish to be guided.

We have had the wrong jury; we have had the wrong group, — no, I will not say the wrong group, but too small a group, — in control of the policies of the United States. The average man has not been consulted, and his heart had begun to sink for fear he never would be consulted again. Therefore, we have got to organize a government whose sympathies will be open to the whole body of the people of the United States, a government which will consult as large a proportion of the people of the United States as possible before it acts.

The average man has not been consulted

Because the great problem of government is to know what the average man is experiencing and is thinking about. Most of us are average men; very few of us rise, except by fortunate accident, above the general level of the community about us; and therefore the man who thinks common thoughts, the man who has had common experiences, is almost always the man who interprets America aright. Isn't that the reason that we are proud of such stories as the story of Abraham Lincoln, — a man who rose out of the ranks and interpreted America better than any man had interpreted it who had risen out of the privileged classes or the educated class of America?

The hope of the United States in the present and in the future is the same that it has always been: it is the hope and confidence that out of unknown homes will come men who will constitute themselves the masters of industry and of politics. The average hopefulness, the average welfare, the average enterprise, the average initiative, of the United States are the only things that make it rich. We are not rich because a few gentlemen direct our industry; we are rich because of our own intelligence and our own industry. America does not consist of men who get their names into the newspapers; America does not consist politically of the men who set themselves up to be political leaders; she does not consist of the men who do most of her talking, — they are important only so far as they speak for that

Out of unknown homes will come men who will be masters of industry and politics

great voiceless multitude of men who constitute the great body and the saving force of the nation. Nobody who cannot speak the common thought, who does not move by the common im-pulse, is the man to speak for America, or for any of her future purposes. Only he is fit to speak who knows the thoughts of the great body of citizens, the men who go about their business every day, the men who toil from morning till night, the men who go home tired in the evenings, the men who are carrying on the things we are so proud of.

You know how it thrills our blood sometimes to think how all the nations of the earth wait to see what America is going to do with her power, her physical power, her enormous resources, her enormous wealth. The nations hold their breath to see what this young country will do with her young unspoiled strength; we cannot help but be proud that we are strong. But what has made us strong? The toil of millions of men, the toil of men who do not boast, who are inconspicuous, but who live their lives humbly from day to day; it is the great body of toilers that constitutes the might of America. It is one of the glories of our land that nobody is able to predict from what family, from what region, from what race, even, the leaders of the country are going to come. The great leaders of this country have not come very often from the established, "successful" families.

I remember speaking at a school not long ago where I understood that almost all the young men

What has made us so strong?

were the sons of very rich people, and I told them I looked upon them with a great deal of pity, because, I said: "Most of you fellows are doomed to obscurity. You will not do anything. You will never try to do anything, and with all the great tasks of the country waiting to be done, probably you are the very men who will decline to do them. Some man who has been 'up against it' some man who has come out of the crowd, somebody who has had the whip of necessity laid on his back, will emerge out of the crowd, will show that he understands the crowd, understands the interests of the nation, united and not separated, and will stand up and lead us."

If I may speak of my own experience, I have found audiences made up of the "common people" quicker to take a point, quicker to understand an argument, quicker to discern a tendency and to comprehend a principle, than many a college class that I have lectured to, — not because the college class lacked the intelligence, but because college boys are not in contact with the realities of life, while "common" citizens are in contact with the actual life of day by day; you do not have to explain to them what touches them to the quick.

Audiences of "common people" are quicker to comprehend a principle

There is one illustration of the value of the constant renewal of society from the bottom that has always interested me profoundly. The only reason why government did not suffer dry rot in the Middle Ages under the aristocratic system

which then prevailed was that so many of the men
who were efficient instruments of government
were drawn from the church, — from that great
religious body which was then the only church,
that body which we now distinguish from other
religious bodies as the Roman Catholic Church.
The Roman Catholic Church was then, as it is
now, a great democracy. There was no peasant so
humble that he might not become a priest, and no
priest so obscure that he might not become Pope
of Christendom; and every chancellery in
Europe, every court in Europe, was ruled by
these learned, trained and accomplished men, —
the priesthood of that great and dominant body.
What kept government alive in the Middle Ages
was this constant rise of the sap from the bottom,
from the rank and file of the great body of the
people through the open channels of the priesthood. That, it seems to me, is one of the most
interesting and convincing illustrations that could
possibly be adduced of the thing that I am talking
about.

The only way that government is kept pure is
by keeping these channels open, so that nobody
may deem himself so humble as not to constitute
a part of the body politic, so that there will constantly be coming new blood into the veins of the
body politic; so that no man is so obscure that he
may not break the crust of any class he may
belong to, may not spring up to higher levels and
be counted among the leaders of the state. Any-

thing that depresses, anything that makes the organization greater than the man, anything that blocks, discourages, dismays the humble man, is against all the principles of progress. When I see alliances formed, as they are now being formed, by successful men of business with successful organizers of politics, I know that something has been done that checks the vitality and progress of society. Such an alliance, made at the top, is an alliance made to depress the levels, to hold them where they are, if not to sink them; and, therefore, it is the constant business of good politics to break up such partnerships, to re-establish and reopen the connections between the great body of the people and the offices of government.

To-day, when our government has so far passed into the hands of special interests; to-day when the doctrine is implicitly avowed that only select classes have the equipment necessary for carrying on government; to-day when so many conscientious citizens, smitten with the scene of social wrong and suffering, have fallen victims to the fallacy that benevolent government can be meted out to the people by kind-hearted trustees of prosperity and guardians of the welfare of dutiful employees — to-day, supremely, does it behoove this nation to remember that a people shall be saved by the power that sleeps in its own deep bosom, or by none; shall be renewed in hope, in conscience, in strength, by waters welling up from its own sweet, perennial springs. Not from above;

A people shall be saved by the power that sleeps in its own deep bosom, or by none not by patronage of its aristocrats. The flower does not bear the root, but the root the flower. Everything that blooms in beauty in the air of heaven draws its fairness, its vigor, from its roots. Nothing living can blossom into fruitage unless through nourishing stalks deep-planted in the common soil. The rose is merely the evidence of the vitality of the root; and the real source of its beauty, the very blush that it wears upon its tender cheek, comes from those silent sources of life that lie hidden in the chemistry of the soil. Up from that soil, up from the silent bosom of the earth, rise the currents of life and energy. Up from the common soil, up from the quiet heart of the people, rise joyously to-day streams of hope and determination bound to renew the face of the earth in glory.

I tell you, the so-called radicalism of our times is simply the effort of nature to release the generous energies of our people. This great American people is at bottom just, virtuous, and hopeful; the roots of its being are in the soil of what is lovely, pure, and of good report, and the need of the hour is just that radicalism that will clear a way for the realization of the aspirations of a sturdy race.

This great American people is at bottom just, virtuous, and hopeful

HERBERT HOOVER

When Herbert C. Hoover (1874–1964) became president in 1928, he was widely regarded as an

American hero. Son of a Quaker blacksmith, he brought to the presidency a well-deserved reputation for public service as an engineer, administrator, and humanitarian. But even though he had ridden into office in 1928 on a wave of optimism, by 1932 his reputation was severely tarnished by his failure to solve the economic problems that brought about America's Great Depression. This disastrous slump in the American economy began on October 29, 1929, with the stock market crash and left fourteen million Americans unemployed before the end of Hoover's first term. Consequently, in his second presidential campaign, Hoover was soundly defeated by Franklin D. Roosevelt.

There is no question that Herbert Hoover was a good man. He led an exemplary life, free of scandal, and performed numerous good works for the country throughout his career. The failure of his presidency cannot be ascribed to any character flaw in the man. Perhaps his political philosophy was inadequate to solve the particular economic problems of the Depression. Or perhaps his inflexibility and unwillingness to change were the cause of his failure. Or perhaps he simply lacked sufficient management skills for a president.

Whatever the reason, in October 1928, when Hoover delivered this speech toward the close of his first presidential campaign, when the economic problems that were soon to engulf the na-

Failure of his presidency could not be ascribed to any character flaw

tion were not readily apparent, the people responded vigorously and positively — as many Americans still do today — to his classic statement of the American conservative philosophy. Hoover regarded free, private enterprise and initiative, a system of "rugged individualism," as the foundations of America's "unparalleled greatness." He believed that government entry into commercial business would destroy political equality, increase corruption, stifle initiative, undermine the development of leadership, extinguish opportunity, and "dry up the spirit of liberty and progress." Here are selected excerpts from that famous speech.

Classic statement of the American conservative philosophy

FROM PRESIDENTIAL CAMPAIGN SPEECH, "THE RUGGED INDIVIDUALISM" OCTOBER 22, 1928

After the war, when the Republican Party assumed administration of the country, we were faced with the problem of determination of the very nature of our national life. Over 150 years we have builded up a form of self-government and we have builded up a social system which is peculiarly our own. It differs fundamentally from all others in the world. It is the American system. It is just as definite and positive a political and social system as has ever been developed on earth. It is founded upon a particular conception that self-

A social system which is peculiarly our own

government can be preserved only by decentralization of Government in the State and by fixing local responsibility; but further than this, it is founded upon the social conception that only through ordered liberty, freedom and equal opportunity to the individual will his initiative and enterprise drive the march of progress.

During the war we turned to the government to solve every difficult economic problem

During the war we necessarily turned to the Government to solve every difficult economic problem — the Government having absorbed every energy of our people for war there was no other solution. For the preservation of the State the Government became a centralized despotism which undertook unprecedented responsibilities, assumed powers, exercised rights, and took over the business of citizens. To large degree we regimented our whole people temporarily into a socialistic state. However justified in time of war if continued in peace time it would destroy not only our system but progress and freedom in our own country and throughout the world. When the war closed the most vital of all issues was whether Governments should continue war ownership and operation of many instrumentalities of production and distribution. We were challenged with the choice of the American system of rugged individualism or the choice of a European system of diametrically opposed doctrines — doctrines of paternalism and state socialism. The acceptance of these ideas would have meant the destruction of self-government through centralization of government; it meant the undermining of the individual initiative and enterprise through which our people have grown to unparalleled greatness.

The Democratic administration cooperated with the Republican Party to demobilize many of her activities and the Republican Party from the beginning of its period of power resolutely turned its face away from these ideas and these war practices, back to our fundamental conception of the state and the rights and responsibilities of the individual. Thereby it restored confidence and hope in the American people, it freed and stimulated enterprise, it restored the Government to its position as an umpire instead of a player in the economic game. For these reasons the American people have gone forward in progress while the rest of the world is halting and some countries have even gone backwards. If anyone will study the causes of retarded recuperation in Europe, he will find much of it due to the stifling of private initiative on one hand, and overloading of the Government with business on the other.

I, regret, however, to say that there has been revived in this campaign a proposal which would be a long step toward the abandonment of our American system, to turn to the idea of government in business. Because the country is faced with difficulty and doubt over certain national problems which we faced — that is, prohibition, farm relief and electrical power — our opponents propose that we must to some degree thrust gov-

I regret there has been revived a proposal to turn the idea of government in business

ernment into these businesses and in effect adopt state socialism as a solution.

There is, therefore, submitted to the American people the question — Shall we depart from the American system and start upon a new road. I wish to make clear my position on the principles involved for they go to the very roots of American life in every act of our Government. I should like to state to you the effect of this projection to the extension of government into business upon our system of self government and our economic system. But even more important is the effect upon the average man. That is the effect on the very basis of liberty and freedom not only for those left outside the fold of expanded bureaucracy but for those embraced within it. . . .

Shall we depart from the American system and start upon a new road?

Bureaucracy is ever desirous of spreading its influence and its power. You cannot give to a government the mastery of the daily working life of a people without at the same time giving it mastery of the peoples' souls and thoughts. Every expansion of government means that government in order to protect itself from political consequences of its errors and wrongs is driven onward without peace to greater and greater control of the country's press and platform. Free speech does not live many hours after free industry and free commerce die.

It is a false liberalism that interprets itself into the Government operation of commercial business. The bureaucratization of our country would poison the very roots of liberalism — that is, free speech, free assembly, free press, political equality and equality of opportunity. It is the road, not to more liberty, but to less liberty. Liberalism should be found not striving to spread bureaucracy, but striving to set bounds to it. True liberalism seeks freedom first in the confident belief that without freedom the pursuit of all other blessings and benefits is vain. That belief is the foundation of all American progress, political as well as economic.

True liberalism seeks freedom first

Liberalism is a force truly of the spirit, a force proceeding from the deep realization that economic freedom cannot be sacrificed if political freedom is to be preserved. Even if governmental conduct of business could give us more efficiency instead of giving us less efficiency, the fundamental objection to it would remain unaltered and unabated. It would destroy political equality. It would cramp and cripple the mental and spiritual energies of our people. It would dry up the spirit of liberty and progress. It would extinguish equality of opportunity, and for these reasons fundamentally and primarily it must be resisted. For a hundred and fifty years liberalism has found its true spirit in the American system, not in the European systems.

I do not wish to be misunderstood in this statement. I am defining a general policy! It does not mean that our Government is to part with one iota of its national resources without complete protection to the public interest. . . .

Nor do I wish to be misinterpreted as believing

that the United States is free-for-all and devil-take-the-hindmost. The very essence of equality of opportunity is that there shall be no domination by any group or trust or combination in this republic, whether it be business or political. It demands economic justice as well as political and social justice. It is no system of laissez faire. . . .

I feel deeply on this subject because during the war I had some practical experience with governmental operation and control. I have witnessed not only at home but abroad the many failures of government in business. I have seen its tyrannies, its injustices, its destructions of self-government, its undermining of the very instincts which carry our people forward to progress. I have witnessed the lack of advance, the lowered standards of living, the depressed spirits of people working under such a system. My objection is based not upon theory or upon a failure to recognize wrong or abuse but I know the adoption of such methods would strike at the very roots of American life and would destroy the very basis of American progress. . . .

I have witnessed the failures of government in business

As a result of our distinctly American system our country has become the land of opportunity to those born without inheritance, not merely because of the wealth of its resources and industry, but because of this freedom of initiative and enterprise. Russia has natural resources equal to ours. Her people are equally industrious, but she has not had the blessings of 150 years of our form

America has become the land of opportunity for those born without inheritance

of government and of our social system. . . . By adherence to the principles of decentralization, self-government, ordered liberty, and opportunity and freedom to the individual, our American experiment has yielded a degree of well-being unparalleled in all the world. It has come nearer to the abolition of poverty, to the abolition of fear of want than humanity has ever reached before. Progress of the last seven years is proof of it. . . . The greatness of America has grown out of a political and social system and a method of control of economic forces distinctly its own — our American system —which has carried this great experiment in human welfare further than ever before in all history. We are nearer today to the ideal of the abolition of poverty and fear from the lives of men and women than ever before in any land. And I again repeat that the departure from our American system by injecting principles destructive to it which our opponents propose will jeopardize the very liberty and freedom of our people, and will destroy equality of opportunity, not alone to ourselves but to our children.

THOMAS WOLFE

Thomas Wolfe (1900–1938) is one of the best of America's twentieth-century novelists. His four great novels are Look Homeward, Angel *(1929),* Of Time and the River *(1935),* The Web and the

Rock (1939), and You Can't Go Home Again *(1940) (the last two published posthumously). Wolfe symbolized in himself, as well as in his work, the "homeless" generation of the 1930s that sought an understanding of the forces that were transforming American life — a generation in search of a faith and a "home." That Wolfe found what he wanted is suggested by the credo that concludes his last novel:*

FROM *YOU CAN'T GO HOME AGAIN*
1940

Credo

I think the true discovery of America is before us. I think the true fulfillment of our spirit, of our people, of our mighty and immortal land, is yet to come. I think the true discovery of our own democracy is still before us. And I think that all these things are certain as the morning, as inevitable as noon. I think I speak for most men living when I say that our America is Here, is Now, and beckons on before us, and that this glorious assurance is not only our living hope, but our dream to be accomplished.

The enemy is here before us with a thousand faces

I think the enemy is here before us, too. But I think we know the forms and faces of the enemy, and in the knowledge that we know him, and shall meet him, and eventually must conquer him is also our living hope. I think the enemy is here before us with a thousand faces, but I think we know that all his faces wear one mask. I think the enemy is single selfishness and compulsive greed. I think the enemy is blind; but has the brutal power of his blind grab. I do not think the enemy was born yesterday, or that he grew to manhood forty years ago, or that he suffered sickness and collapse in 1929, or that we began without the enemy, and that our vision faltered, that we lost the way, and suddenly were in his camp. I think the enemy is old as Time, and evil as Hell, and that he has been here with us from the beginning. I think he stole our earth from us, destroyed our wealth, and ravaged and despoiled our land. I think he took our people and enslaved them, that he polluted the fountains of our life, took unto himself the rarest treasures of our own possession, took our bread and left us with a crust, and, not content, for the nature of the enemy is insatiate — tried finally to take from us the crust.

I think the enemy comes to us with the face of innocence and says to us:

"I am your friend."

I think the enemy deceives us with false words and lying phrases, saying:

"See, I am one of you — I am one of your children, your son, your brother, and your friend. Behold how sleek and fat I have become — and all because I am just one of you, and your friend. Behold how rich and powerful I am — and all because I am one of you — shaped in your way of life, of thinking, of accomplishment. What I am, I am because I am one of you, your humble brother and your friend. "Behold," cries Enemy, "the man I am, the man I have become, the thing I have accomplished — and reflect. Will you destroy this thing? I assure you that it is the most precious thing you have. It is yourselves, the projection of each of you, the triumph of your individual lives, the thing that is rooted in your blood, and native to your stock, and inherent in the traditions of America. It is the thing that all of you may hope to be," says Enemy, "for —" humbly — "am I not just one of you? Am I not just your brother and your son? Am I not the living image of what each of you may hope to be, would wish to be, would desire for his own son? Would you destroy this glorious incarnation of your own heroic self? If you do, then," says Enemy, "you destroy yourselves — you kill the thing that is most gloriously American, and in so killing, kill yourselves."

He lies! And now we know he lies! He is not gloriously, or in any other way, ourselves. He is not our friend, our son, our brother. And he is not American! For, although he has a thousand familiar and convenient faces, his own true face is old as Hell.

Look about you and see what he has done. . . .

E. B. WHITE

E. B. White (1899–1985), was an American essayist, author, and prose stylist. He is known principally as the author of three books — Charlotte's

Web, Stuart Little, *and* The Trumpet of the Swan
*— that have become classics in juvenile litera-
ture, and for his many years as contributor to the
New Yorker. White was awarded the Presidential
Medal of Freedom in 1963 and a special Pulitzer
Prize in 1978. He was a master of the English
language. While honored for his wry wit and humor,
he was equally powerful and persuasive whenever his thoughts turned to more serious matters,
as demonstrated by this famous short essay.*

"FREEDOM"
1940

I have often noticed on my trips up to the city that
people have recut their clothes to follow the fashion. On my last trip, however, it seemed to me
that people had remodeled their ideas too —
taken in their convictions a little at the waist,
shortened the sleeves of their resolve, and fitted
themselves out in a new intellectual ensemble
copied from a smart design out of the very latest
page of history. It seemed to me they had strung
along with Paris a little too long.

I confess to a disturbed stomach. I feel sick
when I find anyone adjusting his mind to the new
tyranny which is succeeding abroad. Because of
its fundamental strictures, fascism does not seem
to me to admit of any compromise or any ratio-
nalization, and I resent the patronizing air of persons who find in my plain belief in freedom a sign

Fascism does not admit of any compromise

of immaturity. If it is boyish to believe that a human being should live free, then I'll gladly arrest my development and let the rest of the world grow up.

I shall report some of the strange remarks I heard in New York. One man told me that he thought perhaps the Nazi ideal was a sounder ideal than our constitutional system "because have you ever noticed what fine alert young faces the young German soldiers have in the news-reel?" He added: "Our American youngsters spend all their time at the movies — they're a mess." That was his summation of the case, his interpretation of the new Europe. Such a remark leaves me pale and shaken. If it represents the peak of our intelligence, then the steady march of despotism will not receive any considerable set-back at our shores.

Another man informed me that our democratic notion of popular government was decadent and not worth bothering about — "because England is really rotten and the industrial towns there are a disgrace." That was the only reason he gave for the hopelessness of democracy; and he seemed mightily pleased with himself, as though he were more familiar than most with the anatomy of decadence, and had detected subtler aspects of the situation than were discernible to the rest of us.

Another man assured me that anyone who took *any* kind of government seriously was a gullible fool. You could be sure, he said, that there is nothing but corruption "because of the way Clemenceau acted at Versailles." He said it didn't make any difference really about this war. It was just another war. Having relieved himself of this majestic bit of reasoning, he subsided.

Another individual, discovering signs of zeal creeping into my blood, berated me for having lost my detachment, my pure skeptical point of view. He announced that he wasn't going to be swept away by all this nonsense, but would prefer to remain in the role of innocent bystander, which he said was the duty of any intelligent person. (I noticed that he phoned later to qualify his remark, as though he had lost some of his innocence in the cab on the way home.)

Those are just a few samples of the sort of talk that seemed to be going round — talk which was full of defeatism and disillusion and sometimes of a too studied innocence. Men are not merely annihilating themselves at a great rate these days. but they are telling one another enormous lies, grandiose fibs. Such remarks as I heard are fearfully disturbing in their cumulative effect. They are more destructive than dive bombers and mine fields, for they challenge not merely one's immediate position but one's main defenses. They seemed to me to issue either from persons who could never have really come to grips with freedom so as to understand her, or from renegades. Where I expected to find indignation, I found paralysis, or a sort of dim acquiescence, as in a child who is duly swallowing a distasteful pill. I was advised of the growing anti-Jewish sentiment by a man who seemed to be watching the phenomenon of intolerance not through tears of shame but with a clear intellectual gaze, as through a well-ground lens.

The least a man can do at such times is to declare himself

The least a man can do at such a time is to declare himself and tell where he stands. I believe in freedom with the same burning delight, the same faith, the same intense abandon which attended its birth on this continent more than a century and a half ago. I am writing my declaration rapidly, much as though I were shaving to catch a train. Events abroad give a man a feeling of being pressed for time. Actually I do not believe I am pressed for time, and I apologize to the reader for a false impression that may be created. I just want to tell, before I get slowed down, that I am in love with freedom and that it is an affair of long standing and that it is a fine state to be in, and that I am deeply suspicious of people who are beginning to adjust to fascism and dictators merely because they are succeeding in war. From such adaptable natures a smell rises. I pinch my nose.

For as long as I can remember I have had a sense of living somewhat freely in a natural world. I don't mean I enjoyed freedom of action, but my existence seemed to have the quality of freeness. I traveled with secret papers pertaining to a divine conspiracy. Intuitively I've always been aware of the vitally important pact which a man has with himself, to be all things to himself, and to be identified with all things, to stand self-reliant, taking advantage of his haphazard connection with a planet, riding his luck, and following his bent with the tenacity of a hound. My first and greatest love affair was with this thing we call freedom, this lady of infinite allure, this dangerous and beautiful and sublime being who restores and supplies us all.

My first and greatest love affair was with this thing we call freedom

It began with the haunting intimation (which I presume every child receives) of his mystical inner life; of God in man; of nature publishing herself through the "I." This elusive sensation is moving and memorable. It comes early in life: a boy, we'll say, sitting on the front steps on a summer night, thinking of nothing in particular, suddenly hearing as with a new perception and as though for the first time the pulsing sound of crickets, overwhelmed with the novel sense of identification with the natural company of insects and grass and night, conscious of a faint answering cry to the universal perplexing question: "What is 'I'?" Or a little girl, returning from the grave of a pet bird leaning with her elbows on the window sill, inhaling the unfamiliar draught of death, suddenly seeing herself as part of the complete story. Or to an older youth, encountering for the first time a great teacher who by some chance word or mood awakens something and the youth beginning to breathe as an individual and con-

scious of strength in his vitals. I think the sensation must develop in many men as a feeling of
identity with God — an eruption of the spirit
caused by allergies and the sense of divine existence as distinct from mere animal existence. This is
the beginning of the affair with freedom.

**Man's free
condition is
in two parts**   But a man's free condition is of two parts: the
instinctive freeness he experiences as an animal
dweller on a planet, and the practical liberties he
enjoys as a privileged member of human society.
The latter is, of the two, more generally understood, more widely admired, more violently challenged and discussed. It is the practical and apparent side of freedom. The United States, almost
alone today, offers the liberties and the privileges
and the tools of freedom. In this land the citizens
are still invited to write plays and books, to paint
their pictures, to meet for discussion, to dissent as
well as to agree, to mount soapboxes in the public square, to enjoy education in all subjects without censorship, to hold court and judge one another, to compose music, to talk politics with their
neighbors without wondering whether the secret
police are listening, to exchange ideas as well as
goods, to kid the government when it needs kid-
ding, and to read real news of real events instead
of phony news manufactured by a paid agent of
the state. This is a fact and should give every person pause.

To be free, in a planetary sense, is to feel that
you belong to earth. To be free, in a social sense,

is to feel at home in a democratic framework. In Adolph Hitler, although he is a freely flowering individual, we do not detect either type of sensibility. From reading his book I gather that his feeling for earth is not a sense of communion but a driving urge to prevail. His feeling for men is not that they coexist, but that they are capable of being arranged and standardized by a superior intellect — that their existence suggests not a fulfillment of their personalities but a submersion of their personalities in the common racial destiny. His very great absorption in the destiny of the German people somehow loses some of its effect when you discover, from his writings, in what vast contempt he holds *all* people. "I learned," he wrote, " . . . to gain an insight into the unbelievably primitive opinions and arguments of the people." To him the ordinary man is a primitive, capable only of being used and led. He speaks continually of people as sheep, halfwits, and impudent fools — the same people from whom he asks the utmost in loyalty, and to whom he promises the ultimate in prizes.

Here in America, where our society is based on belief in the individual, not contempt for him, the free principle of life has a chance of surviving. I believe that it must and will survive. To understand freedom is an accomplishment which all men may acquire who set their minds in that direction; and to love freedom is a tendency which many Americans are born with. To live in the same room with freedom, or in the same hemisphere, is still a profoundly shaking experience for me.

One of the earliest truths (and to him most valuable) that the author of *Mein Kampf* discovered was that it is not the written word, but the spoken word, which in heated moments moves great masses of people to noble or ignoble action. The written word, unlike the spoken word, is something which every person examines privately and judges calmly by his own intellectual standards, not by what the man standing next to him thinks. "I know," wrote Hitler, "that one is able to win people far more by the spoken than by the written word." . . . Later he adds contemptuously: "For let it be said to all knights of the pen and to all the political dandies, especially of today: the greatest changes in this world have never been brought about by a goose quill! No, the pen has always been reserved to motivate these changes theoretically."

Luckily I am not out to change the world — that's being done for me, and at a great clip. But I know that the free spirit of man is persistent in nature; it recurs, and has never successfully been wiped out, by fire or flood. I set down the above remarks merely (in the words of Mr. Hitler) to motivate that spirit, theoretically. Being myself a knight of the goose quill, I am under no misapprehension about "winning people"; but I am inordinately proud these days of the quill, for it has shown itself, historically, to be the hypodermic

The free spirit of man is persistent in nature

which inoculates men and keeps the germ of freedom always in circulation, so that there are individuals in every time in every land who are the
carriers, the Typhoid Marys, capable of infecting
others by mere contact and example. These persons are feared by every tyrant — who shows his
fear by burning the books and destroying the individuals. A writer goes about his task today with
the extra satisfaction which comes from knowing
that he will be the first to have his head lopped off
— even before the political dandies. In my own
case this is a double satisfaction, for if freedom
were denied me by force of earthly circumstance,
I am the same as dead and would infinitely prefer
to go into fascism without my head than with it,
having no use for it any more and not wishing to
be saddled with so heavy an encumberance.

FRANKLIN DELANO ROOSEVELT

*Franklin Delano Roosevelt (1882–1945), thirty-
second president of the United States, is regarded by the majority of the American people as the
leader of the democratic movement of our day.
He was born in Hyde Park, New York, the descendant of an aristocratic family who since colonial days had been prominent landowners, merchants, and capitalists. He was educated at Groton
and Harvard, receiving his A.B. in 1904. He
studied law at Columbia, graduated in 1907, and
practiced until 1910, when he entered politics
and was elected to the New York Senate. From*

1913 to 1920, he was assistant secretary of the Navy. He was elected governor of New York in 1929 and was reelected in 1931.

He was nominated for the presidency by the Democratic Party in 1932 and was swept into office through the revolt of the electorate against the Hoover administration. His first four years in office, marked by liberal reforms in labor, banking, and social legislation (popularly called the New Deal), earned him the love of the masses. In 1940, he became the first president to be elected for a third term. The basis of his third presidential campaign was partly a promise to safeguard the social advances of his first four years in office and partly a promise to try to keep America out of World War II. Early in 1941, however, Roosevelt informed the nation that American aid was essential to a British victory over Germany and that military needs might have to take precedence. Today, this great speech is better remembered for Roosevelt's immortalization of the fundamental rights of a free society, the "Four Freedoms."

The "Four Freedoms" speech

FROM THE STATE
OF THE UNION ADDRESS
JANUARY 6, 1941

I address you, the Members of the Seventy-seventh Congress, at a moment unprecedented in the history of the Union. I use the word "unprecedented," because at no previous time has American security been as seriously threatened from without as it is today. . . .

I suppose that every realist knows that the democratic way of life is at this moment being directly assailed in every part of the world — assailed either by arms, or by secret spreading of poisonous propaganda by those who seek to destroy unity and promote discord in nations that are still at peace. During sixteen long months this assault has blotted out the whole pattern of democratic life in an appalling number of independent nations, great and small. The assailants are still on the march, threatening other nations, great and small.

Therefore, as your President, performing my constitutional duty to "give to the Congress information of the state of the Union," I find it, unhappily, necessary to report that the future and the safety of our country and of our democracy are overwhelmingly involved in events far beyond our borders.

Armed defense of democratic existence is now being gallantly waged in four continents. If that defense fails, all the population and all the resources of Europe, Asia, Africa and Australasia will be dominated by the conquerors. The total of those populations and their resources in those four continents greatly exceeds the sum total of the population and the resources of the whole of the Western Hemisphere — many times over.

In times like these it is immature — and incidentally untrue — for anybody to brag that an unprepared America, single-handed, and with one hand tied behind its back, can hold off the whole world.

No realistic American can expect from a dictator's peace international generosity, or return of true independence, or world disarmament, or freedom of expression, or freedom of religion — or even good business. Such a peace would bring no security for us or for our neighbors. "Those, who would give up essential liberty to purchase a little temporary safety, deserve neither liberty nor safety." As a nation we may take pride in the fact that we are softhearted; but we cannot afford to be soft-headed. We must always be wary of those who with sounding brass and a tinkling cymbal preach the "ism" of appeasement. We must especially beware of that small group of selfish men who would clip the wings of the American eagle in order to feather their own nests.

I have recently pointed out how quickly the tempo of modern warfare could bring into our very midst the physical attack which we must eventually expect if the dictator nations win this war.

There is much loose talk of our immunity from immediate and direct invasion from across the seas. Obviously, as long as the British Navy retains its power, no such danger exists. Even if there were no British Navy, it is not probable that any enemy would be stupid enough to attack us by landing troops in the United States from across

"Those, who would give up essential liberty to purchase a little temporary safety, deserve neither liberty nor safety" thousands of miles of ocean, until it had acquired strategic bases from which to operate. But we learn much from the lessons of the past years in Europe — particularly the lesson of Norway, whose essential seaports were captured by treachery and surprise built up over a series of years. The first phase of the invasion of this Hemisphere would not be the landing of regular troops. The necessary strategic points would be occupied by secret agents and their dupes — and great numbers of them are already here, and in Latin America.

As long as the aggressor nations maintain the offensive, they — not we — will choose the time and the place and the method of their attack. That is why the future of all the American Republics is today in serious danger. That is why this Annual Message to the Congress is unique in our history. That is why every member of the Executive Branch of the Government and every member of the Congress faces great responsibility — and great accountability.

The need of the moment is that our actions and our policy should be devoted primarily — almost exclusively — to meeting this foreign peril. For all our domestic problems are now a part of the great emergency. Just as our national policy in internal affairs has been based upon a decent respect for the rights and the dignity of all our fellow men within our gates, so our national policy in foreign affairs has been based on a decent respect for the rights and dignity of all nations, large and small. And the justice of morality must and will win in the end. Our national policy is this:

Our national policy

First, by an impressive expression of the public will and without regard to partisanship, we are committed to all-inclusive national defense.

Second, by an impressive expression of the public will and without regard to partisanship, we are committed to full support of all those resolute peoples, everywhere, who are resisting aggression and are thereby keeping war away from our Hemisphere. By this support, we express our determination that the democratic cause shall prevail; and we strengthen the defense and the security of our own nation.

Third, by an impressive expression of the public will and without regard to partisanship, we are committed to the proposition that principles of morality and considerations for our own security will never permit us to acquiesce in a peace dictated by aggressors and sponsored by appeasers. We know that enduring peace cannot be bought at the cost of other people's freedom.

In the recent national election there was no substantial difference between the two great parties in respect to that national policy. No issue was fought out on this line before the American electorate. Today it is abundantly evident that American citizens everywhere are demanding and supporting speedy and complete action in recognition of obvious danger. Therefore, the immediate need is a swift and driving increase in our armament production. . . .

Let us say to the democracies: "We Americans are vitally concerned in your defense of freedom. We are putting forth our energies, our resources and our organizing powers to give you the strength to regain and maintain a free world. We shall send you, in ever-increasing numbers, ships, planes, tanks, guns. This is our purpose and our pledge." In fulfillment of this purpose we will not be intimidated by the threats of dictators that they will regard as a breach of international law or as an act of war our aid to the democracies which dare to resist their aggression. Such aid is not an act of war, even if a dictator should unilaterally proclaim it so to be. When the dictators — if the dictators — are ready to make war upon us, they will not wait for an act of war on our part. They did not wait for Norway or Belgium or the Netherlands to commit an act of war. Their only interest is in a new one-way international law, which lacks mutuality in its observance, and, therefore, becomes an instrument of oppression.

The happiness of future generations of Americans may well depend upon how effective and how immediate we can make our aid felt. No one can tell the exact character of the emergency situations that we may be called upon to meet. The Nation's hands must not be tied when the Nation's life is in danger. We must all prepare to make the sacrifices that the emergency — almost

The Nation's hands must not be tied

as serious as war itself — demands. Whatever stands in the way of speed and efficiency in defense preparations must give way to the national need. . . .

As men do not live by bread alone, they do not fight by armaments alone. Those who man our defenses, and those behind them who build our defenses, must have the stamina and the courage which come from unshakable belief in the manner of life which they are defending. The mighty action that we are calling for cannot be based on a disregard of all things worth fighting for.

The Nation takes great satisfaction and much strength from the things which have been done to make its people conscious of their individual stake in the preservation of democratic life in America. Those things have toughened the fibre of our people, have renewed their faith and strengthened their devotion to the institutions we make ready to protect. . . .

A world founded upon four essential human freedoms

In the future days, which we seek to make secure, we look forward to a world founded upon four essential human freedoms.

The first is freedom of speech and expression — everywhere in the world.

The second is freedom of every person to worship God in his own way —- everywhere in the world.

The third is freedom from want — which, translated into world terms, means economic understandings which will secure to every nation a healthy peacetime life for its inhabitants — everywhere in the world.

The fourth is freedom from fear — which, translated into world terms, means a world-wide reduction of armaments to such a point and in such a thorough fashion that no nation will be in a position to commit an act of physical aggression against any neighbor — anywhere in the world.

That is no vision of a distant millennium. It is a definite basis for a kind of world attainable in our own time and generation. That kind of world is the very antithesis of the so-called new order of tyranny which the dictators seek to create with the crash of a bomb.

To that new order we oppose the greater conception — the moral order. A good society is able to face schemes of world domination and foreign revolutions alike without fear.

Since the beginning of our American history, we have been engaged in change — in a perpetual peaceful revolution — a revolution which goes on steadily, quietly adjusting itself to changing conditions — without the concentration camp or the quick-lime in the ditch. The world order which we seek is the cooperation of free countries, working together in a friendly, civilized society.

This nation has placed its destiny in the hands and heads and hearts of its millions of free men and women; and its faith in freedom under the guidance of God. Freedom means the supremacy

A good society is able to face schemes of world domination without fear

of human rights everywhere. Our support goes to those who struggle to gain those rights or keep them. Our strength is our unity of purpose.

Our strength is our unity of purpose

To that high concept there can be no end save victory.

EARL WARREN

Earl Warren (1891–1974) reached the zenith of his career with his appointment as the fourteenth chief justice of the United States by President Eisenhower in 1953. Before that time, he had been attorney general of California, governor of California (for three terms), and an unsuccessful candidate for vice president on the Republican ticket, in 1948.

He led the Supreme Court in numerous landmark civil rights decisions

Warren, a liberal activist, led the Court in handing down a number of landmark decisions in the fields of civil rights and individual liberties, including such celebrated decisions as Brown v. Board of Education *(abolition of segregation in public schools, 1954),* Mapp v. Ohio *(search and seizure, 1961),* Betts v. Brady *(right to counsel, 1961),* Gideon v. Wainwright *(right to counsel, 1963),* New York Times v. Sullivan *(freedom of the press, 1964),* Escobedo v. Illinois *(right to counsel, 1964), and* Miranda v. Arizona *(rights of the accused, 1966).*

Brown v. Board of Education [of Topeka, Kansas] *is the case in which the Supreme Court* struck down the "separate but equal" doctrine of Plessy v. Ferguson[17] for public education and required the desegregation of schools throughout the country. Many observers regard the case as the Court's most important decision of the twentieth century.

At the time of the decision, seventeen southern states and the District of Columbia required that public schools be racially segregated. A few northern and western states, including Kansas, left the issue of integration up to local school boards. Although most of the schools in Kansas were integrated in 1954, those in Topeka were not.

In Topeka, an African American third grader named Linda Brown had to walk one mile through a railroad switchyard to reach her elementary school, even though a white elementary school was only seven blocks from her home. Linda's father tried to enroll her in the white school, but the principal of the school refused. Brown (and other parents similarly aggrieved) filed suit in the U.S. District Court, asking for an injunction that would forbid the segregation of Topeka's schools.

The defense put forward by the Topeka Board of Education was that because segregation in Topeka pervaded many other aspects of life, segregated schools served the worthy purpose of preparing African American children for the seg-

[17] See page 277.

regation they would face during adulthood, and moreover, that segregated schools were not necessarily harmful, as these schools had produced great black leaders such as Frederick Douglass and George Washington Carver. Finally, the board argued that the Court should follow, and indeed the Court did follow, the precedent of Plessy v. Ferguson *and rule in favor of the defendant school board.*

On appeal (where the Topeka case was joined with similar cases from other states), in the majority opinion written by Chief Justice Warren, the Supreme Court reversed the lower court decision, as follows:

FROM MAJORITY OPINION IN
BROWN V. BOARD OF EDUCATION
1954

These cases come to us from the States of Kansas, South Carolina, Virginia, and Delaware. They are premised on different facts and different local conditions, but a common legal question justifies their consideration together in this consolidated opinion.

In each of these cases, minors of the Negro race, through their legal representatives, seek the aid of the courts in obtaining admission to the public schools of their community on a nonsegregated basis. In each instance, they had been denied admission to schools attended by white children under laws requiring or permitting segregation according to race. This segregation was alleged to deprive the plaintiffs of the equal protection of the laws under the Fourteenth Amendment. In each of the cases other than the Delaware case, a three-judge federal district court denied relief to the plaintiffs on the so-called "separate but equal" doctrine announced by this Court in *Plessy v. Ferguson*. Under that doctrine, equality of treatment is accorded when the races are provided substantially equal facilities, even though these facilities are separate. . . .

The plaintiffs contend that segregated public schools are not "equal" and cannot be made "equal," and that hence they are deprived of the equal protection of the laws. Because of the obvious importance of the question presented, the Court took jurisdiction. . . .

Reargument was largely devoted to the circumstances surrounding the adoption of the Fourteenth Amendment in 1868. It covered exhaustively consideration of the Amendment in Congress, ratification by the states, then existing practices in racial segregation, and the views of proponents and opponents of the Amendment. This discussion and our own investigation convince us that, although these sources cast some light, it is not enough to resolve the problem with which we are faced. At best, they are inconclusive. The most avid proponents of the post-War Amendments undoubtedly intended them to

Discussion of the 14th Amendment

remove all legal distinctions among "all persons born or naturalized in die United States." Their opponents, just as certainly, were antagonistic to both the letter and the spirit of the Amendments and wished them to have the most limited effect. What others in Congress and the state legislatures had in mind cannot be determined with any degree of certainty.

An additional reason for the inconclusive nature of the Amendment's history, with respect to segregated schools, is the status of public education at that time. In the South, the movement toward free common schools, supported by general taxation, had not yet taken hold. Education of white children was largely in the hands of private groups. Education of Negroes was almost nonexistent, and practically all of the race were illiterate. In fact, any education of Negroes was forbidden by law in some states. Today, in contrast, many Negroes have achieved outstanding success in the arts and sciences as well as in the business and professional world. It is true that public school education at the time of the Amendment had advanced further in the North, but the effect of the Amendment on Northern States was generally ignored in the congressional debates. Even in the North the conditions of public education did not approximate those existing today. The curriculum was usually rudimentary; un-graded schools were common in rural areas; the school term was but three months a year in many states;

In the South, free common schools, supported by taxation, had not yet taken hold

and compulsory school attendance was virtually unknown. As a consequence, it is not surprising that there should be so little in the history of the Fourteenth Amendment relating to its intended effect on public education.

In the first cases in this Court construing the Fourteenth Amendment, decided shortly after its adoption, the Court interpreted it as proscribing all state-imposed discriminations against the Negro race. The doctrine of "separate but equal" did not make its appearance in this Court until 1896 in the case of *Plessy v. Ferguson,* involving not education but transportation. American courts have since labored with the doctrine for over half a century. . . .

American courts have labored with the doctrine of "separate but equal" for over half a century

In the instant cases, that question is directly presented. Here . . . there are findings below that the Negro and white schools involved have been equalized, or are being equalized, with respect to buildings, curricula, qualifications and salaries of teachers, and other "tangible" factors. Our decision, therefore, cannot turn on merely a comparison of these tangible factors in the Negro and white schools involved in each of the cases. We must look instead to the effect of segregation itself on public education.

In approaching this problem, we cannot turn the clock back to 1868 when the Amendment was adopted, or even to 1896 when *Plessy v. Ferguson* was written. We must consider public education in the light of its full development and its present place in American life throughout the Nation. Only in this way can it be determined if segregation in public schools deprives these plaintiffs of the equal protection of the laws.

Today, education is perhaps the most important function of state and local governments. Compulsory school attendance laws and the great expenditures for education both demonstrate our recognition of the importance of education to our democratic society. It is required in the performance of our most basic public responsibilities, even service in the armed forces. It is the very foundation of good citizenship. Today it is a principal instrument in awakening the child to cultural values, in preparing him for later professional training, and in helping him to adjust normally to his environment. In these days, it is doubtful that any child may reasonably be expected to succeed in life if he is denied the opportunity of an education. Such an opportunity, where the state has undertaken to provide it, is a right which must be made available to all on equal terms.

Education is the very foundation of good citizenship

We come then to the question presented: Does segregation of children in public schools solely on the basis of race, even though the physical facilities and other "tangible" factors may be equal, deprive the children of the minority group of equal educational could not opportunities? We believe that it does

In *Sweatt v. Painter* . . . in finding that a segregated law school for Negroes provide them equal educational opportunities, this Court relied in large part on "those qualities which are incapable of objective measurement but which make for greatness in a law school." In *McLaurin v. Oklahoma State Regents* . . . the Court, in requiring that a Negro admitted to a white graduate school be treated like all other students, again resorted to intangible considerations: ". . . his ability to study, to engage in discussions and exchange views with other students, and, in general, to learn his profession." Such considerations apply with added force to children in grade and high schools. To separate them from others of similar age and qualifications solely because of their race generates a feeling of inferiority as to their status in the community that may affect their hearts and minds in a way unlikely ever to be undone. The effect of this separation on their educational opportunities was well stated by a finding in the Kansas case by a court which nevertheless felt compelled to rule against the Negro plaintiffs:

Separation creates a feeling of inferiority

> Segregation of white and colored children in public schools has a detrimental effect upon the colored children. The impact is greater when it has the sanction of the law; for the policy of separating the races is usually interpreted as denoting the inferiority of the negro group. A sense of inferiority affects the motivation of a child to learn. Segregation with the sanction of law, therefore, has

a tendency to [retard] the educational and mental development of negro children and to deprive them of some of the benefits they would receive in a racial[ly] integrated school system.

Whatever may have been the extent of psychological knowledge at the time of *Plessy v. Ferguson*, this finding is amply supported by modern authority. Any language in *Plessy v. Ferguson* contrary to this finding is rejected.

"Separate but equal" has no place in public education

We conclude that in the field of public education the doctrine of "separate but equal" has no place. Separate educational facilities are inherently unequal. Therefore, we hold that the plaintiffs and others similarly situated for whom the actions have been brought are, by reason of the segregation complained of, deprived of the equal protection of the laws guaranteed by the Fourteenth Amendment. . . .

JOHN F. KENNEDY

Most Americans are well acquainted with the career of John F. Kennedy (1917–1963), privileged son of a wealthy Boston family, graduate of the exclusive Choate Academy and Harvard University, war hero, congressman, senator, Pulitzer Prize–winning author, and, finally, our thirty-fifth president, the youngest ever elected and ever to die in office. Kennedy and his wife and family

were handsome, photogenic, and extremely pop-
ular with the American public. His brief, roughly
thousand-day presidency, abruptly terminated
by his dramatic and controversial assassination,
has served to make of his life a legend. Ken-
nedy's political philosophy was well represented
by his inaugural address and its famous exhorta-
tion: "My fellow Americans: ask not what your
country can do for you — ask what you can do for
your country. My fellow citizens of the world: ask
not what America will do for you, but what togeth-
er we can do for the freedom of man."

INAUGURAL ADDRESS
JANUARY 20, 1961

We observe today not a victory of party but a
celebration of freedom — symbolizing an end as
well as a beginning — signifying renewal as well as
change. For I have sworn before you and Almighty
God the same solemn oath our forebears prescribed nearly a century and three-quarters ago.

The world is very different now. For man holds
in his mortal hands the power to abolish all forms
of human poverty and all forms of human life. And
yet the same revolutionary beliefs for which our forebears fought are still at issue around the globe —
the belief that the rights of man come not from the
generosity of the state but from the hand of God.

We dare not forget today that we are the heirs
of that first revolution. Let the word go forth from
this time and place, to friend and foe alike, that

The torch has been passed to a new generation of Americans

the torch has been passed to a new generation of Americans — born in this century, tempered by war, disciplined by a hard and bitter peace, proud of our ancient heritage — and unwilling to witness or permit the slow undoing of those human rights to which this nation has always been committed, and to which we are committed today at home and around the world.

Let every nation know, whether it wishes us well or ill, that we shall pay any price, bear any burden, meet any hardship, support any friend, oppose any foe, to assure the survival and the success of liberty.

This much we pledge — and more

This much we pledge — and more.

To those old allies whose cultural and spiritual origins we share, we pledge the loyalty of faithful friends. United, there is little we cannot do in a host of cooperative ventures. Divided, there is little we can do — for we dare not meet a powerful challenge at odds and split asunder.

To those new states whom we welcome to the ranks of the free, we pledge our word that one form of colonial control shall not have passed away merely to be replaced by a far more iron tyranny. We shall not always expect to find them supporting our view. But we shall always hope to find them strongly supporting their own freedom — and to remember that in the past, those who foolishly sought power by riding the back of the tiger ended up inside.

To those peoples in the huts and villages of half

the globe struggling to break the bonds of mass misery, we pledge our best efforts to help them help themselves, for whatever period is required — not because the Communists may be doing it, not because we seek their votes, but because it is right. If a free society cannot help the many who are poor, it cannot save the few who are rich.

To our sister republics south of our border, we offer a special pledge — to convert our good words into good deeds — in a new alliance for progress — to assist free men and free governments in casting off the chains of poverty. But this peaceful revolution of hope cannot become the prey of hostile powers. Let all our neighbors know that we shall join with them to oppose aggression or subversion anywhere in the Americas. And let every other power know that this Hemisphere intends to remain the master of its own house.

To that world assembly of sovereign states, the United Nations, our last best hope in an age where the instruments of war have far outpaced the instruments of peace, we renew our pledge of support — to prevent it from becoming merely a forum for invective — to strengthen its shield of the new and the weak — and to enlarge the area in which its writ may run.

Finally, to those nations who would make themselves our adversary, we offer not a pledge but a request: that both sides begin anew the quest for peace, before the dark powers of destruction unleashed by science engulf all humanity in planned or accidental self-destruction.

We dare not tempt them with weakness

We dare not tempt them with weakness. For only when our arms are sufficient beyond doubt can we be certain beyond doubt that they will never be employed.

But neither can two great and powerful groups of nations take comfort from our present course — both sides overburdened by the cost of modern weapons, both rightly alarmed by the steady spread of the deadly atom, yet both racing to alter that uncertain balance of terror that stays the hand of mankind's final war.

So let us begin anew

So let us begin anew — remembering on both sides that civility is not a sign of weakness, and sincerity is always subject to proof. Let us never negotiate out of fear. But let us never fear to negotiate.

Let both sides explore what problems unite us instead of belaboring those problems which divide us.

Let both sides, for the first time, formulate serious and precise proposals for the inspection and control of arms — and bring the absolute power to destroy other nations under the absolute control of all nations.

Let both sides seek to invoke the wonders of science instead of its terrors. Together let us explore the stars, conquer the deserts, eradicate disease, tap the ocean depths, and encourage the arts and commerce.

Let both sides unite to heed in all corners of the earth the command of Isaiah — to "undo the heavy burdens . . . [and] let the oppressed go free."

And if a beachhead of cooperation may push back the jungle of suspicion, let both sides join in creating a new endeavor, not a new balance of power, but a new world of law, where the strong are just and the weak secure and the peace preserved.

All this will not be finished in the first one hundred days. Nor will it be finished in the first one thousand days, nor in the life of this Administration, nor even perhaps in our lifetime on this planet. But let us begin.

In your hands, my fellow citizens, more than mine, will rest the final success or failure of our course. Since this country was founded, each generation of Americans has been summoned to give testimony to its national loyalty. The graves of young Americans who answered the call to service surround the globe.

Now the trumpet summons us again — not as a call to bear arms, though arms we need — not as a call to battle, though embattled we are — but as a call to bear the burden of a long twilight struggle, year in and year out, "rejoicing in hope, patient in tribulation" — a struggle against the common enemies of man: tyranny, poverty, disease, and war itself.

Now the trumpet summons us again

Can we forge against these enemies a grand and global alliance, North and South, East and West, that can assure a more fruitful life for all mankind? Will you join in that historic effort?

In the long history of the world, only a few generations have been granted the role of defending freedom in its hour of maximum danger. I do not shrink from this responsibility — I welcome it. I do not believe that any of us would exchange places with any other people or any other generation. The energy, the faith, the devotion which we bring to this endeavor will light our country and all who serve it — and the glow from that fire can truly light the world.

And so, my fellow Americans: ask not what your country can do for you — ask what you can do for your country.

Ask not what your country can do for you — ask what you can do for your country

My fellow citizens of the world: ask not what America will do for you, but what together we can do for the freedom of man.

Finally, whether you are citizens of America or citizens of the world, ask of us here the same high standards of strength and sacrifice which we ask of you. With a good conscience our only sure reward, with history the final judge of our deeds, let us go forth to lead the land we love, asking His blessing and His help, but knowing that here on earth God's work must truly be our own.

MARTIN LUTHER KING, JR.

An exemplar for those who subscribe to the "great man" theory of history

Martin Luther King, Jr. (1929–1968), is an exemplar for those who subscribe to the "great men" theory of history — that is, that the course of history is primarily determined not by events or the evolution of ideas but by the effect of influential individuals. Surely King stands as the most influential African American leader in American history. And regrettably, we will never know just how much more rapid and how much greater would have been the progress of his people had he lived his life for a full term.

The son of a Baptist minister in Atlanta, King was ordained in 1948 at age nineteen and became assistant pastor at Atlanta's Ebenezer Baptist Church, where his father was pastor. In 1954, one year before receiving his Ph.D. in theology from Boston University, King became pastor of Dexter Avenue Baptist Church in Montgomery, Alabama, the city in which he was to lead the famous bus boycotts of 1955 and 1956. Thereafter, he was instrumental in the founding of the Southern Christian Leadership Conference and the Student Nonviolent Coordinating Committee, taking part — in most instances in a leadership role — in the protest boycotts and marches of the 1960s. In 1964, he became the youngest recipient of the Nobel Peace Prize, and he is honored today in America by the national celebration of Martin Luther King Day on the third Monday of January each year.

While perhaps not possessed of the majestic vocabulary of other famous orators who are represented in this primer, such as Edmund Burke or Thomas Jefferson or Daniel Webster, King stirred the concern and sparked the conscience of an entire generation of Americans through his

He sparked the conscience of an entire generation of Americans

writings and speeches, contributing immeasurably to the cause of American freedom. Here are two of the most famous.

FROM LETTER FROM A BIRMINGHAM CITY JAIL
APRIL 16, 1963

My Dear Fellow Clergymen:

While confined here in the Birmingham City Jail, I came across your recent statement calling our present activities "unwise and untimely." Seldom, if ever, do I pause to answer criticism of my work and ideas. . . . But since I feel you are men of genuine good will and your criticisms are sincerely set forth, I would like to answer your statements in what I hope will be patient and reasonable terms.

I think I should give the reason for my being in Birmingham, since you have been influenced by the argument of "outsiders coming in.". . . I am here, along with several members of my staff, because we were invited here. I am here because I have basic organizational ties here.

I am in Birmingham because injustice is here

Beyond this, I am in Birmingham because injustice is here. Just as the eighth century prophets left their little villages and carried their "thus saith the Lord" far beyond the boundaries of their hometowns; and just as the Apostle Paul left his little village of Tarsus and carried the gospel of Jesus Christ to practically every hamlet and city of the Graeco-Roman world, I too am compelled to carry the gospel of freedom beyond my particular home town. . . .

Moreover, I am cognizant of the interrelatedness of all communities and states. I cannot sit idly by in Atlanta and not be concerned about what happens in Birmingham.

Injustice anywhere is a threat to injustice everywhere. We are caught in an inescapable network of mutuality, tied in a single garment of destiny. Whatever affects one directly affects all indirectly. Never again can we afford to live with the narrow, provincial "outside agitator" idea. Anyone who lives in the United States can never be considered an outsider anywhere in this country.

Injustice anywhere is a threat to injustice everywhere

You deplore the demonstrations taking place in Birmingham. But I am sorry that your statement fails to express a similar concern for the conditions that brought the demonstrations into being. I am sure that each of you would want to go beyond the superficial social analyst who looks merely at effects, and does not grapple with underlying causes. I would not hesitate to say that it is unfortunate that so-called demonstrations are taking place in Birmingham at this time, but I would say in more emphatic terms that it is even more unfortunate that the white power structure of this city left the Negro community with no other alternative.

In any nonviolent campaign there are four basic steps:

The four
steps of a
nonviolent
campaign

1) collection of the facts to determine whether injustices are alive; 2) negotiation; 3) self-purification; and 4) direct action. We have gone through all of these steps in Birmingham. There can be no gainsaying of the fact that racial injustice engulfs this community. Birmingham is probably the most thoroughly segregated city in the United States. Its ugly record of police brutality is known in every section of this country. Its unjust treatment of Negroes in the courts is a notorious reality. There have been more unsolved bombings of Negro homes and churches in Birmingham than any city in this nation. These are the hard, brutal, and unbelievable facts. On the basis of these conditions Negro leaders sought to negotiate with the city fathers. But the political leaders consistently refused to engage in good faith negotiation.

Then came the opportunity last September to talk with leaders of Birmingham's economic community. In these negotiating sessions certain promises were made by the merchants — such as the promise to remove humiliating racial signs from the stores. On the basis of these promises, the Reverend Shuttlesworth and the leaders of the Alabama Christian Movement for Human Rights agreed to a moratorium on any type of demonstrations. As the weeks and months unfolded we realized that we were the victims of a broken promise. The signs remained. Like so many experiences of the past we were confronted with blasted hopes, and the dark shadow of a deep disappointment settled upon us. We had no alternative except that of preparing for direct action, whereby we would present our very bodies as means of laying our case before the conscience of the local and the national community. . . .

You may well ask: "Why direct action? Why sit-ins, marches, etc.? Isn't negotiation a better path?" You are exactly right in your call for negotiation. Indeed, this is the very purpose of direct action. Nonviolent direct action seeks to create such a crisis and establish such creative tension that a community that has constantly refused to negotiate is forced to confront the issue. It seeks so to dramatize the issue that it can no longer be ignored. . . .

Isn't negotiation a better path?

So the purpose of the direct-action program is to create a situation so crisis-packed that it will inevitably open the door to negotiation. We, therefore, concur with you in your call for negotiation. Too long has our beloved Southland been bogged down in the tragic attempt to live in monologue rather than dialogue.

One of the basic points in your statement is that our acts are untimely. Some have asked: "Why didn't you give this new administration time to act?" The only answer that I can give to this query is that the new administration must be prodded about as much as the outgoing one before it acts. . . . My friends, I must say to you

We have not made a single gain in civil rights without determined legal and nonviolent pressure

that we have not made a single gain in civil rights without determined legal and nonviolent pressure. History is the long and tragic story of the fact that privileged groups seldom give up their privileges voluntarily. Individuals may see the moral light and voluntarily give up their unjust posture; but, as Reinhold Niebuhr has reminded us, groups tend to be more immoral than individuals.

Freedom must be demanded by the repressed

We know through painful experience that freedom is never voluntarily given by the oppressor; it must be demanded by the oppressed. Frankly, I have never yet engaged in a direct-action movement that was "well timed," according to the timetable of those who have not suffered unduly from the disease of segregation. For years now, I have heard the word "Wait!" It rings in the ear of every Negro with piercing familiarity. This "Wait" has almost always meant 'Never."... We must come to see with the distinguished jurist of yesterday, that "justice too long delayed is justice denied."

We have waited 340 years for our rights

We have waited for more than 340 years for our constitutional and God-given rights. . . . I guess it is easy for those who have never felt the stinging darts of segregation to say, "Wait." But when you have seen vicious mobs lynch your mothers and fathers at will and drown your sisters and brothers at whim; when you have seen hate-filled policemen curse, kick, brutalize and even kill your black brothers and sisters with impunity;

when you see the vast majority of your twenty million Negro brothers smothering in an airtight cage of poverty in the midst of an affluent society; when you suddenly find your tongue twisted and your speech stammering as you seek to explain to your six-year-old daughter why she can't go to the public amusement park that has just been advertised on television, and her little eyes when she is told that Funtown is closed to colored children, and see the depressing clouds of inferiority beginning to form in her little mental sky, and see her begin to distort her little personality by unconsciously developing a bitterness toward white people; when you have to concoct an answer for a five-year-old son asking in agonizing pathos: "Daddy, why do white people treat colored people so mean?"; when you take a cross-country drive and find it necessary to sleep night after night in the uncomfortable corners of your automobile because no motel will accept you; when you are humiliated day in and day out by nagging signs reading "white" and "colored"; when your first name becomes "nigger," your middle name becomes "boy" (however old you are) and your last name becomes "John," and when your wife and mother are never given the respected title "Mrs."; when you are harried by day and haunted by night by the fact that you are a Negro living constantly at tiptoe stance never quite knowing what to expect next, and are plagued with inner fears and outer resentments; when you are forev-

"Daddy, why do white people treat colored people so mean?"

er fighting a degenerating sense of "nobodiness";
then you will understand why we find it difficult
to wait. There comes a time when the cup of
endurance runs over, and men are no longer willing to be plunged into an abyss of injustice where
they experience the blackness of corroding
despair. I hope, sirs, you can understand our legitimate and unavoidable impatience.

There comes
a time when
the cup of
endurance
runs over

You express a great deal of anxiety over our
willingness to break laws. This is certainly a legitimate concern. Since we so diligently urge people
to obey the Supreme Court's decision of 1954
outlawing segregation in the public schools, it is
rather strange to find us consciously breaking
laws. One may well ask: "How can you advocate
breaking some laws and obeying others?" The
answer lies in the fact that there are two types of
laws: there are *just* and there are *unjust* laws. I
would agree with Saint Augustine that "An unjust
law is no law at all."

Now what is the difference between the two?
How does one determine whether a law is just or
unjust? A just law is a man-made code that
squares with the moral law or the law of God. An
unjust law is a code that is out of harmony with
the moral law. To put it in the terms of Saint
Thomas Aquinas, an unjust law is a human law
that is not rooted in eternal and natural law. Any
law that uplifts human personality is just. Any
law that degrades human personality is unjust.
All segregation statutes are unjust because segregation distorts the soul and damages the person-

An unjust
law is a code
that is out of
harmony
with the
moral law

ality. It gives the segregator a false sense of superiority, and the segregated a false sense of inferiority. . . . Thus it is that I can urge men to obey the 1954 decision of the Supreme Court, for it is morally right; and I can urge them to disobey segregation ordinances, for they are morally wrong.

Let us turn to a more concrete example of just and unjust laws. An unjust law is a code that a majority inflicts on a minority that is not binding on itself. This is difference made legal. On the other hand a just law is a code that a majority compels a minority to follow and that it is willing to follow itself. This is sameness made legal.

Let me give another explanation. A law is unjust is a code inflicted upon a minority which that minority had no part in enacting or creating because they did not have the unhampered right to vote. Who can say that the legislature of Alabama which set up that state's segregation laws was democratically elected? Throughout the state of Alabama all types of conniving methods are used to prevent Negroes from becoming registered voters and there are some counties without a single Negro registered to vote despite the fact that the Negro constitutes a majority of the population. Can any law set up in such a state be considered democratically structured?

These are just a few examples of unjust and just laws. There are some instances when a law is just on its face and unjust in its application. For instance, I was arrested on Friday on arrested on a charge of parading without a permit. Now, there is nothing wrong in having an ordinance which requires a permit for a parade, but when the ordinance is used to preserve segregation and to deny citizens the First Amendment privilege of peaceful assembly and peaceful protest, then it becomes unjust.

I hope you can see the distinction I am trying to point out. In no sense do I advocate evading or defying the law, as the rabid segregationist would do. That would lead to anarchy. One who breaks an unjust law must do so *openly*, *lovingly* . . . and with a willingness to accept the penalty. I submit that an individual who breaks a law that conscience tells him is unjust, and willingly accepts the penalty of staying in jail in order to arouse the conscience of the community over its injustice, is in reality expressing the highest respect for law.

One who breaks an unjust law must do so *openly, lovingly*

Of course, there is nothing new about this kind of civil disobedience. It was seen sublimely in the refusal of Shadrach, Meshach and Abednego to obey the laws of Nebuchadnezzar because a higher moral law was at involved. It was practiced superbly by the early Christians who were willing to face hungry lions and the excruciating pain of chopping blocks, before submitting to certain unjust laws of the Roman Empire. To a degree academic freedom is a reality today be-cause Socrates practiced civil disobedience. . . .

In your statement you assert that our actions, even though peaceful, must be condemned because they precipitate violence. But can this assertion be logically made? Isn't this like condemning a robbed man because his possession of money precipitated the evil act of robbery? Isn't this like condemning Socrates because his unswerving commitment to truth and his philosophical delvings precipitated the misguided popular mind to make him drink the hemlock? Isn't this like condemning Jesus because His God-consciousness and never-ceasing devotion to His will precipitated the evil act of crucifixion? We must come to see, as federal courts have consistently affirmed, that it is immoral to urge an individual to withdraw his efforts to gain his basic constitutional rights because the quest precipitates violence. Society must protect the robbed and punish the robber. . . .

You spoke of our activity in Birmingham as extreme. At first I was rather disappointed that fellow clergymen would see my nonviolent efforts as those of an extremist. I started thinking about the fact that I stand in the middle of two opposing forces in the Negro community. One is a force of complacency made up in part of Negroes who, as a result of long years of oppression, have been so completely drained of self-respect and a sense of "somebodiness" that they have adjusted to segregation, and, of a few Negroes who, because of a degree of academic and economic security, and because at points they profit by segregation, have unconsciously become insensitive to the problems of the masses. The other force is one of bitterness and hatred, and comes perilously close to advocating violence. It is expressed in the various black nationalist groups that are springing over the nation, the largest and best-known being Elijah Muhammad's Muslim movement. This movement is nourished by the Negro's contemporary frustration over the continued existence of racial discrimination. It is made up of people who have lost faith in America, who have absolutely repudiated Christianity, and who have concluded that the white man is an incorrigible "devil." I have tried to stand between these two forces, saying that we need not follow the "do-nothingism" of the complacent nor the hatred and despair of the black nationalist. There is the more excellent way of love and nonviolent protest. I'm grateful to God that, through the Negro church, the dimension of nonviolence entered our struggle. If this philosophy had not emerged, I am convinced that by now many streets of the South would be flowing with floods of blood. And I am further convinced that if our white brothers dismiss as "rabble-rousers" and "outside agitators" those of us who employ nonviolent direct action and refuse to support our nonviolent efforts, millions of Negroes will, out of frustration and despair, seek solace and security in black nationalist ideologies, a development that will lead inevitably to a frightening racial nightmare.

Oppressed people cannot remain oppressed forever. The urge for freedom will eventually

I have tried to stand between these two forces

The urge for freedom will eventually come

come. This is what happened to the American Negro. Something within has reminded him of his birthright of freedom, and something without has reminded him that he can gain it. Consciously or unconsciously . . . [he] is moving with a sense of cosmic urgency toward the promised land of racial justice. Recognizing this vital urge that has engulfed the Negro community, one should readily understand public demonstrations. The Negro has many pent-up resentments and latent frustrations. He has to get them out. So let him march sometime; let him make prayer pilgrimages to the city hall; understand why he must have sit-ins and freedom rides. If his repressed emotions do not come out in these nonviolent ways, they will come out in ominous expressions of violence. This is not a threat; it is a fact of history. So I have not said to my people: "get rid of your discontent." But I have tried to say that this normal and healthy discontent can be channeled through the creative outlet of nonviolent direct action. Now this approach is being dismissed as extremist. I must admit that I was initially disappointed in being so categorized.

But as I continued to think about the matter I gradually gained a bit of satisfaction from the label. Was not Jesus an extremist for love — "Love your enemies, bless them that curse you, pray for them which despitefully use you." Was not Amos an extremist for justice — "Let justice roll down like waters and righteousness like a

Was not Jesus an extremist for love?

mighty stream." Was not Paul an extremist for the gospel of Jesus Christ — "I bear in my body the marks of the Lord Jesus." Was not Martin Luther an extremist — "Here I stand; I can do no other so help me God." Was not John Bunyan an extremist — "I will stay in jail to the end of my days before I make a butchery of my conscience." Was not Abraham Lincoln an extremist — "This nation cannot survive half slave and half free." Was not Thomas Jefferson an extremist — "We hold these truths to be self-evident, that all men are created equal." So the question is not whether we will be extremist but what kind of extremist we will be. Will we be extremists for hate or will we be extremists for love? Will we be extremists for the preservation of injustice — or will we be extremists for the cause of justice? In that dramatic scene on Calvary's hill, three men were crucified. We must not forget that all three were crucified for the same crime — the crime of extremism. Two were extremists for immorality, and thusly fell below their environment. The other, Jesus Christ, was an extremist for love, truth and goodness, and thereby rose above his environment. So, after all, maybe the South, the nation and the world are in dire need of creative extremists.

I had hoped that the white moderate would see this need. Maybe I was too optimistic. Maybe I expected too much. I guess I should have realized that few members of a race that has oppressed another race can understand or appreciate the deep groans and the passionate yearnings of those that have been oppressed and still fewer have the vision to see that injustice must be rooted out by strong, persistent and determined action. . . .

Let me rush on to mention my other disappointment. I have been so greatly disappointed with the white church and its leadership. . . .

I had this strange feeling when I was suddenly catapulted into the leadership of the bus protest in Montgomery several years ago that we would have the support of the white church. I felt that the white ministers, priests and rabbis of the South would be some of our strongest allies. Instead, some have been outright opponents, refusing to understand the freedom movement and misrepresenting its leader; all too many others have been more cautious than courageous and have remained silent behind the anesthetizing security of the stained-glass windows.

In spite of my shattered dreams of the past, I came to Birmingham with the hope that the white religious leadership of this community would see the justice of our cause, and with deep moral concern, serve as the channel through which our just grievances would get to the power structure. I had hoped that each of you would understand. But again I have been disappointed. I have heard

I have been greatly disappointed with the white church

southern religious leaders of the South call upon their worshipers to comply with a desegregation decision because it is the *law*, but I have longed to hear white ministers say: "Follow this decree because integration is morally *right* and because the Negro is your brother." In the midst of blatant injustices inflicted upon the Negro, I have watched white churchmen stand on the sideline and mouth pious irrelevancies and sanctimonious trivialities. In the midst of a mighty struggle to rid our nation of racial and economic injustice, I have heard many ministers say: "Those are social issues, with which the gospel has no real concern.". . .

In deep disappointment I have wept over the laxity of the church. . . .

I hope the church as a whole will meet the challenge of this decisive hour. But even if the church does not come to the aid of justice, I have no despair about the future. I have no fear about the outcome of our struggle in Birmingham, even if our motives are presently misunderstood. We will reach the goal of freedom in Birmingham and all over the nation, because the goal of America is freedom. Abused and scorned though we may be, our destiny is tied up with the destiny of America. Before the pilgrims landed at Plymouth we were here. Before the pen of Jefferson etched across the pages of history the majestic words of the Declaration of Independence, we were here.

I have no despair about the future

For more than two centuries our foreparents labored in this country without wages; they made cotton king; and they built the homes of their masters in the midst of brutal injustice and shameful humiliation — and yet out of a bottomless vitality they continued to thrive and develop. If the inexpressible cruelties of slavery could not stop us, the opposition we now face will surely fail. We will win our freedom because the sacred heritage of our nation and the eternal will of God are embodied in our echoing demands. . . .

Never before have I written a letter this long. I'm afraid it is much too long to take your precious time. . . .

If I have said anything in this letter that is an overstatement of the truth and indicative of an unreasonable impatience, I beg you to forgive me. If I have said anything in this letter that is an understatement of the truth and is indicative of my having a patience that makes me patient with anything less than brotherhood, I beg God to forgive me.

I hope this letter finds you strong in the faith. I also hope that circumstances will soon make it possible for me to meet each of you, not as an integrationist or a civil rights leader, but as a fellow clergyman and a Christian brother. Let us all hope that the dark clouds of racial prejudice will soon pass away and the deep fog of misunderstanding will be lifted from our fear-drenched

Let us hope that the dark clouds of racial injustice will soon pass away

communities and in some not too distant tomorrow the radiant stars of love and brotherhood will shine over our great nation with all their scintillating beauty.

> Yours for the cause of Peace
> and Brotherhood,
> Martin Luther King, Jr.

SPEECH AT THE MARCH ON WASHINGTON, "I HAVE A DREAM" AUGUST 28, 1963

Five score years ago, a great American, in whose symbolic shadow we stand today, signed the Emancipation Proclamation. This momentous decree came as a great beacon light of hope to millions of Negro slaves who had been seared in the flames of withering injustice. It came as a joyous daybreak to end the long night of captivity.

But one hundred years later, the Negro is still not free. One hundred years later, the life of the Negro is still sadly crippled by the manacles of segregation and the chains of discrimination. One hundred years later, the Negro lives on a lonely island of poverty in the midst of a vast ocean of material prosperity. One hundred years later, the Negro is still languishing in the corners of American society and finds himself an exile in his own land. So we have come here today to dramatize an appalling condition.

In a sense we have come to our nation's Cap-

The Negro lives on a lonely island of poverty

ital to cash a check. When the architects of our republic wrote the magnificent words of the Constitution and the Declaration of Independence, they were signing a promissory note to which every American was to fall heir. This note was a promise that all men, yes, black men as well as white men, would be guaranteed the "unalienable Rights of Life, Liberty, and the Pursuit of Happiness." It is obvious today that America has defaulted on this promissory note insofar as her citizens of color are concerned. Instead of honoring this sacred obligation, America has given the Negro people a bad check; a check which has come back marked "insufficient funds."

But we refuse to believe that the bank of justice is bankrupt. We refuse to believe that there are insufficient funds in the great vaults of opportunity of this nation. So we have come to cash this check, a check that will give us upon demand the riches of freedom and the security of justice.

We have come to our nation's Capital to cash a check

We have also come to this hallowed spot to remind America of the fierce urgency of now. This is not time to engage in the luxury of cooling off or to take the tranquilizing drug of gradualism. Now is the time to make real the promises of democracy. Now is the time to rise from the dark and desolate valley of segregation to the sunlit path of racial justice. Now is the time to lift our nation from the quicksands of racial injustice to the solid rock of brotherhood. Now is the time to make justice a reality for all of God's children.

It would be fatal for the nation to overlook the

urgency of the moment. This sweltering summer of the Negro's legitimate discontent will not pass until there is an invigorating autumn of freedom and equality. Nineteen sixty-three is not an end, but a beginning. And those who hope that the Negro needed to blow off steam and will now be content will have a rude awakening if the nation returns to business as usual. There will be neither rest nor tranquillity in America until the Negro is granted his citizenship rights. The whirlwinds of revolt will continue to shake the foundations of our nation until the bright day of justice emerges.

1963 is not an end, but a beginning

But there is something that I must say to my people who stand on the warm threshold which leads into the palace of justice. In the process of gaining our rightful place, we must not be guilty of wrongful deeds. Let us not seek to satisfy our thirst for freedom by drinking from the cup of bitterness and hatred. We must forever conduct our struggle on the high plane of dignity and discipline. We must not allow our creative protest to degenerate into physical violence. Again and again, we must rise to the majestic heights of meeting physical force with soul force. The marvelous new militancy which has engulfed the Negro community must not lead us to a distrust of all white people, for many of our white brothers, as evidenced by their presence here today, have come to realize that their freedom is inextricably bound to our freedom. We cannot walk alone.

Let us not satisfy our thirst for freedom by drinking from the cup of bitterness

And as we walk, we must make the pledge that we shall march ahead. We cannot turn back. There are those who are asking the devotees of civil rights, "When will you be satisfied?"

We can never be satisfied as long as the Negro is the victim of the unspeakable horrors of police brutality. We can never be satisfied as long as our bodies, heavy with the fatigue of travel, cannot gain lodging in the motels of the highways and the cities. We cannot be satisfied as long as our children are stripped of their selfhood and robbed of their dignity by signs stating "for whites only." We cannot be satisfied as long as the Negro's basic mobility is from a smaller ghetto to a larger one. We can never be satisfied as long as a Negro in Mississippi cannot vote and a Negro in New York believes he has nothing for which to vote. No, no, we are not satisfied, and we will not be satisfied until justice rolls down like waters and righteousness like a mighty stream.

I am not unmindful that some of you have come here out of great trials and tribulations. Some of you have come fresh from narrow jail cells. Some of you have come from areas where your quest for freedom left you battered by the storms of persecution and staggered by the winds of police brutality. You have been the veterans of creative suffering. Continue to work with the faith that unearned suffering is redemptive.

Go back to Mississippi, go back to Alabama, go back to South Carolina, go back to Georgia, go back to Louisiana, go back to the slums and ghettos of our Northern cities, knowing that somehow this situation can and will be changed. Let us not wallow in the valley of despair.

I say to you today, my friends, that in spite of the difficulties and frustrations of the moment I still have a dream. It is a dream deeply rooted in the American dream.

I have a dream that one day this nation will rise up and live out the true meaning of its creed: "We hold these truths to be self-evident; that all men are created equal."

I have a dream that one day on the red hills of Georgia the sons of former slaves and the sons of former slaveowners will be able to sit down together at the table of brotherhood.

I have a dream that one day even the state of Mississippi, a desert state sweltering with the heat of injustice and oppression, will be transformed into an oasis of freedom and justice.

I have a dream that my four little children will one day live in a nation where they will not be judged by the color of their skin but by the content of their character.

I have a dream today.

I have a dream that one day the state of Alabama, whose governor's lips are presently dripping with the words of interposition and nullification, will be transformed into a situation where little black boys and black girls will be able to join hands with little white boys and girls and walk together as sisters and brothers.

> **Let us not wallow in the valley of despair**

> **I have a dream**

I have a dream today.

I have a dream that one day every valley shall be exalted, every hill and mountain shall be made low, the rough places will be made plain, and the crooked places will be made straight, and the glory of the Lord shall be revealed, and all flesh shall see it together.

This is our hope. This is the faith with which I return to the South. With this faith we will be able to hew out of the mountain of despair a stone of hope. With this faith we will be able to transform the jangling discords of our nation into a beautiful symphony of brotherhood.

With this faith we will be able to work together, to pray together, to struggle together, to go to jail together, to stand up for freedom together, knowing that we will be free one day.

This will be the day when all of God's children will be able to sing with new meaning, "My country 'tis of thee, sweet land of liberty, of thee I sing. Land where my father died, land of the Pilgrims' pride, from every mountainside, let freedom ring."

And if America is to be a great nation, this must become true. So let freedom ring from the prodigious hilltops of New Hampshire. Let freedom ring from the mighty mountains of New York. Let freedom ring from the heightening Alleghenies of Pennsylvania!

So let freedom ring

Let freedom ring from the snowcapped Rockies of Colorado! Let freedom ring from the curvaceous peaks of California! But not only that;

let freedom ring from Stone Mountain of Georgia! Let freedom ring from Lookout Mountain of Tennessee!

Let freedom ring from every hill and molehill of Mississippi. From every mountainside, let freedom ring.

When we let freedom ring, when we let it ring from every village and every hamlet, from every state and every city, we will be able to speed up that day when all of God's children, black men and white men, Jews and Gentiles, Protestants and Catholics, will be able to join hands and sing in the words of the old Negro spiritual, "Free at last! Free at last! Thank God Almighty, we are free at last!"

Free at last! Thank God Almighty, we are free at last!

LYNDON B. JOHNSON

The great Shakespearean character of our presidential history

Lyndon Baines Johnson (1908–1973) is surely the great Shakespearean character of our presidential history. It was said of Johnson that like Julius Caesar, "he doth bestride the narrow world like a Colossus." Indeed, President Johnson was a character larger than life, a compulsive overachiever who realized several great victories . . . but suffered one catastrophic defeat.

When Johnson began his career in politics in the 1930s, he was influenced by the liberal programs of Franklin Delano Roosevelt and the New Deal. During his presidency, he oversaw the enactment of a number of new liberal reform programs on the liberal agenda; Johnson described them, in a 1964 speech, as part of a "Great Society." Included were the "War on Poverty," the Medicare and Medicaid programs, and the Higher Education and Elementary and Secondary Education Acts, which provided federal aid to local schools. Two laws that Johnson pushed through Congress — the Civil Rights Act of 1964 (an initiative started in the Kennedy administration) and the Voting Rights Act of 1965 — are reckoned by many observers to be the most important legislation enacted in this country since the passage of the Fourteenth Amendment in the mid-1800s.

Introduced the "Great Society"

But Johnson's unyielding advocacy of the Vietnam War, which resulted in the death of fifty-eight thousand Americans and more than two million North and South Vietnamese, ranks as one of the grossest miscalculations in history. It earned him the enduring condemnation — and frequently the vilification — of a large number of Americans: "Hey, hey, LBJ, how many kids have you killed today?"

Whatever one's opinion of his politics or foreign policies, one cannot help being fascinated by this controversial, so very American man.

A so very American man

It is undeniable that for his entire life, Lyndon Johnson deeply believed in and earnestly fought for American freedoms. Here are two examples of LBJ at his finest.

FROM SPECIAL MESSAGE
TO THE CONGRESS
MARCH 15, 1965

I speak tonight for the dignity of man

I speak tonight for the dignity of man and the destiny of Democracy.

I urge every member of both parties, Americans of all religions and of all colors, from every section of this country, to join me in that cause.

At times history and fate meet at a single time in a single place to shape a turning point in man's unending search for freedom. So it was at Lexington and Concord. So it was a century ago at Appomattox. So it was last week in Selma, Alabama.

There, long suffering men and women peacefully protested the denial of their rights as Americans. Many were brutally assaulted. One good man, a man of God, was killed.

There is no cause for pride in what has happened in Selma. There is no cause for self-satisfaction in the long denial of equal rights of millions of Americans. But there is cause for hope and for faith in our democracy in what is happening here tonight.

For the cries of pain and the hymns and protests of oppressed people have summoned into convocation all the majesty of this great Government — the Government of the greatest Nation on earth.

Our mission is at once the oldest and the most

basic of this country — to right wrong, to do justice, to serve man.

Our mission is at once the oldest and the most basic of this country

In our time we have come to live with moments of great crisis. Our lives have been marked with debate about great issues; issues of war and peace, issues of prosperity and depression. But rarely in any time does an issue lay bare the secret heart of America itself. Rarely are we met with a challenge, not to our growth or abundance, our welfare or our security, but rather to the values and the purposes and the meaning of our beloved nation.

The issue of equal rights for American Negroes is such an issue. And should we defeat every enemy, should we double our wealth and conquer the stars, and still be unequal to this issue, then we will have failed as a people and as a nation.

For with a country as with a person, "What is a man profited, if he shall gain the whole world, and lose his own soul?"

There is no Negro problem. There is no Southern problem. There is no Northern problem. There is only an American problem. And we are met here tonight as Americans — not as Democrats or Republicans — we are met here as Americans to solve that problem.

We are met here as Americans to solve the problem of equal rights for American negroes

This was the first nation in the history of the world to be founded with a purpose. The great phrases of that purpose still sound in every American heart, North and South: "All men are created equal" — "government by consent of the gov-

erned" — "give me liberty or give me death."
Well, those are not just clever words, or those are
not just empty theories. In their name Americans
have fought and died for two centuries, and
tonight around the world they stand there as
guardians of our liberty, risking their lives.

Every citizen shall share in the dignity of man

Those words are a promise to every citizen
that he shall share in the dignity of man. This dignity cannot be found in a man's possessions; it
cannot be found in his power, or in his position. It
really rests on his right to be treated as a man
equal in opportunity to all others. It says that he
shall share in freedom, he shall choose his leaders, educate his children, and provide for his family according to his ability and his merits as a
human being.

To apply any other test — to deny a man his
hopes because of his color or race, his religion or
the place of his birth — is not only to do injustice,
it is to deny America and to dishonor the dead
who gave their lives for American freedom.

The Right to Vote

Our fathers believed that if this noble view of
the rights of man was to flourish, it must be rooted in democracy. The most basic right of all was
the right to choose your own leaders. The history
of this country, in large measure, is the history of
the expansion of that right to all of our people.

Many of the issues of civil rights are very complex and most difficult. But about this there can
and should be no argument. Every American cit-

izen must have an equal right to vote. There is no reason which can excuse the denial of that right. There is no duty which weighs more heavily on us than the duty we have to ensure that right.

Every American citizen must have an equal right to vote

Yet the harsh fact is that in many places in this country men and women are kept from voting simply because they are Negroes.

Every device of which human ingenuity is capable has been used to deny this right. The Negro citizen may go to register only to be told that the day is wrong, or the hour is late, or the official in charge is absent. And if he persists, and if he manages to present himself to the registrar, he may be disqualified because he did not spell out his middle name or because he abbreviated a word on the application.

And if he manages to fill out an application he is given a test. The registrar is the sole judge of whether he passes this test. He may be asked to recite the entire Constitution, or explain the most complex provisions of State law. And even a college degree cannot be used to prove that he can read and write.

For the fact is that the only way to pass these barriers is to show a white skin.

Experience has clearly shown that the existing process of law cannot overcome systematic and ingenious discrimination. No law that we now have on the books — and I have helped to put three of them there — can ensure the right to vote when local officials are determined to deny it.

In such a case our duty must be clear to all of

us. The Constitution says that no person shall be kept from voting because of his race or his color. We have all sworn an oath before God to support and to defend that Constitution. We must now act in obedience to that oath.

Wednesday I will send to Congress a law designed to eliminate illegal barriers to the right to vote. . . .

This bill will strike down restrictions to voting in all elections — Federal, State, and local — which have been used to deny Negroes the right to vote.

This bill will establish a simple, uniform standard which cannot be used, however ingenious the effort, to flout our Constitution.

It will provide for citizens to be registered by officials of the United States Government if the State officials refuse to register them.

It will eliminate tedious, unnecessary lawsuits which delay the right to vote. Finally, this legislation will ensure that properly registered individuals are not prohibited from voting.

I will welcome the suggestions from all of the Members of Congress — I have no doubt that I will get some — on ways and means to strengthen this law and to make it effective. But experience has plainly shown that this is the only path to carry out the command of the Constitution.

To those who seek to avoid action by their National Government in their own communities; who want to and who seek to maintain purely local control over elections, the answer is simple:

Open your polling places to all your people. Allow men and women to register and vote whatever the color of their skin. Extend the rights of citizenship to every citizen of this land.

Open your polling places to all your people

There is no constitutional issue here. The command of the Constitution is plain.

There is no moral issue. It is wrong — deadly wrong — to deny any of your fellow Americans the right to vote in this country.

There is no issue of States rights or national rights. There is only the struggle for human rights.

. . .

We Shall Overcome

But even if we pass this bill, the battle will not be over. What happened in Selma is part of a far larger movement which reaches into every section and State of America. It is the effort of American Negroes to secure for themselves the full blessings of American life.

Their cause must be our cause too. Because it is not just Negroes, but really it is all of us, who must overcome the crippling legacy of bigotry and injustice.

And we shall overcome.

As a man whose roots go deeply into Southern soil I know how agonizing racial feelings are. I know how difficult it is to reshape the attitudes and the structure of our society.

But a century has passed, more than a hundred years, since the Negro was freed. And he is not fully free tonight.

It was more than a hundred years ago that Abraham Lincoln, a great President of another party, signed the Emancipation Proclamation, but emancipation is a proclamation and not a fact.

A century has passed, more than a hundred years, since equality was promised. And yet the Negro is not equal.

A century has passed since the day of promise. And the promise is unkept.

The time of justice has now come

The time of justice has now come. I tell you that I believe sincerely that no force can hold it back. It is right in the eyes of man and God that it should come. And when it does, I think that day will brighten the lives of every American.

For Negroes are not the only victims. How many white children have gone uneducated, how many white families have lived in stark poverty, how many white lives have been scarred by fear, because we have wasted our energy and our substance to maintain the barriers of hatred and terror?

So I say to all of you here and to all in the Nation tonight, that those who appeal to you to hold on to the past do so at the cost of denying you your future.

This great, rich, restless country can offer opportunity and education and hope to all: black and white, North and South, sharecropper and city dweller. These are the enemies: poverty,

ignorance, disease. They are the enemies and not
our fellow man, not our neighbor. And these enemies too, poverty, disease and ignorance, we shall
overcome. . . .

An American Problem

Now let none of us in any sections look with
prideful righteousness on the troubles in another
section, or on the problems of our neighbors.
There is really no part of America where the
promise of equality has been fully kept. In Buffa-
lo as well as in Birmingham, in Philadelphia as
well as in Selma, Americans are struggling for the
fruits of freedom.

This is one Nation. What happens in Selma or
in Cincinnati is a matter of legitimate concern to
every American. But let each of us look within
our own hearts and our own communities, and let
each of us put our shoulder to the wheel to root
out injustice wherever it exists.

This is one nation

As we meet here in this peaceful, historic
chamber tonight, men from the South, some of
whom were at Iwo Jima, men from the North who
have carried Old Glory to far corners of the world
and brought it back without a stain on it, men
from the East and from the West, are all fighting
together without regard to religion, or color, or
region, in Vietnam. Men from every region fought
for us across the world 20 years ago.

And in these common dangers and these common sacrifices the South made its contribution of

honor and gallantry no less than any other region of the great Republic — and in some instances, a great many of them, more.

And I have not the slightest doubt that good men from everywhere in this country, from the Great Lakes to the Gulf of Mexico, from the Golden Gate to the harbors along the Atlantic, will rally together now in this cause to vindicate the freedom of all Americans. For all of us owe this duty; and I believe that all of us will respond to it.

All of us owe this duty

Your President makes that request of every American.

Progress Through the Democratic Process

The real hero of this struggle is the American Negro. His actions and protests, his courage to risk safety and even to risk his life, have awakened the conscience of this Nation. His demonstrations have been designed to call attention to injustice, designed to provoke change, designed to stir reform.

He has called upon us to make good the promise of America. And who among us can say that we would have made the same progress were it not for his persistent bravery, and his faith in American democracy.

Equality depends on respect for law and order

For at the real heart of battle for equality is a deep-seated belief in the democratic process. Equality depends not on the force of arms or tear gas but upon the force of moral right; not on recourse to violence but on respect for law and order.

There have been many pressures upon your President and there will be others as the days come and go. But I pledge you tonight that we intend to fight this battle where it should be fought: in the courts, and in the Congress, and in the hearts of men.

We must preserve the right of free speech and the right of free assembly. But the right of free speech does not carry with it, as has been said, the right to holler fire in a crowded theater. We must preserve the right to free assembly, but free assembly does not carry with it the right to block public thoroughfares to traffic.

We do have a right to protest, and a right to march under conditions that do not infringe the constitutional rights of our neighbors. And I intend to protect all those rights as long as I am permitted to serve in this office.

We will guard against violence, knowing it strikes from our hands the very weapons which we seek — progress, obedience to law, and belief in American values.

In Selma as elsewhere we seek and pray for peace. We seek order. We seek unity. But we will not accept the peace of stifled rights, or the order imposed by fear, or the unity that stifles protest. For peace cannot be purchased at the cost of liberty.

We will not accept the peace of stifled rights

In Selma tonight, as in every — and we had a

good day there — as in every city, we are working for just and peaceful settlement. We must all
remember that after this speech I am making
tonight, after the police and the FBI and the
Marshals have all gone, and after you have
promptly passed this bill, the people of Selma and
the other cities of the Nation must still live and
work together. And when the attention of the
Nation has gone elsewhere they must try to heal
the wounds and to build a new community.

This cannot be easily done on a battleground
of violence, as the history of the South itself
shows. It is in recognition of this that men of both
races have shown such an outstandingly impressive responsibility in recent days — last Tuesday,
again today.

Rights Must Be Opportunities

The bill that I am presenting to you will be
known as a civil rights bill. But, in a larger sense,
most of the program I am recommending is a civil
rights program. Its object is to open the city of
hope to all people of all races.

Because all Americans just must have the
right to vote. And we are going to give them that
right.

All Americans must have the privileges of citizenship regardless of race. And they are going to
have those privileges of citizenship regardless of
race.

But I would like to caution you and remind

you that to exercise these privileges takes much more than just legal right. It requires a trained mind and a healthy body. It requires a decent home, and the chance to find a job, and the opportunity to escape from the clutches of poverty.

Of course, people cannot contribute to the Nation if they are never taught to read or write, if their bodies are stunted from hunger, if their sickness goes untended, if their life is spent in hopeless poverty just drawing a welfare check.

So we want to open the gates to opportunity. But we are also going to give all our people, black and white, the help that they need to walk through those gates.

We want to open the gates to opportunity

The Purpose of the Government

My first job after college was as a teacher in Cotulla, Texas, in a small Mexican-American school. Few of them could speak English, and I couldn't speak much Spanish. My students were poor and they often came to class without breakfast, hungry. They knew even in their youth the pain of prejudice. They never seemed to know why people disliked them. But they knew it was so, because I saw it in their eyes. I often walked home late in the afternoon, after the classes were finished, wishing there was more that I could do. But all I knew was to teach them the little that I knew, hoping that it might help them against the hardships that lay ahead.

Somehow you never forget what poverty and

hatred can do when you see its scars on the hopeful face of a young child.

I never thought then, in 1928, that I would be standing here in 1965. It never even occurred to me in my fondest dreams that I might have the chance to help the sons and daughters of those students and to help people like them all over this country.

But now I do have that chance — and I'll let you in on a secret — I mean to use it. And I hope that you will use it with me.

This is the richest and most powerful country which ever occupied the globe. The might of past empires is little compared to ours. But I do not want to be the President who built empires, or sought grandeur, or extended dominion.

I want to be the President who educated young children to the wonders of their world. I want to be the President who helped to feed the hungry and to prepare them to be taxpayers instead of taxeaters.

I want to be the President who helped the poor to find their own way and who protected the right of every citizen to vote in every election.

I want to be the President who helped to end hatred among his fellow men and who promoted love among the people of all races and all regions and all parties.

I want to be the President who helped to end war among the brothers of this earth.

And so. . . . I came down here to ask you to share this task with me and to share it with the

I do not
want to be
the President who
built empires

people that we both work for. I want this to be the Congress, Republicans and Democrats alike, which did all these things for all these people.

Beyond this great chamber, out yonder in 50 States, are the people that we serve. Who can tell what deep and unspoken hopes are in their hearts tonight as they sit there and listen. We all can guess, from our own lives, how difficult they often find their own pursuit of happiness, how many problems each little family has. They look most of all to themselves for their futures. But I think that they also look to each of us.

Above the pyramid on the great seal of the United States it says — in Latin "God has favored our undertaking."

God will not favor everything that we do. It is rather our duty to divine His will. But I cannot help believing that He truly understands and that He really favors the undertaking that we begin here tonight.

FROM SPEECH AT
HOWARD UNIVERSITY
JUNE 4, 1965

In far too many ways American Negroes have been another nation; deprived of freedom, crippled by hatred, the doors of opportunity closed to hope.

In our time change has come to this nation. The American Negro, acting with impressive restraint, has peacefully protested and marched, entered the courtrooms and the seats of government, demanding a justice that has long been denied. The voice of the Negro was the call to action. But it is a tribute to America that, once aroused, the courts and the Congress, the President and most of the people, have been the allies of progress.

Thus we have seen the high court of the country declare that discrimination based on race was repugnant to the Constitution, and therefore void. We have seen in 1957, and 1960, and again in 1964, the first civil rights legislation in this Nation in almost an entire century. . . .

The voting rights bill will be the latest, and among the most important, in a long series of victories. But this victory — as Winston Churchill said of another triumph for freedom — "is not the end. It is not even the beginning of the end. But it is, perhaps, the end of the beginning."

The barriers to that freedom are tumbling down

That beginning is freedom; and the barriers to that freedom are tumbling down. Freedom is the right to share, share fully and equally, in American society — to vote, to hold a job, to enter a public place, to go to school. It is the right to be treated in every part of our national life as a person equal in dignity and promise to all others.

But freedom is not enough. You do not wipe away the scars of centuries by saying: Now you are free to go where you want, and do as you desire, and choose the leaders you please.

You do not take a person who, for years, has

been hobbled by chains and liberate him, bring him up to the starting line of a race and then say, "you are free to compete with all the others," and still justly believe that you have been completely fair.

Thus it is not enough just to open the gates of opportunity. All our citizens must have the ability to walk through those gates.

It is not enough just to open the gates of opportunity

This is the next and the more profound stage of the battle for civil rights. We seek not just freedom but opportunity. We seek not just legal equity but human ability, not just equality as a right and a theory but equality as a fact and equality as a result.

For the task is to give 20 million Negroes the same chance as every other American to learn and grow, to work and share in society, to develop their abilities —physical, mental and spiritual, and to pursue their individual happiness.

To this end equal opportunity is essential, but not enough, not enough. Men and women of all races are born with the same range of abilities. But ability is not just the product of birth. Ability is stretched or stunted by the family that you live with, the neighborhood you live in — by the school you go to and the poverty or the richness of your surroundings. It is the product of a hundred unseen forces playing upon the little infant, the child, and finally the man. . . .

Of course Negro Americans as well as white Americans have shared in our rising national abundance. But the harsh fact of the matter is that in the battle for true equality too many — far too many — are losing ground every day.

We are not completely sure why this is. We know the causes are complex and subtle. But we do know the two broad basic reasons. And we do know that we have to act.

First, Negroes are trapped — as many whites are trapped — in inherited, gateless poverty. They lack training and skills. They are shut in, in slums, without decent medical care. Private and public poverty combine to cripple their capacities.

We are trying to attack these evils through our poverty program, through our education program, through our medical care and our other health programs, and a dozen more of the Great Society programs that are aimed at the root causes of this poverty.

We will increase our attack on poverty until this most enduring of foes yields to our unyielding will

We will increase, and we will accelerate, and we will broaden this attack in years to come until this most enduring of foes finally yields to our unyielding will.

But there is a second cause — much more difficult to explain, more deeply grounded, more desperate in its force. It is the devastating heritage of long years of slavery; and a century of oppression, hatred, and injustice.

Negro poverty is not white poverty

For Negro poverty is not white poverty. Many of its causes and many of its cures are the same. But there are differences — deep, corrosive, obstinate differences — radiating painful roots into the community, and into the family, and the nature of the individual.

These differences are not racial differences. They are solely and simply the consequence of ancient brutality, past injustice, and present prejudice. They are anguishing to observe. For the Negro they are a constant reminder of oppression. For the white they are a constant reminder of guilt. But they must be faced and they must be dealt with and they must be overcome, if we are ever to reach the time when the only difference between Negroes and whites is the color of their skin.

Nor can we find a complete answer in the experience of other American minorities. They made a valiant and a largely successful effort to emerge from poverty and prejudice.

The Negro, like these others, will have to rely mostly upon his own efforts. But he just cannot do it alone. For they did not have the heritage of centuries to overcome, and they did not have a cultural tradition which had been twisted and battered by endless years of hatred and hopelessness, nor were they excluded — these others — because of race or color — a feeling whose dark intensity is matched by no other prejudice in our society.

Nor can these differences be understood as isolated infirmities. They are a seamless web. They cause each other. They result from each other. They reinforce each other.

Much of the Negro community is buried under a blanket of history and circumstance. It is not a lasting solution to lift just one corner of that blanket. We must stand on all sides and we must raise the entire cover if we are to liberate our fellow citizens. . . .

Perhaps most important — its influence radiating to every part of life — is the breakdown of the Negro family structure. For this, most of all, white America must accept responsibility. It flows from centuries of oppression and persecution of the Negro man. It flows from the long years of degradation and discrimination, which have attacked his dignity and assaulted his ability to produce for his family. . . .

The breakdown of the negro family structure

The family is the cornerstone of our society. More than any other force it shapes the attitude, the hopes, the ambitions, and the values of the child. And when the family collapses it is the children that are usually damaged. When it happens on a massive scale the community itself is crippled.

So, unless we work to strengthen the family, to create conditions under which most parents will stay together, all the rest — schools, and playgrounds, and public assistance, and private concern — will never be enough to cut completely the circle of despair and deprivation.

There is no single easy answer to all of these problems.

Jobs are part of the answer. They bring the income which permits a man to provide for his family.

Decent homes in decent surroundings and a chance to learn — an equal chance to learn — are part of the answer.

Welfare and social programs better designed to hold families together are part of the answer.

Care for the sick is part of the answer.

An understanding heart by all Amerians is another big part of the answer. . . .

So, it is the glorious opportunity of this generation to end the one huge wrong of the American Nation, and, in so doing, to find America for ourselves, with the same immense thrill of discovery which gripped those who first began to realize that here, at last, was a home for freedom.

The glorious opportunity of this generation is to end the one huge wrong of the American nation

All it will take is for all of us to understand what this country is and what this country must become.

The Scripture promises: "I shall light a candle of understanding in thine heart, which shall not be put out."

Together, and with millions more, we can light that candle of understanding in the heart of all America.

And once lit, it will never again go out.

RONALD REAGAN

Historians caution that it is too early to fully evaluate the effectiveness of the presidency of our fortieth president, Ronald Reagan (1911–   ). However, there is support in many quarters for the assessment that his major contribution to the preservation of American freedoms was his 1983 proposal of the Strategic Defense Initiative (the so-called Star Wars systems). This initiative

He is perhaps best remembered for the "Star Wars" initiative

called for a comprehensive and intense research and development program by the United States to eliminate the threat of strategic nuclear missiles, thereby (according to those who subscribe to the assessment) pushing the Soviet Union into an exceedingly expensive arms race that destroyed its economy and brought about the fall of its communist regime.

Author of two fine speeches on the meaning of American freedom

Two of President Reagan's most moving declarations about American freedom are his speech at Moscow State University in 1988 — "Go to any American town. . . . Go into any schoolroom. . . . Go into any courtroom. . . . Go to any university campus. . . . Turn on the television. . . . March in any demonstration. . . . Go into any union hall . . ." — and his farewell address in 1989 — "How stands [America] on this winter night? . . . She's still a beacon, still a magnet for all who must have freedom, for all the pilgrims from all the lost places who are hurtling through darkness, toward home."

FROM SPEECH AT
MOSCOW STATE UNIVERSITY
MAY 31, 1988

We Americans make no secret of our belief in freedom. In fact, it's something of a national pastime. Every four years the American people choose a new president, and 1988 is one of those years. At one point there were 13 major candidates running in the two major parties, not to mention all the others, including the Socialist and

Libertarian candidates — all trying to get my job. About 1,000 local television stations, 8,500 radio stations, and 1,700 daily newspapers, each one an independent, private enterprise, fiercely independent of the government, report on the candidates, grill them in interviews, and bring them together for debates. In the end, the people vote — they decide who will be the next president.

But freedom doesn't begin or end with elections. Go to any American town, to take just an example, and you'll see dozens of churches, representing many different beliefs — in many places synagogues and mosques — and you'll see families of every conceivable nationality, worshipping together.

Freedom doesn't begin or end with elections

Go into any schoolroom, and there you will see children being taught the Declaration of Independence, that they are endowed by their Creator with certain inalienable rights — among them life, liberty, and the pursuit of happiness — that no government can justly deny — the guarantees in their Constitution for freedom of speech, freedom of assembly, and freedom of religion.

Go into any courtroom and there will preside an independent judge, beholden to no government power. There every defendant has the right to a trial by a jury of his peers, usually 12 men and women — common citizens, they are the ones, the only ones, who weigh the evidence and decide on guilt or innocence. In that court, the accused is innocent until proven guilty, and the word of a policeman, or any official, has no greater legal standing than the word of the accused.

Go to any university campus, and there you'll find an open, sometimes heated discussion of the problems in American society and what can be done to correct them. Turn on the television, and you'll see the legislature conducting the business of government right there before the camera, debating and voting on the legislation that will become the law of the land. March in any demonstration, and there are many of them — the people's right of assembly is guaranteed in the Constitution and protected by the police. Go into any union hall where the members know their right to strike is protected by law. . . .

But freedom is even more than this: Freedom is the right to question, and change the established way of doing things. It is the continuing revolution of the marketplace. It is the understanding that allows us to recognize shortcomings and seek solutions. It is the right to put forth an idea, scoffed at by the experts, and watch it catch fire among the people. It is the right to follow your dream, to stick to your conscience, even if you're the only one in a sea of doubters.

Freedom is the recognition that no single person, no single authority or government has a monopoly on the truth, but that every individual life is infinitely precious, that every one of us put on this earth has been put here for a reason and has something to offer. . . .

Freedom, it has been said, makes people selfish and materialistic, but Americans are one of the most religious peoples on Earth. Because they know that liberty, just as life itself, is not earned but a gift from God, they seek to share with the world. "Reason and experience," said George Washington in his Farewell Address, "both forbid us to expect that national morality can prevail in exclusion of religious principle. And it is substantially true, that a virtue or morality is a necessary spring of popular government." Democracy is less a system of government than it is a system to keep government limited, unintrusive: A system of constraints on power to keep politics and government secondary to the important things in life, the true sources of value found only in family and faith.

But I hope you know I go on about these things not simply to extol the virtues of my own country, but to speak to the true greatness of the heart and soul of your land. Who, after all, needs to tell the land of Dostoevsky about the quest for truth, the home of Kandinsky and Scriabin about imagination, the rich and noble culture of the Uzbek man of letters, Alisher Navio, about beauty and heart? The great culture of your diverse land speaks with a glowing passion to all humanity. Let me cite one of the most eloquent contemporary passages on human freedom. It comes not from the literature of America, but from this country, from one of the greatest writers of the twentieth century, Boris Pasternak, in the novel *Dr. Zhivago*. He writes, "I think that if the beast who sleeps in man could be held down by threats — any kind of threat, whether of jail or of retribution after death — then the highest emblem of humanity would be the lion tamer in the circus with his whip, not the prophet who sacrificed himself. But this is just the point — what has for centuries raised man above the beast is not the cudgel, but an inward music — the irresistible power of unarmed truth.". . .

"The irresistible power of unarmed truth"

FROM FAREWELL ADDRESS
JANUARY 11, 1989

My fellow Americans: This is the 34th time I'll speak to you from the Oval Office and the last. We've been together eight years now, and soon it'll be time for me to go. But before I do, I wanted to share some thoughts, some of which I've been saving for a long time. . . .

One of the things about the Presidency is that you're always somewhat apart. You spend a lot of time going by too fast in a car someone else is driving, and seeing the people through tinted glass — the parents holding up a child, and the wave you saw too late and couldn't return. And so many times I wanted to stop and reach out from behind the glass, and connect. Well, maybe I can do a little of that tonight. . . .

You know, down the hall and up the stairs from this office is the part of the White House where the President and his family live. There are a few favorite windows I have up there that I like to stand and look out of early in the morning. The view is over the grounds here to the Washington Monument, and then the Mall and the Jefferson Memorial. But on mornings when the humidity is low, you can see past the Jefferson to the river, the Potomac, and the Virginia shore. Someone said that's the view Lincoln had when he saw the smoke rising from the Battle of Bull Run. I see more prosaic things: the grass on the banks, the morning traffic as people make their way to work, now and then a sailboat on the river.

I've been thinking a bit at that window. I've been reflecting on what the past eight years have meant and mean. And the image that comes to mind like a refrain is a nautical one — a small story about a big ship, and a refugee, and a sailor. It was back in the early eighties, at the height of the boat people. And the sailor was hard at work on the carrier *Midway*, which was patrolling the South China Sea. The sailor, like most American servicemen, was young, smart, and fiercely observant. The crew spied on the horizon a leaky little boat. And crammed inside were refugees from Indochina hoping to get to America. The *Midway* sent a small launch to bring them to the ship and safety. As the refugees made their way through the choppy seas, one spied the sailor on deck, and stood up, and called out to him. He yelled, "Hello, American sailor. Hello, freedom man."

"Hello, American sailor. Hello, freedom man."

A small moment with a big meaning, a moment the sailor, who wrote it in a letter, couldn't get out of his mind. And, when I saw it, neither could I. Because that's what it was to be an American in the 1980's. We stood, again, for freedom. I know we always have, but in the past few years the world again — and in a way, we ourselves — rediscovered it. . . .

In all of that time I won a nickname, "The Great Communicator." But I never thought it was my style or the words I used that made a difference: It was the content. I wasn't a great communicator, but I communicated great things, and they didn't spring full bloom from my brow, they came from the heart of a great nation — from our experience, our wisdom, and our belief in the principles that have guided us for two centuries. They called it the Reagan revolution. Well, I'll accept that, but for me it always seemed more like the great rediscovery, a rediscovery of our values and our common sense. . . .

A rediscovery of our values and our common sense.

[B]ecause we're a great nation, our challenges seem complex. It will always be this way. But as long as we remember our first principles and believe in ourselves, the future will always be ours. And something else we learned: Once you begin a great movement, there's no telling where it will end. We meant to change a nation, and instead, we changed a world.

Countries across the globe are turning to free markets and free speech and turning away from the ideologies of the past. For them, the great rediscovery of the 1980's has been that, lo and behold, the moral way of government is the practical way of government: Democracy, the profoundly good, is also the profoundly productive. . . .

Finally, there is a great tradition of warnings in Presidential farewells, and I've got one that's been on my mind for some time. But oddly enough it starts with one of the things I'm proudest of in the past eight years: the resurgence of national pride that I called the new patriotism. This national feeling is good, but it won't count for much, and it won't last unless it's grounded in thoughtfulness and knowledge.

The new patriotism

An informed patriotism is what we want. And are we doing a good enough job teaching our children what America is and what she represents in the long history of the world? Those of us who are over 35 or so years of age grew up in a different America. We were taught, very directly, what it means to be an American. And we absorbed, almost in the air, a love of country and an appreciation of its institutions. If you didn't get these things from your family you got them from the neighborhood, from the father down the street who fought in Korea or the family who lost someone at Anzio. Or you could get a sense of patriotism from school. And if all else failed you could get a sense of patriotism from the popular culture. The movies celebrated democratic values and implicitly reinforced the idea that America was special. TV was like that, too, through the mid-sixties.

But now, we're about to enter the nineties, and some things have changed. Younger parents aren't sure that an unambivalent appreciation of America is the right thing to teach modern children. And as for those who create the popular culture, well-grounded patriotism is no longer the style. Our spirit is back, but we haven't reinstitutionalized it. We've got to do a better job of getting across that America is freedom — freedom of speech, freedom of religion, freedom of enterprise. And freedom is special and rare. It's fragile; it needs [protection].

We've got to teach history based not on what's in fashion but what's important

So, we've got to teach history based not on what's in fashion but what's important — why the Pilgrims came here, who Jimmy Doolittle was, and what those 30 seconds over Tokyo meant. You know, four years ago on the 40th anniversary of D-Day, I read a letter from a young woman writing to her late father, who'd fought on Omaha Beach. . . . [S]he said, "we will always remember, we will never forget what the boys of Normandy did." Well, let's help her keep her word. If we forget what we did, we won't know who we are. I'm warning of an eradication of the American memory that could result, ultimately, in an erosion of the American spirit. Let's start with some basics: more attention to American history and a greater emphasis on civic ritual.

And let me offer lesson number one about America: All great change in America begins at the dinner table. So, tomorrow night in the kitchen I hope the talking begins. And children, if your parents haven't been teaching you what it means to be an American, let 'em know and nail 'em on it. That would be a very American thing to do.

All great change in America begins at the dinner table

And that's about all I have to say tonight, except for one thing. The past few days when I've been at the window upstairs, I've thought a bit of the "shining city upon a hill." The phrase comes from John Winthrop, who wrote it to describe the America he imagined. What he imagined was important because he was an early Pilgrim, an early freedom man. He journeyed here on what today we'd call a little wooden boat; and like the other Pilgrims, he was looking for a home that would be free.

I've spoken of the shining city all my political life, but I don't know if I ever quite communicated what I saw when I said it. But in my mind it was a tall, proud city built on rocks stronger than oceans, wind-swept, God-blessed, and teeming with people of all kinds living in harmony and peace; a city with free ports that hummed with commerce and creativity. And if there had to be city walls, the walls had doors and the doors were open to anyone with the will and the heart to get here. That's how I saw it, and see it still.

And how stands the city on this winter night? More prosperous, more secure, and happier than

How stands the city on this winter night?

it was eight years ago. But more than that: After 200 years, two centuries, she still stands strong and true on the granite ridge, and her glow has held steady no matter what storm. And she's still a beacon, still a magnet for all who must have freedom, for all the pilgrims from all the lost places who are hurtling through the darkness, toward home.

We've done our part. And as I walk off into the city streets, a final word to the men and women of the Reagan revolution, the men and women across America who for eight years did the work that brought America back. My friends: We did it. We weren't just marking time. We made a difference. We made the city stronger, we made the city freer, and we left her in good hands. All in all, not bad, not bad at all.

And so, Good-bye, God bless you, and God bless the United States of America.

APPENDIX

THE CONSTITUTION OF THE UNITED STATES

September 17, 1787

WE, the people of the United States, in order to form a more perfect Union, establish justice, insure domestic tranquillity, provide for the common defence, promote the general welfare, and secure the blessings of liberty to ourselves and our posterity, do ordain and establish this Constitution for the United States of America.

ARTICLE I. § 1. All legislative powers herein granted, shall be vested in a Congress of the United States, which shall consist of a Senate and House of Representatives.

§ 2. The House of Representatives shall be composed of members chosen every second year by the people of the several States; and the electors in each State shall have the qualifications requisite for electors of the most numerous branch of the State Legislature.

No person shall be a representative who shall not have attained to the age of twenty-five years, and been seven years a citizen of the United States, and who shall not, when elected, be an inhabitant of that State in which he shall be chosen.

Representatives and direct taxes shall be apportioned among the several States which may be included within this

Union, according to their respective numbers, which shall be determined by adding to the whole number of free persons, including those bound to service for a term of years, and excluding Indians not taxed, three fifths of all other persons. The actual enumeration shall be made within three years after the first meeting of the Congress of the United States, and within every subsequent term of ten years, in such manner as they shall by law direct. The number of representatives shall not exceed one for every thirty thousand, but each State shall have at least one representative, and until such enumeration shall be made, the state of New Hampshire shall be entitled to choose three, Massachusetts eight, Rhode Island and Providence Plantations one, Connecticut five, New York six, New Jersey four, Pennsylvania eight, Delaware one, Maryland six, Virginia ten, North Carolina five, South Carolina five, and Georgia three.

When vacancies happen in the representation from any State, the Executive authority thereof shall issue writs of election to fill such vacancies.

The House of Representatives shall choose their speaker and other officers; and shall have the sole power of impeachment.

§ 3. The Senate of the United States shall be composed of two Senators from each State, chosen by the Legislature thereof, for six years; and each Senator shall have one vote.

Immediately after they shall be assembled, in consequence of the first election, they shall be divided as equally as may be into three classes. The seats of the Senators of the first class shall be vacated at the expiration of the second year, of the second class at the expiration of the fourth year, and of the third class at the expiration of the sixth year, so that one third may be chosen every second year; and if vacancies happen by resignation, or otherwise, during the recess of the Legislature of any State, the Executive thereof may make temporary appointments until the next meeting of the Legislature, which shall then fill such vacancies.

No person shall be a Senator who shall not have attained to the age of thirty years, and been nine years a citizen of the United States, and who shall not, when elected, be an inhabitant of that State for which he shall be chosen.

The Vice President of the United States shall be president of the Senate, but shall have no vote, unless they be equally divided.

The Senate shall choose their other officers, and also a president *pro tempore*, in the absence of the Vice President, or when he shall exercise the office of President of the United States.

The Senate shall have the sole power to try all impeachments. When sitting for that purpose, they shall be on oath or affirmation. When the President of the United States is tried, the Chief Justice shall preside; and no person shall be convicted without the concurrence of two thirds of the members present.

Judgment in cases of impeachment shall not extend further than to removal from office, and disqualification to hold and enjoy any office of honour, trust or profit, under the United States; but the party convicted shall nevertheless be liable and subject to indictment, trial, judgment, and punishment according to law.

§ 4. The times, places and manner of holding elections for Senators and Representatives, shall be prescribed in each State by the Legislature thereof; but the Congress may at any time by law make or alter such regulations, except as to the places of choosing Senators. The Congress shall assemble at least once in every year, and such meeting shall be on the first Monday in December, unless they shall by law appoint a different day.

§ 5. Each House shall be the judge of the elections, returns, and qualifications of its own members, and a majority of each shall constitute a quorum to do business; but a smaller number may adjourn from day to day, and may be authorized to compel the attendance of absent members, in such manner, and under such penalties, as each House may provide.

Each House may determine the rules of its proceedings, punish its members for disorderly behaviour, and, with the concurrence of two thirds, expel a member.

Each House shall keep a journal of its proceedings, and from time to time publish the same, excepting such parts as may, in their judgment, require secrecy; and the yeas and nays of the members of either House on any question, shall, at the desire of one fifth of those present, be entered on the journal.

Neither House, during the session of Congress, shall, without the consent of the other, adjourn for more than three days, nor to any other place than that in which the two Houses shall be sitting.

§ 6. The Senators and Representatives shall receive a compensation for their services, to be ascertained by law, and paid out of the Treasury of the United States. They shall, in all cases, except treason, felony, and breach of the peace, be privileged from arrest during their attendance at the session of their respective Houses, and in going to, and returning from, the same; and for any speech or debate in either House, they shall not be questioned in any other place.

No Senator or Representative shall, during the time for which he was elected, be appointed to any civil office under the authority of the United States, which shall have been created, or the emoluments whereof shall have been increased during such time; and no person holding any office under the United States, shall be a member of either House during his continuance in office.

§ 7. All bills for raising revenue shall originate in the House of Representatives; but the Senate may propose or concur with amendments as on other bills.

Every bill which shall have passed the House of Representatives and the Senate, shall, before it become a law, be presented to the President of the United States; if he approve he shall sign it, but if not he shall return it, with his objections, to that House in which it shall have originated, who shall enter the objections at large on their journal, and proceed to reconsider it. If after such reconsideration two thirds of that House shall agree to pass the bill, it shall be sent, together with the objections, to the other House, by which it shall likewise be reconsidered, and if approved by two thirds of that House, it shall become a law. But in all such cases the votes of both Houses shall be determined by yeas and nays, and the names of the persons voting for and against the bill shall be entered on the journal of each House respectively. If any bill shall not be returned by the President within ten days, (Sundays excepted,) after it shall have been presented to him, the same shall be a law, in like manner as if he had signed it, unless the Congress by their adjournment prevent its return, in which case it shall not be a law.

Every order, resolution, or vote, to which the concurrence of the Senate and House of Representatives may be necessary, (except on a question of adjournment,) shall be presented to the President of the United States; and before the same shall take effect, shall be approved by him, or being disapproved by him, shall be re-passed by two thirds of the Senate and House of Representatives, according to the rules and limitations prescribed in the case of a bill.

§ 8. The Congress shall have power: To lay and collect taxes, duties, imposts and excises, to pay the debts, and provide for the common defence and general welfare of the United States; but all duties, imposts, and excises shall be uniform throughout the United States:

To borrow money on the credit of the United States:

To regulate commerce with foreign nations, and among the several States, and with the Indian tribes:

To establish an uniform rule of naturalization, and uniform laws on the subject of bankruptcies throughout the United States:

To coin money, regulate the value thereof, and of foreign coin, and fix the standard of weights and measures:

To provide for the punishment of counterfeiting the securities and current coin of the United States:

To establish post-offices and post-roads:

To promote the progress of science and useful arts, by securing, for limited times, to authors and inventors, the exclusive right to their respective writings and discoveries:

To constitute tribunals inferior to the Supreme Court:

To define and punish piracies and felonies committed on the high seas, and offences against the law of nations:

To declare war, grant letters of marque and reprisal, and make rules concerning captures on land and water:

To raise and support armies: but no appropriation of money to that use shall be for a longer term than two years:

To provide and maintain a navy:

To make rules for the government and regulation of the land and naval forces:

To provide for calling forth the militia to execute the laws of the Union, suppress insurrections and repel invasions:

To provide for organizing, arming, and disciplining the militia, and for governing such part of them as may be employed in the service of the United States, reserving to the States respectively, the appointment of the officers, and the authority of training the militia according to the discipline prescribed by Congress.

To exercise exclusive legislation, in all cases whatsoever, over such district (not exceeding ten miles square) as may by cession of particular States, and the acceptance of Congress, become the seat of the government of the United States, and to exercise like authority over all places purchased by the consent of the legislature of the State in which the same shall be, for the erection of forts, magazines, arsenals, dock-yards, and other needful buildings. And,

To make all laws which shall be necessary and proper for carrying into execution the foregoing powers, and all other powers vested by this Constitution in the government of the United States, or in any department or officer thereof.

§ 9. The migration or importation of such persons as any of the States now existing shall think proper to admit, shall not be prohibited by the Congress prior to the year one thousand eight hundred and eight; but a tax or duty may be imposed on such importation, not exceeding ten dollars for each person.

The privilege of the writ of *habeas corpus* shall not be suspended, unless when in cases of rebellion or invasion the public safety may require it.

No bill of attainder or *ex post facto* law shall be passed.

No capitation, or other direct tax, shall be laid, unless in proportion to the *census* or enumeration herein before directed to be taken.

No tax or duty shall be laid on articles exported from any State. No preference shall be given by any regulation of commerce or revenue to the ports of one State over those of another; nor shall vessels bound to, or from, one State be obliged to enter, clear, or pay duties in another.

No money shall be drawn from the treasury, but in consequence of appropriations made by law; and a regular statement and account of the receipts and expenditures of all public money shall be published from time to time.

No title of nobility shall be granted by the United States; and no person holding any office of profit or trust under them, shall, without the consent of the Congress, accept of any present, emolument, office, or title of any kind whatever, from any king, prince, or foreign state.

§ 10. No State shall enter into any treaty, alliance, or confederation; grant letters of marque and reprisal; coin money; emit bills of credit; make any thing but gold and silver coin a tender in payment of debts; pass any bill of attainder, *ex post facto* law, or law impairing the obligation of contracts, or grant any title of nobility.

No State shall, without the consent of the Congress, lay any imposts or duties on imports or exports, except what may be absolutely necessary for executing its inspection laws; and the net produce of all duties and imposts, laid by any State on imports or exports, shall be for the use of the treasury of the United States; and all such laws shall be subject to the revision and control of the Congress. No State shall, without the consent of Congress, lay any duty of tonnage, keep troops, or ships of war, in time of peace, enter into any agreement or compact with another State, or with a foreign power, or engage in war, unless actually invaded, or in such imminent danger as will not admit of delay.

ARTICLE II. § 1. The executive power shall be vested in a President of the United States of America. He shall hold his office during the term of four years, and together with the Vice President, chosen for the same term, be elected as follows:

Each State shall appoint, in such manner as the legislature thereof may direct, a number of electors equal to the whole number of Senators and Representatives to which the State may be entitled in the Congress; but no Senator or Representative, or person holding an office of trust or profit under the United States, shall be appointed an elector.

The electors shall meet in their respective States, and vote by ballot for two persons, of whom one at least shall not be an inhabitant of the same State with themselves. And they shall make a list of all the persons voted for, and of the number of votes for each; which list they shall sign and certify, and transmit sealed to the seat of the government of the United States, directed to the President of the Senate. The President of the Senate shall, in the presence of the Senate and House of Representatives, open all the certificates, and the votes shall then be counted. The person having the greatest number of votes shall be the President, if such number be a majority of the whole number of electors appointed; and if there be more than one who have such majority, and have an equal number of votes, then the House of Representatives shall immediately choose by ballot one of them for President; and if no person have a majority, then from the five highest on the list the said House shall in like manner choose the President. But in choosing the President, the votes shall be taken by States, the representation from each State having one vote; a quorum for this purpose shall consist of a member or members from two thirds of the States, and a majority of all the States shall be necessary to a choice. In every case, after the choice of the President, the person having the greatest number of votes of the electors shall be the Vice President. But if there should remain two or more who have equal votes, the Senate shall choose from them by ballot the Vice President.

The Congress may determine the time of choosing the electors, and the day on which they shall give their votes; which day shall be the same throughout the United States.

No person except a natural born citizen, or a citizen of the United States, at the time of the adoption of this Constitution, shall be eligible to the office of President; neither shall any person be eligible to that office who shall not have attained to the age of thirty-five years, and been fourteen years a resident within the United States.

In case of the removal of the President from office, or of his death, resignation, or inability to discharge the powers and duties of the said office, the same shall devolve on the Vice President, and the Congress may by law provide for the case of removal, death, resignation, or inability, both of the President and Vice President, declaring what officer shall then act as President, and such officer shall act accordingly until the disability be removed, or a President shall be elected.

The President shall at stated times, receive for his services, a compensation, which shall neither be increased nor diminished during the period for which he shall have been elected, and he shall not receive within that period any other emolument from the United States or any of them.

Before he enter on the execution of his office, he shall take the following oath or affirmation:

"I do solemnly swear, (or affirm,) that I will faithfully execute the office of President of the United States, and will, to the best of my ability, preserve, protect, and defend the Constitution of the United States."

§ 2. The President shall be commander-in-chief of the army and navy of the United States, and of the militia of the several States, when called into the actual service of the United States; he may require the opinion, in writing, of the principal officer in each of the executive departments, upon any subject relating to the duties of their respective offices, and he shall have power to grant reprieves and pardons for offences against the United States, except in cases of impeachment.

He shall have power, by and with the advice and consent of the Senate, to make treaties, provided two thirds of the Senators present concur; and he shall nominate, and by and with the advice and consent of the Senate, shall appoint ambassadors, other public ministers and consuls, judges of the Supreme Court, and all other officers of the United States, whose appointments are not herein otherwise provided for, and which shall be established by law. But the Congress may by law vest the appointment of such inferior officers, as they think proper, in the President alone, in the courts of law, or in the heads of departments.

The President shall have power to fill up all vacancies that may happen during the recess of the Senate, by granting commissions which shall expire at the end of their session.

§ 3. He shall, from time to time, give to the Congress information of the state of the Union, and recommend to their consideration such measures as he shall judge necessary and expedient. He may on extraordinary occasions, convene both Houses, or either of them; and in case of disagreement between them, with respect to the time of adjournment, he may adjourn them to such time as he shall think proper. He shall receive ambassadors and other public ministers. He shall take care that the laws be faithfully executed; and shall commission all the officers of the United States.

§ 4. The President, Vice President, and all civil officers of the United States, shall be removed from office on impeachment for, and conviction of, treason, bribery, or other high crimes and misdemeanors.

ARTICLE III. § 1. The judicial power of the United States shall be vested in one Supreme Court, and in such inferior courts as the Congress may, from time to time, ordain and establish. The judges, both of the Supreme and inferior courts, shall hold their offices during good behaviour; and shall, at stated times, receive for their services, a compensation, which shall not be diminished during their continuance in office.

§ 2. The judicial power shall extend to all cases, in law and equity, arising under this Constitution, the laws of the United States, and treaties made, or which shall be made, under their authority; to all cases affecting ambassadors, other public ministers, and consuls; to all cases of admiralty and maritime jurisdiction; to controversies to which the United States shall be a party; to controversies between two or more States, between a State and citizens of another State, between citizens of different States, between citizens of the same State claiming lands under grants of different States, and between a State, or the citizens thereof, and foreign States, citizens or subjects.

In all cases affecting ambassadors, other public ministers and consuls, and those in which a State shall be party, the Supreme Court shall have original jurisdiction. In all the other cases before mentioned, the Supreme Court shall have appellate jurisdiction, both as to law and fact, with such exceptions, and under such regulations, as the Congress shall make.

The trial of all crimes, except in cases of impeachment, shall be by jury; and such trial shall be held in the State where the said crimes shall have been committed; but when not committed within any State, the trial shall be at such place or places as the Congress may by law have directed.

§ 3. Treason against the United States, shall consist only in levying war against them, or in adhering to their enemies, giving them aid and comfort. No person shall be convicted of treason unless on the testimony of two witnesses to the same overt act, or on confession in open court.

The Congress shall have power to declare the punishment of treason, but no attainder of treason shall work corruption of blood, or forfeiture, except during the life of the person attainted.

ARTICLE IV. § 1. Full faith and credit shall be given in each State to the public acts, records, and judicial proceedings of every other State. And the Congress may by general laws prescribe the manner in which such acts, records, and proceedings shall be proved, and the effect thereof.

§ 2. The citizens of each State shall be entitled to all privileges and immunities of citizens in the several States.
A person charged in any State with treason, felony, or other crime, who shall flee from justice, and be found in another State, shall, on demand of the executive authority of the State from which he fled, be delivered up, to be removed to the State having jurisdiction of the crime.

No person held to service or labour in one State, under the laws thereof, escaping into another, shall, in consequence of any law or regulation therein, be discharged from such service or labour, but shall be delivered up on claim of the party to whom such service or labour may be due.

§3. New States may be admitted by the Congress into this Union; but no new State shall be formed or erected within the jurisdiction of any other State; nor any State be formed by the junction of two or more States, or parts of States, without the consent of the legislatures of the States concerned, as well as of the Congress.

The Congress shall have power to dispose of and make all needful rules and regulations respecting the territory or other property belonging to the United States; and nothing in this Constitution shall be so construed as to prejudice any claims of the United States, or of any particular State.

§ 4. The United States shall guarantee to every State in this Union a republican form of government, and shall protect each of them against invasion; and on application of the legislature, or of the executive, (when the legislature cannot be convened) against domestic violence.

ARTICLE V. The Congress, whenever two thirds of both Houses shall deem it necessary, shall propose amendments to this Constitution, or, on the application of the legislatures of two thirds of the several States, shall call a convention for proposing amendments, which, in either case, shall be valid to all intents and purposes, as part of this Constitution, when ratified by the legislatures of three fourths of the several States, or by conventions in three fourths thereof, as the one or the other mode of ratification may be proposed by the Congress; provided, that no amendment, which may be made prior to the year one thousand eight hundred and eight, shall in any manner affect the first and fourth clauses in the ninth section of the first article; and that no State, without its consent, shall be deprived of its equal suffrage in the Senate.

ARTICLE VI. All debts contracted, and engagements entered into, before the adoption of this Constitution, shall be as valid against the United States, under this Constitution, as under the confederation.

This Constitution, and the laws of the United States which shall be made in pursuance thereof, and all treaties made, or which shall be made, under the authority of the

United States, shall be the supreme law of the land: and the judges, in every State, shall be bound thereby, any thing in the Constitution or laws of any State to the contrary notwithstanding.

The Senators and Representatives before mentioned, and the members of the several State legislatures, and all executive and judicial officers, both of the United States and of the several States, shall be bound, by oath or affirmation, to support this Constitution; but no religious test shall ever be required as a qualification to any office or public trust under the United States.

ARTICLE VII. The ratification of the conventions of nine States, shall be sufficient for the establishment of this Constitution between the States so ratifying the same.

Done in Convention, by the unanimous consent of the States present, the seventeenth day of September, in the year of our Lord one thousand seven hundred and eighty-seven, and of the independence of the United States of America the twelfth. In witness whereof we have hereunto subscribed our names.

GEORGE WASHINGTON, PRESIDENT,
and Deputy from Virginia.

New Hampshire.—John Langdon, Nicholas Gilman.
Massachusetts.—Nathaniel Gorham, Rufus King.
Connecticut.—William Samuel Johnson, Roger Sherman.
New York.—Alexander Hamilton.

New Jersey.—William Livingston, David Brearley, William
    Paterson, Jonathan Dayton.

Pennsylvania.—Benjamin Franklin, Thomas Mifflin,
    Robert Morris, George Clymer, Thomas Fitzsimons, Jared
    Ingersoll, James Wilson, Gouverneur Morris.

Delaware.—George Read, Gunning Bedford, Jun., John
    Dickinson, Richard Bassett, Jacob Broom.

Maryland.—James M'Henry, Daniel of St. Thomas Jenifer,
    Daniel Carroll.

Virginia.—John Blair, James Madison, Jun.

North Carolina.—William Blount, Richard Dobbs Spaight,
    Hugh Williamson

South Carolina.—John Rutledge, Charles Cotesworth
    Pinckney, Charles Pinckney, Pierce Butler.

Georgia.—William Few, Abraham Baldwin.

                          Attest: WILLIAM JACKSON, *Secretary.*

AMENDMENTS

AMENDMENT I

Congress shall make no law respecting an establishment of religion, or prohibiting the free exercise thereof; or abridging the freedom of speech, or of the press, or the right of the people peaceably to assemble, and to petition the Government for a redress of grievances.

AMENDMENT II

A well regulated Militia, being necessary to the security of a free State, the right of the people to keep and bear Arms, shall not be infringed.

AMENDMENT III

No Soldier shall, in time of peace be quartered in any house, without the consent of the Owner, nor in time of war, but in a manner to be prescribed by law.

AMENDMENT IV

The right of the people to be secure in their persons, houses, papers, and effects, against unreasonable searches and seizures, shall not be violated, and no Warrants shall issue, but upon probable cause, supported by Oath or affirmation, and particularly describing the place to be searched, and the persons or things to be seized.

AMENDMENT V

No person shall be held to answer for a capital, or otherwise infamous crime, unless on a presentment or indictment of a Grand Jury, except in cases arising in the land or naval forces, or in the Militia, when in actual service in time of War or public danger; nor shall any person be subject for the same offence to be twice put in jeopardy of life or limb, nor shall be compelled in any criminal case to be a witness against himself, nor be deprived of life, liberty, or property, without due process of law; nor shall private property be taken for public use, without just compensation.

AMENDMENT VI

In all criminal prosecutions, the accused shall enjoy the right to a speedy and public trial, by an impartial jury of the State and district wherein the crime shall have been committed, which district shall have been previously ascertained by law, and to be informed of the nature and cause of the accusation; to be confronted with the witnesses against him; to have compulsory process for obtaining witnesses in his favor, and to have the assistance of counsel for his defence.

AMENDMENT VII

In Suits at common law, where the value in controversy shall exceed twenty dollars, the right of trial by jury shall be preserved, and no fact tried by a jury, shall be otherwise re-examined in any Court of the United States, than according to the rules of the common law.

AMENDMENT VIII

Excessive bail shall not be required, nor excessive fines imposed, nor cruel and unusual punishments inflicted.

AMENDMENT IX

The enumeration in the Constitution, of certain rights, shall not be construed to deny or disparage others retained by the people.

AMENDMENT X

The powers not delegated to the United States by the Constitution, nor prohibited by it to the States, are reserved to the States respectively, or to the people.

AMENDMENT XI

The Judicial power of the United States shall not be construed to extend to any suit in law or equity, commenced or prosecuted against one of the United States by Citizens of another State, or by Citizens or Subjects of any Foreign State.

AMENDMENT XII

The Electors shall meet in their respective states, and vote by ballot for President and Vice-President, one of whom, at least, shall not be an inhabitant of the same state with themselves; they shall name in their ballots the person voted for as President, and in distinct ballots the person voted for as Vice-President, and they shall make distinct lists of all persons voted for as President, and of all persons voted for as Vice-President, and of the number of votes for each, which lists they shall sign and certify, and transmit sealed to the seat of the government of the United States, directed to the President of the Senate;—The President of the Senate shall, in the presence of the Senate and House of Representatives, open all the certificates and the votes shall then be counted;—The person having the greatest number of votes for President, shall be the President, if such number be a majority of the whole number of Electors appointed; and if no person have such majority, then from the persons having the highest numbers not exceeding three on the list of those voted for as President, the House of Representatives shall choose immediately, by ballot, the President. But in choosing the President, the votes shall be taken by states, the representation from each state having one vote; a quorum for this purpose shall consist of a member or members from two-thirds of the states, and a majority of all the states shall be necessary to a choice. And if the House of Representatives shall not choose a President whenever the right of choice shall devolve upon them, before the fourth day of March next following, then the Vice-President shall act as President, as in the case of the death or other constitutional disability of the President— The person having the greatest number of votes as Vice-President, shall be the Vice-President, if such number be a majority of the whole number of Electors appointed, and if no person have a majority, then from the two highest numbers on the list, the Senate shall choose the Vice-President; a quorum for the purpose shall consist of two-thirds of the whole number of Senators, and a majority of the whole number shall be necessary to a choice. But no person constitutionally ineligible to the office of President shall be eligible to that of Vice-President of the United States.

AMENDMENT XIII

Section 1. Neither slavery nor involuntary servitude, except as a punishment for crime whereof the party shall have been duly convicted, shall exist within the United States, or any place subject to their jurisdiction.

Section 2. Congress shall have power to enforce this article by appropriate legislation

AMENDMENT XIV

Section 1. All persons born or naturalized in the United States and subject to the jurisdiction thereof, are citizens of the United States and of the State wherein they reside. No State shall make or enforce any law which shall abridge the privileges or immunities of citizens of the United States; nor shall any State deprive any person of life, liberty, or property, without due process of law; nor deny to any person within its jurisdiction the equal protection of the laws.

Section 2. Representatives shall be apportioned among the several States according to their respective numbers, counting the whole number of persons in each State, excluding Indians not taxed. But when the right to vote at any election for the choice of electors for President and Vice-President of the United States, Representatives in Congress, the Executive and Judicial officers of a State, or the members of the Legislature thereof, is denied to any of the male inhabitants of such State, being twenty-one years of age, and citizens of the United States, or in any way abridged, except for participation in rebellion, or other crime, the basis of representation therein shall be reduced in the proportion which the number of such male citizens shall bear to the whole number of male citizens twenty-one years of age in such State.

Section 3. No person shall be a Senator or Representative in Congress, or elector of President and Vice-President, or hold any office, civil or military, under the United States, or under any State, who, having previously taken an oath, as a member of Congress, or as an officer of the United States, or as a member of any State legislature, or as an executive or judicial officer of any State, to support the Constitution of the United States, shall have engaged in insurrection or rebellion against the same, or given aid or comfort to the enemies thereof. But Congress may by a vote of two-thirds of each House, remove such disability.

Section 4. The validity of the public debt of the United States, authorized by law, including debts incurred for payment of pensions and bounties for services in suppressing insurrection or rebellion, shall not be questioned. But neither the United States nor any State shall assume or pay any debt or obligation incurred in aid of insurrection or rebellion against the United States, or any claim for the loss or emancipation of any slave; but all such debts, obligations and claims shall be held illegal and void.

Section 5. The Congress shall have power to enforce, by appropriate legislation, the provisions of this article..

AMENDMENT XV

Section 1. The right of citizens of the United States to vote shall not be denied or abridged by the United States or by any State on account of race, color, or previous condition of servitude.

Section 2. The Congress shall have power to enforce this article by appropriate legislation.

AMENDMENT XVI

The Congress shall have power to lay and collect taxes on incomes, from whatever source derived, without apportionment among the several States, and without regard to any census or enumeration.

AMENDMENT XVII

The Senate of the United States shall be composed of two Senators from each State, elected by the people thereof, for six years; and each Senator shall have one vote. The electors in each State shall have the qualifications requisite for electors of the most numerous branch of the State legislatures.

When vacancies happen in the representation of any State in the Senate, the executive authority of such State shall issue writs of election to fill such vacancies: *Provided,* That the legislature of any State may empower the executive thereof to make temporary appointments until the people fill the vacancies by election as the legislature may direct.

This amendment shall not be so construed as to affect the election or term of any Senator chosen before it becomes valid as part of the Constitution.

AMENDMENT XVIII

Section 1. After one year from the ratification of this article the manufacture, sale, or transportation of intoxicating liquors within, the importation thereof into, or the exportation thereof from the United States and all territory subject to the jurisdiction thereof for beverage purposes is hereby prohibited.

Section 2. The Congress and the several States shall have concurrent power to enforce this article by appropriate legislation.

Section 3. This article shall be inoperative unless it shall have been ratified as an amendment to the Constitution by the legislatures of the several States, as provided in the Constitution, within seven years from the date of the submission hereof to the States by the Congress.

AMENDMENT XIX

The right of citizens of the United States to vote shall not be denied or abridged by the United States or by any State on account of *sex.*

Congress shall have power to enforce this article by appropriate legislation.

AMENDMENT XX

Section 1. The terms of the President and Vice-President shall end at noon on the 20th day of January, and the terms of Senators and Representatives at noon on the 3d day of January, of the years in which such terms would have ended if this article had not been-ratified; and the terms of their successors shall then begin.

Section 2. The Congress shall assemble at least once in every year, and such meeting shall begin at noon on the 3d day of January, unless they shall by law appoint a different day.

Section 3. If, at the time fixed for the beginning of the term of the President, the President elect shall have died, the Vice-President elect shall become President. If a President shall not have been chosen before the time fixed for the beginning of his term, or if the President elect shall have failed to qualify, then the Vice-President elect shall act as President until a President shall have qualified; and the Congress may by law provide for the case wherein neither a

President elect nor a Vice-President elect shall have qualified, declaring who shall then act as President, or the manner in which one who is to act shall be selected, and such person shall act accordingly until a President or Vice-President shall have qualified.

Section 4. The Congress may by law provide for the case of the death of any of the persons from whom the House of Representatives may choose a President whenever the right of choice shall have devolved upon them, and for the case of the death of any of the persons from whom the Senate may choose a Vice-President whenever the right of choice shall have devolved upon them.

Section 5. Sections 1 and 2 shall take effect on the 15th day of October following the ratification of this article.

Section 6. This article shall be inoperative unless it shall have been ratified as an amendment to the Constitution by the legislatures of three-fourths of the several States within seven years from the date of its submission.

AMENDMENT XXI

Section 1. The eighteenth article of amendment to the Constitution of the United States is hereby repealed.

Section 2. The transportation or importation into any State, Territory, or possession of the United States for delivery or use therein of intoxicating liquor in violation of the laws thereof, is hereby prohibited.

Section 3. This article shall be inoperative unless it shall have been ratified an amendment to the Constitution by conventions in the several States, provided in the Constitution, within seven years from the date of the submission hereof to the States by the Congress.

AMENDMENT XXII

Section 1. No person shall be elected to the office of the President more than twice, and no person who has held the office of President, or acted as President, for more than two years of a term to which some other person was elected President shall be elected to the office of the President more than once. But this Article shall not apply to any person holding the office of President when this Article was proposed by the Congress, and shall not prevent any person who may be holding the office of President, or acting as President, during the term within which this Article becomes operative from holding the office of President or acting as President during the remainder of such term.

Section 2. This article shall be inoperative unless it shall have been ratified as an amendment to the Constitution by the legislatures of three-fourths of the several States within seven years from the date of its submission to the States by the Congress.

AMENDMENT XXIII

Section 1. The District constituting the seat of Government of the United States shall appoint in such manner as the Congress may direct: A number of electors of President and Vice-President equal to the whole number of Senators and Representatives in Congress to which the District would be entitled if it were a State, but in no event more than the least populous State; they shall be in addition to those appointed by the States, but they shall be considered, for the purposes of the election of President and Vice-President, to be electors appointed by a State; and they shall meet in the District and perform such duties as provided by the twelfth article of amendment.

Section 2. The Congress shall have power to enforce this article by appropriate legislation.

AMENDMENT XXIV

Section 1. The right of citizens of the United States to vote in any primary or other election for President or Vice-President, for electors for President or Vice-President, or for Senator or Representative in Congress, shall not be denied or abridged by the United States or any State by reason of failure to pay any poll tax or other tax.

Section 2. The Congress shall have power to enforce this article by appropriate legislation.

AMENDMENT XXV

Section 1. In case of the removal of the President from office or of his death or resignation the Vice-President shall become President.

Section 2. Whenever there is a vacancy in the office of the Vice-President, the President shall nominate a Vice-President who shall take office upon confirmation by a majority vote of both Houses of Congress.

Section 3. Whenever the President transmits to the President pro tempore of the Senate and the Speaker of the House of Representatives his written declaration that he is unable to discharge the powers and duties of his office, and until he transmits to them a written declaration to the contrary, such powers and duties shall be discharged by the Vice-President as Acting President.

Section 4. Whenever the Vice-President and a majority of either the principal officers of the executive departments or of such other body as Congress may by law provide, transmit to the President pro tempore of the Senate and the Speaker of the House of Representatives their written declaration that the President is unable to discharge the powers and duties of his office, the Vice- President shall immediately assume the powers and duties of the office as Acting President.

Thereafter, when the President transmits to the President pro tempore of the Senate and the Speaker of the House of Representatives his written declaration that no inability exists, he shall resume the powers and duties of his office unless the Vice-President and a majority of either the principal officers of the executive department or of such other body as Congress may by law provide, transmit within four days to the President pro tempore of the Senate and the Speaker of the House of Representatives their written declaration that the President is unable to discharge the powers and duties of his office. Thereupon Congress shall decide the issue, assembling within forty-eight hours for that purpose if not in session. If the Congress, within twenty-one days after receipt of the latter written declaration, or, if Congress is not in session, within twenty-one days after Congress is required to assemble, determines by two-thirds vote of both Houses that the President is unable to discharge the powers and duties of his office, the Vice-President shall continue to discharge the same as Acting President; otherwise, the President shall resume the powers and duties of his office.

AMENDMENT XXVI

Section 1. The right of citizens of the United States, who are eighteen years of age or older, to vote shall not be denied or abridged by the United States or by any State on account of age.

Section 2. The Congress shall have power to enforce this article by appropriate legislation.

AMENDMENT XXVII

No law, varying the compensation for the services of the Senators and Representatives, shall take effect, until an election of Representatives shall have intervened.

INDEX OF CONTRIBUTORS

ABOUT THE AUTHOR

Les Adams was a lawyer, publisher, writer, and chairman of Palladium Press. His academic degrees include a B.A. in English from the University of North Carolina; an M.A. in English from Columbia University; a J.D. *cum laude,* from the Cumberland School of Law of Samford University, where he was editor-in-chief of the law review; and an honorary doctorate of law (LL.D.) from William Penn College. He is the author of *The Second Amendment Primer,* and co-author (with Akhil Amar) of *The Bill of Rights Primer.* He was a member of the Alabama Bar Association, The American Bar Association, and the National Rifle Association.